A LAMBING SEASON
IN
IRELAND

A LAMBING SEASON
IN
IRELAND

MARIA COFFEY

McArthur & Company

Toronto

Canadian Cataloguing in Publication Data

Coffey, Maria, 1952 –
A lambing season in Ireland: tales of a vet's wife

ISBN 1-55278-140-2

1. Goering, Dag. 2. Coffey, Maria, 1952 – . 3. Veterinarians – Ireland – Dingle Region – Biography. 4. Lambs – Ireland – Dingle Region. 5. Sheep – Parturition – Ireland – Dingle Region. I. Title

SF613.G637C63 2000   636.3′089′092   C00-930300-6

Composition & Design by *Michael P. Callaghan*
Cover Design by *Mad Dog Design Connection Inc.*
Typeset at *Moons of Jupiter, Inc.* (Toronto)
Printed in Canada by *Transcontinental Printing Inc.*

McArthur & Company
322 King Street West, Suite 402
Toronto, ON, M5V 1J2

10 9 8 7 6 5 4 3 2 1

The publisher wishes to acknowledge the financial support of the Government of Canada through the Book Publishing Industry Development Program (BPIDP) for our publishing activities.

For my mother, Bee,

and in memory of my father, Tom,

with thanks for your love and this life

Author's Note

In the hope of providing privacy and anonymity where they are required, I have changed the names of many of the characters in this story, renamed all the townlands, and in some instances altered people's geographical locations and the chronology of events. Also, so there is no confusion within the text as to my name, I should mention that the Irish locals called me Marie.

✢

CHAPTER ONE

The sheep were still on the high mountain slopes when we arrived in County Kerry. It was mid-February, too early yet for the shepherds and their dogs to herd the pregnant ewes down to lower, richer pastures in readiness for lambing. As we followed the winding road that skirts the Iveragh Peninsula, we could see them above us, tiny white dots in a wild tapestry of brown, prune and gold, crisscrossed by stone walls and shot through with gleaming ribbons of streams and waterfalls.

"How do the shepherds ever manage to find all their sheep up there?" I asked Dag.

"They know where to look."

Sheep learn the terrain of a mountain, he told me, and have favourite places to shelter from the wind and rain. They sense changes in the weather and move to more protected spots ahead of storms. Ewes pass this on to their lambs, and family groups keep to certain areas, from one generation to another.

We crossed the Fingras River, then took a sharp turn to follow its valley. Ahead of us, on the brow of a small hill, four massive, rectangular stones rose from the earth. Patches of pale green lichen covered their rounded surfaces. They stood endup in a line, leaning at slight angles like drunken sentinels. They had stood there for three thousand years, since the Bronze Age. As we drove on, I watched them shrink against a backdrop of hills and sky.

"Do you think the people who erected those stones kept sheep?"

Dag laughed.

"Don't ask me. I'm a vet, not a historian."

He turned his gaze from the road to catch glimpses of the rain-misted landscape: deep, glaciated valleys carving through the mountains, sweeps of lonely bog, sheer cliffs and jagged offshore islands pounded by a wind-churned, silver-lit sea. Of the five peninsulas that reach like long fingers from southwest Ireland into the Atlantic Ocean, the Iveragh is the biggest, the highest, the most remote, and has the greatest concentration of sheep. We were on our way to Cahersiveen, on its northern side, where Dag would spend the next few months assisting the O'Leary veterinary practice. Cows were already calving and the lambing season was soon to begin. It was the busiest time of the year in rural Ireland.

The road passed through several small, pleasing settlements, all bristling with Bed and Breakfast signs. Kenmare had a prosperous air, with craft shops and expensive restaurants inhabiting many of its lovely old buildings. Sneem's colourfully painted houses and neat gardens gave credence to the sign boasting that it had once won Ireland's Tidy Town Award. In Castle Cove and Caherdaniel there were quaint, historic pubs, and Waterville gazed out to a long shingle beach and expansive ocean views. Beyond Waterville, however, things changed. The mountains receded and for ten miles or so the landscape became monotonous and oppressive. Muddy cows grazed in rough, boggy fields. Stark bungalows popped up, with big square windows like empty eyes. We passed a small industrial estate surrounded by a chain-link fence and billboards proudly announcing a sock factory and a sweater factory. A squat weather station was festooned with scores of aerials and satellite dishes; beyond it was a sprawling grey hospital and an ugly pink hotel.

"This must be Cahersiveen," I said quietly.

The misty rain had turned into a downpour; through the swishing of the windscreen wipers we saw the settlement ahead. Rows of gloomy terraced houses flanked the narrow road, smoke hanging low over their chimneys. Cars parked along both curbs left barely one lane free, and a tractor was puttering along, slowing the traffic. I registered abandoned shopfronts, with whitewashed windows and paint peeling from walls. Outside a hardware store, wheelbarrows, spades and bags of fertilizer were displayed on the sidewalk. A group of teenagers in grey school uniforms huddled in the doorway of a small supermarket, eating doughnuts and ice-creams.

"At least this isn't a tourist trap," said Dag, with forced brightness. "It seems—"

He shrugged, searching for the right word. A Jack Russell terrier dashed out into the road, narrowly missing our wheels. It crossed to a butcher's shop, where it lifted its leg against the frame of the open door.

"It seems pretty real," Dag concluded lamely, then we both fell into silence.

CHAPTER TWO

"You're on the ball, up so bright and early," said the post office clerk. Stifling a yawn, he slid a book of stamps across the counter to me. "You'd make a great postman, alright."

It was nine-thirty, yet there was hardly a soul along Cahersiveen's Main Street, and most of the shops still had faded blinds pulled down over their windows. I had just left the Sive Hostel, where Dag and I were staying for a few days while we looked for a house to rent. He was in the vets' surgery, starting his first day of work; I had the morning to kill before meeting him for lunch.

Aimlessly, I wandered down the street, in the direction of the huge, hulking grey church which dominated the village. People had begun emerging from its lofty doorways, on their way out from morning Mass. A chilly wind was blowing; the men pulled up their collars and adjusted their hats, the women knotted headscarves under their chins. I passed by a butcher's shop; its fluorescent lights were burning brightly, and the man inside gave me a friendly wave, then beckoned me in. After a moment's hesitation, I pushed open the door, activating a bell which pinged loudly. There was a strong, disquieting smell of blood in the shop. Neatly arranged inside a glass-fronted, refrigerated display case were purple cow tongues, pale, plucked chickens, slabs of slick, brown liver and fat pink curls of homemade sausage. On top of the case, next to a large pottery bowl filled with fresh eggs, were several cardboard collection boxes.

Emblazoned with smiling black faces, they awaited donations for the soul-saving work of The Missionary Sisters of the Sacred Heart in Papua New Guinea, The Holy Ghost Missionaries in Nigeria and Saint Antony's Missionaries in Cork.

The butcher was a young man with closely cropped hair. He stood behind a wooden block, chopping up a chicken with such gusto that bits of flesh flew into the air from his blade.

"Are your eggs free-range?" I asked.

"You mean run-around? They are of course. This bird here was a run-around hen too, not like those awful scrawny things in plastic bags you buy across in the supermarket. Will you have a dozen eggs? Today's a fair day, so I'll be sold out by eleven."

He wiped his hands on his white coat, and began carefully filling up an egg box from the bowl.

"Are you here from England on your holidays?"

"I'm from Canada. My husband's going to be working with the O'Learys for a few months."

"The new vet? I heard talk of him." He gave me a sly look. "We must be very advanced in Ireland now, if it's worth his while to come all this way only for a few months of work."

It was a question rather than a statement. I told him that Dag liked to work in small rural communities, where people had close connections to the land and their animals. He particularly enjoyed working with sheep, especially mountain sheep, tough little creatures left to run semi-wild for much of the year. It wasn't money that had drawn him to Cahersiveen.

The butcher was staring at me, the stout fingers of one hand clasped around a delicate egg.

"Don't tell me," he said, his voice tinged with disbelief, "that he's come all this way, only for the *sheep*?"

The door pinged again, and a young, dark-eyed woman came in, pulling a baby in a buggy behind her.

5

"Are you open, Michael?"

"I am, Mary. I'll be with you right away."

He handed me the box of eggs and took the coins I offered. "Enjoy your holidays!" he called, as I left his shop.

Through the plate-glass window of a café, I saw three men working on plates of bacon, eggs, sausage, black pudding, baked beans, fried tomatoes and soda bread. I went inside and ordered coffee and a warm scone. When I sat down at the table next to the men, they gave me sidelong looks. I leaned over and asked if I could borrow the newspapers lying on a empty chair.

"Read away," one offered. "But there's nothing in there that's worth knowing about."

"Pervert Gets Five Years For Sexual Abuse of Daughter" screamed the headline on *The Kerryman*. Inside there were stories about a scandal involving a nearby local council, an account of a fashion show recently held at the pink hotel on the edge of Cahersiveen and in-depth articles about the progress of Kerry's school football teams. *The Irish Independent* offered lurid details from the trial of a priest accused of sodomy and dedicated several column inches on page three to the brutal murder of a woman in West Cork. After scanning them, I folded up the papers and returned them to their owner.

"You were right," I told him.

"'Tis terrible indeed what is happening in the world," he said. "People have lost their morals altogether."

Gloomily, I began picking at my scone. It had been Dag's idea to come to Ireland, and I'd agreed to it only after much persuasion and with great reluctance. I already felt all too familiar with the place, for it had inhabited the years of my childhood. I grew up among a tightly knit Irish Catholic community in the English Midlands. The words "home" and "Ireland" were synonymous to my parents and their friends; as recent emigrants, they clung resolutely to their culture and their religion. My upbringing was secure and happy, but in my teens I began to feel stifled by small-town life and and the strictures of the Catholic Church, and as soon as I was old enough I raced away to discover the rest of the world. But I couldn't escape Murphy's Law. When I moved to Canada I fell in love with a veterinarian whose dream was to live and work in Ireland. Our marriage made him eligible for Irish citizenship, thus enabling him to realize his dream and bringing me back to the point where I began: a small community under the shadow of a great church.

I finished my scone, and pushed currants and crumbs around my plate, wondering if I'd ever escape again.

Sudden activity on the street pulled me away from my thoughts. Vans were driving up and double-parking, burly men were jumping out, opening the back doors and pulling out trestle tables and brightly striped tarpaulins. By the time I'd finished my second cup of coffee, a market was in progress. I paid up and went out to look at the stalls. An array of goods was on offer: farmers' overalls, tin buckets, waxed jackets, towels, sheets, duvet covers, women's and children's clothing, night dresses, pyjamas, underwear, potted plants, seedling cabbages, sacks of potatoes, toilet seat covers, rugs and carpets. Women wearing flat, sensible shoes and carrying plastic shopping baskets stood about in tight groups, exchanging gossip. Men sat on the ledges of shop windows, smoking cigarettes and narrowing their eyes as they inhaled. I stopped at a stall selling shoes and boots. It was set up in front of a van with a *COFFEY'S* sign written in large letters on its side. A ruddy-faced man leaned against the stall, staring into space.

"Are you a Coffey?" I asked him, hoping to strike up a conversation.

He eyed me suspiciously.

"I am, I suppose."

"I'm a Coffey, too."

"Is that so?" he replied, with obvious disinterest.

I examined the green Wellingtons he had on offer.

"Eight pounds is the best price I can give you, now," he warned, as I picked out my size. "I can't sell them to you for any less."

Clutching my box of eggs and my newly purchased Wellingtons, I crossed the road to the library, a flat-roofed building painted cream with brown trim. On the small square outside it was a bust of the late Clifford Sigerson, a local author and poet. Close by, a bronze statue of a rifle-bearing soldier stood atop a plinth. Listed underneath were the names of those who had died in the fight for Irish freedom. The set of dates had been left ominously open-ended: "1916 to 19 — ."

Inside was one large room, the walls lined with shelves and stacks arranged haphazardly across the floor. Close to the door, the librarian sat behind a three-sided counter. As she looked up from sorting through cards, her phone rang.

"Excuse me a minute," she said, reaching for the receiver.

Beyond her desk, by the far wall, was the children's section, where a woman was reading to a couple of boisterous preschoolers. In the middle of the room, a man slept soundly on one of several low chairs arranged around a coffee table.

"I did, Martina, I heard they set a date," the librarian was saying. "Three hundred and fifty they're having to the reception. Ah, no, there's no place here big enough for that number. I'd say it will be held in Tralee or Killarney. Hold on a minute there, Martina, I have someone here to see to."

She smiled at me again.

"Can I help you?"

I shrugged and gazed about. I didn't really know what I wanted.

"Most tourists have an interest in the local history," she suggested.

She steered me past the sleeping man towards a shelf in the history section, and then returned to her conversation.

"Ah, no Martina, they've plenty of money. I'd say there's no worries in that department."

I settled down in one of the low chairs and began paging through Barrington's *Discovering Kerry*. In painstaking detail, he described how the Irish had suffered under English rule: feudalism in the 1200s, total conquest by the 1500s, dispossession of land under Cromwell and "planters," religious persecution during Penal Times, the Great Hunger in the 1840s and the ongoing struggle for independence.

It didn't make for easy or comfortable reading, particularly when I got around to the Troubles. Con Keating from Cahersiveen died while taking part in the 1916 Easter Rising. Thomas Ashe, another Kerryman, went on a hunger strike and died of neglect while under British guard. On March 12, 1923, during the Civil War, five local men were shot in the legs by the military, tied to a landmine just outside Cahersiveen, and blown to bits. *Discovering Kerry* was an unsparing account of a painful history.

An elderly couple came into the library, conversing loudly. The woman wore a belted mackintosh and a cotton headscarf tied under her chin. She was carrying several bulging shopping bags.

"I was there when he was born, Dan," she was saying, as she made her way towards the chairs. "He had a lovely mother, God have mercy on her."

"Oh heaven," agreed the man, as he followed her. "She was a nice woman, she was, Mary."

"She'd go mad if she knew what was happening now," she said, sinking heavily onto a chair close to mine.

"Oh God, she would."

"Was she an aunt of Johnnie Hegan's?"

"Oh Christ, she might have been."

"She'd crack a joke with anyone."

"She would, she would indeed, God rest her soul."

There was a pause in their conversation, while the woman rifled through the newspapers on the table.

"Jesus, Mary and Joseph!" She was staring at the front page of *The Kerryman*. "Where in God's name do they find all these perverts? Do you think there were as many perverts in our day, Dan, only we didn't know about them?"

Dan seemed more interested in the contents of Mary's shopping bags than in the perverts of Kerry.

"That's a great head of cabbage you have there, Mary."

"It is, Dan. I bought it from Johnny Apple this morning. I love a cabbage. Only the other day I was thinking of when we were children and our mothers sent us out to pick the nettles and dandelion leaves, and we boiled them together and we thought they were grand. Do you remember that, Dan?"

"I do indeed, Mary. I ate many the top of a nettle in the springtime. But I've had enough of them now."

"Our people ate too many nettles in the hungry times. They were forced to eat them and that's why we have no interest in them anymore. But they're still good for you all the same, Dan."

"They are, Mary. They are."

The sleeping man gave a sudden snort, his head snapped up and he looked around in confusion.

"Did you wake yourself up, Paudie?" asked Mary.

"I did, I suppose," he mumbled. "Who's this girl with you?"

"And how would I know that, Paudie? I've never met this girl before in my life."

She turned to me. "Are you a stranger in these parts?"

"I'm from Canada," I said.

She fixed me with a searching gaze. "Canada? That's odd now, for to me you sound like someone English-born."

Only a week before, we had been in Manchester to visit my mother, Bee. She had been born and brought up in Galway, and she expressed misgivings about our plans to live for a few months in Kerry.

"It's a wild place," she had warned us. "People there have long memories."

"Memories about what?" I asked.

Ignoring this, she continued, "When you're in Kerry, now, *don't* be English. Tell people that you're Irish, and that your name is Patricia Maria Carmel Philomena Coffey. Tell them that your father was from Tipperary and your mother's from Galway, and that you attended a convent school run by Our Lady of Mercy nuns, and that you spent your summers as a child on your uncle's farm in County Longford and—"

Her voice rose as she stressed the finale of this litany.

"—TELL THEM THAT YOU TOOK IRISH DANCING LESSONS!"

Self-consciously, I began to relay this information to Mary, but mercifully I didn't get very far before Dan butted in.

"Did you hear that, Mary?" he cried, after the bit about my father. "This girl is a Coffey, too, from Tipperary. You can tell it by looking at her. She has Irish eyes and Irish bones."

Mary seemed unimpressed.

"We Coffeys were all from Tipperary. We were thrown off our land by the English in Cromwell's time and we became tinkers."

"Don't be telling her that now," said Dan, looking embarrassed. "Not every Coffey was a tinker."

"Indeed they were, Dan. Coffeys the Tinkers, that's how we were known. We made pots and pans, and we came down west after they threw us off our land. That's the history and there's no denying it."

"Tinker isn't a name you should call anyone, Mary. The priest said as much in his sermon."

"And what kind of nonsense is that?" she snapped.

"I just met a Coffey in the market," I ventured. "I bought these Wellingtons from him."

"Ah, he's not a tinker, he's from a travelling family," said Dan. "That's different."

This only riled Mary anew.

"There is no difference!" She stood up, collecting her bags. "All this lather you hear from the pulpit and in the newspapers about tinker being a bad word, 'tis nothing but nonsense. We Coffeys don't need any other name because tinkers is what we are and we shouldn't be ashamed of it. Do you remember old Batty Coffey, God rest his soul, and how he played his concertina at the crossroads on market day? Listen to me, Dan, do you remember him?"

"I do, Mary." Dan had obviously given up the fight; he was sitting back in his chair, his hands across his paunch and his eyes half-closed.

"Batty wasn't ashamed to call himself a tinker, and neither should we be!"

As she leaned down towards me, I caught a strong whiff of sherry.

"We'll meet again," she whispered dramatically. "We're Coffeys, girl, and we're tinkers, and we'll stand together."

✦

CHAPTER THREE

At noon, I walked up to the surgery, a small pebble-dashed bungalow at the top of a steep lane. Above it rose Bentee Mountain, clad in russet bracken and winter-grey heather, its summit hidden by clouds. Several cars and trailers were parked outside the surgery, and a group of men hung around the doorway. They stood back to make way for me, and I stepped straight from the pavement into a small, square reception room. Floor to ceiling shelves were stacked with scour powders, deworming agents, sheep dip, milk replacer, dog food, cat food and flea powders. On one wall, a large poster depicted a black-faced ram dressed in green silky shorts and boxing gloves, standing on its back legs and striking a fighting pose. "KNOCK OUT BLOWFLY IN 9 SECONDS!" screamed the caption above.

Just inside the door, Frank O'Leary leaned against a counter, deep in conversation with a farmer. He was a fit-looking man in his early sixties, with silvery hair and kind blue eyes. Dressed in corduroy trousers, and a fine woollen sweater over his shirt and tie, he had an air of elegance about him, and a demeanour more suited to that of a diplomat than a veterinary surgeon who had worked in rural Ireland for thirty years. On the far side of the counter, his son Mike was talking to Ann, who sat in front of a computer. They all turned to greet me as I walked in.

"I'll say you're ready for your dinner, Marie, but it will be delayed a little, I'm afraid," said Frank apologetically. "Dag's working on a calf in the back and the O'Sullivan brothers are coming in with another for him soon. It's always busy on fair day, so he's in at the deep end already."

As Frank went out with the farmer to one of the trailers, the back door of the reception room opened and Dag appeared, looking worried. His shirt sleeves were rolled up, a stethoscope hung from the pocket of his waxed sleeveless jacket and he had a smear of dung on his cheek.

"John Falvey's out there with a four-day-old calf that hasn't stood up yet," he told Mike. "It doesn't have a suck reflex so he's been feeding it with a stomach tube. The navel is swollen and its mucosal membranes are bright red and now it's starting to scour—"

"It's got HEFT," Mike interrupted him. "It's a common enough ailment in Ireland. Did you not see it in the latest edition of *Baillieres Veterinary Dictionary*?"

Dag stared at him, obviously dumbfounded.

"HEFT?" he repeated, his face flushing with embarrassment. "I've never heard of it."

"Ah well, it's an acronym that you maybe don't use much in Canada," said Mike. "It stands for 'Has Every Fucking Thing.'"

Through the surgery window, I saw a rust-eaten, mud-splattered Ford Fiesta roll up and stutter to a halt outside.

"Patsy and Florence O'Sullivan are here," Ann announced.

"They're a pair of mountainy old men," added Mike. "You'll have fun with them."

Both brothers wore black suits, shiny with grease, and the fraying cuffs of their thin sweaters poked out the ends of their sleeves.

"Who are you?" the frailer of the two called out querulously, as Dag walked towards them.

"I'm the new vet," he replied.

The man scowled at him. His brother piped up, "A *new* vet, Patsy! And a fine big man he is, too."

"Alright, so." Patsy cocked a thumb towards the car. "I have a calf in here with a fierce scour."

Stretched across the back seat of the Ford Fiesta, atop a heap of stained newspapers, was a brown and white calf. Its eyes were dull and sunken and its tail was caked in a brown pasty diarrhea. Gazing at the animal through the window, Dag asked about its age, how long it had been scouring, if its mother was healthy, how the other calves in the pen were doing and so on.

"OK, let's have a look at the little fellow," he said finally, opening the car door.

There wasn't much room in the back of the small vehicle for a calf and a man of Dag's height. Folding himself practically double, he squeezed in next to the animal, took its rectal temperature, put a finger in its mouth to check the suck reflex and listened to its chest through his stethoscope. The car rocked slightly as he shifted his weight. Leaning in through the doors, the two brothers watched him intently.

"He's badly dehydrated," Dag told them, as he eased backwards out of the car and unfolded himself. "We should put him on a drip to replace the lost fluids and to counteract the acid in his blood."

"Work away, so," instructed Florence.

While Dag was getting what he needed from the surgery, Florence flirted good-naturedly with me.

"You're a nice, healthy girl," he said, flashing me a wide, gummy smile. "By God you are. I could be happy with a girl like you. By God I could."

Patsy, however, seemed uneasy in my presence, and stared into the middle distance while I tried to strike up a conversation.

"How many cows do you have?"

"I have five and my brother has three."

"Do you live together?"

"Close enough. In the same townland."

"And which townland is that?"

"Ballynakilly."

"Is it far from here?"

"Far enough."

Dag returned with a large syringe between his teeth, and his hands full of bottles, needles and flexible plastic tubing. Jamming himself between the back and front seats of the car, he inserted a long, thick needle into a vein in the calf's neck. Blood spurted out, running down his fingers and along the back of his hands. He attached one end of the flexible tubing to the needle, and the other end onto a bottle of electrolyte solution. He passed the bottle through the car window, asking me to hold it aloft. Ten minutes later, when the solution had drained through, he attached a fresh bottle. By the time it was empty, the calf's ears were twitching.

"The little fellow is brighter already," said Patsy admiringly, when the third infusion was complete and Dag was standing on the pavement trying to straighten his back. "And there was I, thinking I'd have to carry him all the way to Lourdes and ask Saint Bernadette for a miracle."

A car pulled up alongside us and a man with a full-moon face and a grizzly chin rolled down his window.

"How are you, John?" Patsy greeted him. "Is it the vet you're after? I have the new man here and he has a way with animals."

"I've a ewe that's gaining, but her lamb won't come," said the man, getting out of the car.

Opening the lid of the boot, he revealed a swollen Suffolk ewe, one of the lowland breeds that were beginning to lamb already. She was lying on her side, panting hard and in obvious distress.

"How long has she been gaining?" asked Dag.

"I'd say she started around breakfast time."

"Poor old girl. Let's get her round back and I'll have a look."

Behind the surgery, a small patch of lawn doubled as an operating room. A metal table stood against the end wall of the building, with a hose pipe and several buckets next to it. Scattered over the grass were bits of bloody membrane, the remnants of other surgical procedures done during the morning. In the garden of the next door house a woman was hanging out washing, keeping her eyes averted from our direction.

While Dag helped John hoist the ewe out of the car and onto the table, he sent me to fetch two buckets of warm water, some soap and a bottle of disinfectant from the back room of the surgery. This room was multi-purpose: as well as being used for examining and operating on small animals, it provided storage for drugs, boxes of plastic gloves, surgical tools, suture materials and the alarming-looking equipment used for calvings, castrations and dehornings. It was also the refreshment centre, and I found Ann in one corner, next to a stack of mugs, a box of tea bags and several packets of biscuits, waiting for the kettle to boil. Young and slender, she had a fashionable haircut and was dressed in a short, tight skirt, sheer black stockings and high-heeled shoes.

"You're very brave, offering to help," she said, as I hauled out a couple of buckets from beneath the sink. "I won't go anywhere near the blood."

"I don't intend to, either," I told her.

"I'll have a cup of tea ready for you, so," she called, as I hurried out.

With a soapy hand, Dag felt around inside the ewe.

"Her cervix isn't dilated," he told John. "Ring womb—isn't that what you call it here? I'll try to massage the cervix to get it open, but this one is very tight. It could have to be a Caesarean."

For a couple of minutes he worked with his hand plunged deeply inside the ewe and his face set in concentration. Then he looked up at John.

"This isn't getting us anywhere. We'll have to cut her open."

"Ann's making me some tea," I announced. "I'll see you inside."

"Can you hang around here for a bit?" asked Dag. "We might need your help."

Nervously, I watched him tie up the ewe's feet, use shears to clip away a patch of fleece the size of a tea tray on her side, then shave the skin underneath with a razor.

"I'll shave you next," he teased John.

"And then me and your missus will do you," John retorted, "but we'll have to tie you down by the feet, like we did the sheep, before we get that big thatch of a beard off your face."

He winked a lot as he talked, and between sentences he pursed his lips to spit neatly on the ground. When Dag began injecting the ewe with a local anaesthetic, John pulled a face and stared up at the sky.

"Isn't it fine weather we're having?" he chattered. "'Tis a pity the clouds are moving in. They say there is a change coming and I was hoping this dry spell would last, for the wet is no good for the lambs."

Dag pressed his scalpel against the shaved patch on the ewe's side, and I shut my eyes. When next I looked, blood was flowing from the fresh incision, and pooling on the grass. There was a sucking sound, as he reached through the opening and into the jumble of pink and greyish coils inside.

"The uterus is pretty dry and tight," he said. "That always makes things a little tricky."

The ewe lay in silence with a glassy-eyed stare. John held her head, stroking her face with one hand.

"Sheep are tough little animals," he murmured, "the way they suffer so."

The uterus Dag pulled into view was a red, glistening sack, steaming a little in the cold air. When he cut into it, watery, blood-streaked fluids gushed from the incision, and a pale blue, transparent membrane appeared.

"Here we go," he said, slitting open the membrane and revealing a yellowish-white limb. Grasping hold of its front feet, he pulled the lamb into the world. The slimy body looked lifeless, but Dag swung it hard to and fro from the back legs, like a pendulum, then laid it on the grass and squeezed the snout to clear away mucus. The lamb shook its head and snorted.

"It's a boy," Dag announced, after a quick examination.

"And he's a fierce horse of a lamb, too," cried John happily.

But the job was far from over. While John held the long fleece back from the area of the wound with his big, rough hands, Dag began stitching the ewe using a long curved needle and lengths of cat gut. He worked first on the uterus, which suddenly began to contract and disappear amongst the other organs.

"Press hard on her side, Maria," said Dag tersely. "Right here on this shaved patch. I want to get all the fluid out."

I pressed, and the blood and fluids that had spilled from the uterus into the ewe's body cavity welled up through the incision, and flowed over my hands. Before I had time to react to this, Dag asked me to scrub up. I fished about for the brush in the bucket of disinfected water, fearful of what I might have to do next. By the time I returned to the operating table, he had pulled the shrinking uterus out into view again.

"Hold this, would you?" he asked.

I'd never touched the insides of a live animal before. All I could think, as I grasped the slick uterus, was *warm*. Not only warm, but so alive that it seemed to be pulling itself back into the body, making me strain to keep it exposed. When Dag's needle pushed into the flesh—the living flesh I held in my hands—the world began to spin slightly. I shut my eyes, and took several deep breaths.

"She doesn't complain," I heard John say.

Opening my eyes again, I gave him a grateful smile, but when he carried on I realized he was talking about the ewe.

"Sheep are always that way. The old people used to say it's because they're so bold. When you go to kill a cow or a pig or a goat, they'll squeal and bellow. But a sheep won't make a noise, they'll never show you their fear. They have principles, you might say."

Once Dag had finished stitching the uterus in two layers, I let it slip back inside the body cavity. Then he set to work with his needle and cat gut on the ewe's abdominal muscles. By now the lamb was breathing normally and trying to struggle up onto his skinny, wobbly legs, which promptly collapsed beneath him. He shook his head, opened his mouth and gave his first high, reedy bleat, to which his mother, still on the operating table, immediately responded. When at last the job was done, the two men carried her to the boot of the car. John gathered up the clipped fleece from the grass, made a nest of it next to the new mother and gently laid the lamb on top. The ewe sniffed her baby, then began to nuzzle and lick.

"Now then," said John to his animals. "You'll both be happy now."

Dag turned to me. "Ready for some lunch?"

✜

CHAPTER FOUR

The East End Bar, named after its geographical position on Main Street, was in the front room of an old terraced house. Its walls and ceiling were painted in sombre shades of yellow and maroon. Artificial coals, fuelled by gas, glowed in a cast-iron fireplace, but did little to pierce the damp coolness. Several men stood along the counter, with pints of stout in front of them. They were freshly shaven and smartly turned-out, with ties knotted tightly at the necks of pressed shirts and hair slicked into place with grease. They nodded solemnly to Dag in greeting, then murmured to each other.

We'd been in Cahersiveen for barely a week, yet news of the arrival of the "big Canadian vet" had already spread. One of the men put down his pint and stepped forward, extending a hand to Dag. Small and wiry, the man had dark, shining eyes, and his hair was teased into an exaggerated duck-tail.

"You're very welcome in this pub, sir!" he cried.

Turning to his companions, he declaimed, "You would not believe what this gentleman did to my ewe today!"

Dag raised his eyebrows, as if alarmed at what the farmer might say next.

"The way he looked after her prolapse," he continued, "it was *wonderful*. In all my thirty years as a farmer, I've never seen anything like it."

"And my brother's calf," another much older man chipped in. "Christ, he was bad, but this man got him right in no time."

Dag's face had flushed with a mixture of pride and confusion.

"I'm sorry, Ted, I didn't recognize you at first," he told the duck-tail man.

"That is to be expected, for you saw me in my farm clothes first, and I'm a different character altogether in those."

"I'll wager you don't recognize me either," chipped in the old man, who I now realized was Florence O'Sullivan. "There are many of us around these parts but only the one of you and you'll have a mighty fierce time keeping our names and faces in your head."

"I know your wife," another man told Dag, as if I wasn't in the room with him. "I saw her in the café last week, reading a newspaper."

Ted Donnelly ushered us over to a table and ordered drinks that he insisted on paying for.

"It is quite a thing to see a vet and his wife in this bar," he said, sitting down next to us. "They usually frequent the golf club or some such place. But you're very welcome, and we're delighted to have you with us. Now tell me sir, where did you learn such things about sheep?"

For the next hour, he and Dag talked intensely of ewes, rams and lambs, and medical problems with names like naval ill and watery mouth. Ted had a flock of several hundred Scotch Blackface, and he was pleased to hear that Dag preferred mountain sheep to the lowland breeds.

"They look delicate, but they're tough little creatures," said Dag.

Ted nodded.

"They have to be tough. They do! For it is hard country around here and the sheep farmer has to know what he's about. Frank O'Leary hates to see me coming with a sheep, for he knows that if I bring a ewe in to him, there's a big problem with it. He told me that himself. You see, we sheep farmers know many a cure ourselves."

Before long I was soon so bored that my head was nodding and my eyelids were beginning to droop. A tap on my shoulder started me awake, and I looked up to see the woman from behind the bar standing next to me with a mug of coffee and a plate of biscuits.

"I thought this might keep you going," she said with a sympathetic grin.

We had walked into her pub that evening simply because it was opposite the Sive Hostel, where we were staying while we looked for a house to rent. Noreen, in her thirites, was small and effervescent, with a generous grin and hair pulled back into a girlish ponytail. She told me that she got quite a lot of trade from the hostel during the summer season, but that her regular customers were farmers who lived on the east side of town. Farmers on the west side frequented places like Tom's Tavern or the Skellig Rock, those from "Over the Water," the name given to the area across the River Fertha, drank at the Townlands pub, the workers from the sock factory on the edge of town tended to congregate at Mike Murts, teenagers headed to the disco in the Harp every Saturday night, the footballers met up at the Daniel O'Connell and professional types and golfers gathered at The Point.

These were broad generalizations, of course, because there were twenty-six pubs in Cahersiveen, although this was a paltry number compared with the days when the town had a thriving fishing industry and a passenger railway that linked it with Tralee and Dublin. Fifty-two pubs were open then, one for every twenty-three people in town, but after the closure of the railway line in 1960 a good half of them called last orders for good. The East End Bar had been one of the survivors; Noreen's husband, John, was born here almost forty years ago and had inherited the business from his parents. But the pub didn't provide them with a full living; John worked for the council and they also kept lowland sheep on some land along the banks of the River Fertha.

"We're glad to see your husband here," said Noreen. "We'll be calling on him soon enough when the lambs start coming."

I asked Noreen if she knew of any houses for rent. We had hoped to find a small, traditional cottage close to the sea, but such places seemed to be in short supply. Instead, several modern bungalows had been offered to us. We arrived at one to find its owner with a tank strapped to his back, spraying insecticide over the gravel driveway. The squat, yellow bungalow stood on land that had been flattened by bulldozers and effectively cleared of all vegetation. Standing in front of it, a forlorn Yorkshire terrier stared disconsolately into the distance, perhaps wondering where he could cock his leg. The majority of such places were holiday homes that were rented out in summer months and usually sat empty over the winter. Their owners were proud of them and seemed rather hurt when we declined to move in.

"Are you telling me you're not interested?" said one woman huffily, after we'd viewed and rejected her riverside bungalow. "It's only a hundred pounds a week!"

There had been no shortage of help offered to us as we searched for somewhere to live. While we were picking up some groceries in a supermarket, Dag met a couple of farmers who leaned on their shopping carts for ten minutes, discussing the matter of our accommodation with the cashier. Finally, they reached a consensus that we should talk to John Quirke, who lived a little way up the road and who knew everyone and everything to do with houses. Minutes after we'd knocked at his door, John was making phone calls on our behalf while his wife served us fresh cream cakes and cups of tea. Then they were driving us to see an old farmhouse high on a hill. We were delighted with the place, but it had no phone and was so far from the nearest pole that a connection would take weeks. Without a phone, Dag couldn't work, so we were back where we started, in the Sive Hostel.

The welcoming, homey atmosphere of the hostel was due in large part to Paul, its gregarious American manager. One evening he half-jokingly suggested to me that we should stay on there, and that I could help him run the place when things got busier. The sociability of such a job was appealing, and for a couple of hours I seriously considered it. Then Dag came back from the surgery and reminded us that he'd soon be on night call, the phone would be ringing at all hours, farmers would be arriving at the front door with ewes in labour, and that after a lambing or a caesarean he'd be washing his blood-stained hands and surgical equipment in the communal kitchen sink. We agreed that it probably wasn't such a good idea after all.

Noreen could offer us long-term bed and breakfast, but knew of no place for rent, and neither did the two women who had joined us at the table. Both were middle-aged farmers' wives who had a similar, rather severe style: hair cut short and clipped close to the temples and neck, skirts and blazers in plain dark colours and worn with high-buttoned blouses, court shoes and lots of gold accessories.

"Did you enjoy yourself at John Quirke's?" one of them asked, in a way that told me she was acknowledging the fact I had been there, rather than asking for information.

"He was very kind," I said. "Do you know him well?"

"I wouldn't say so, not exactly. My cousin's husband's friend is married to an in-law of his, and my neighbour is related to the people who own the house he took you up to."

"I see," I said, though I didn't at all.

"Mary Casey's house wasn't quite right for you?"

"Mary Casey?" I cast my mind over the people we'd met and the places for rent we'd seen over the past few days.

"She has a lovely bungalow down by the river. The tourists are mad for it in the summer, I hear they queue up to give her two hundred pounds a week."

"God, it's a beautiful place," her friend chipped in, giving me a narrow-eyed look. "The view is magnificent. I can't imagine a person not wanting to live there."

"It was too big for just Dag and myself," I hurriedly explained. "I think Mary was upset that we didn't take it—did she say anything to you?"

"Ah no, not a word, Mary would never speak ill of anyone," said the woman, and reached for her lemonade.

"She wouldn't, no," agreed her friend. "She's the nicest woman you could meet, is Mary."

For fifty pounds I had bought a second-hand bicycle, and I decided to take it out on a test run to look at some of the local sights. Heading east out of town, I followed the Ring of Kerry road, which hugs the Fertha Estuary before veering away from the river to climb a low mountain pass. I freewheeled down the first hill, then crossed the Carhan bridge. Below it, along the banks of the quietly flowing river, stood some ivy-covered ruins. This was the birthplace of Daniel O'Connell, the famous "Liberator," who in 1829 secured emancipation for the Catholics of Ireland. He'd barely lived here. As a small boy he was fostered out with country people, then was adopted by his rich uncle, Maurice O'Connell, who paid for his education in Dublin, England and France.

A farmer I'd met in the East End pub had told me not to worry about cycling along the Ring of Kerry.

"Drivers are used to people going home from the pubs on their bikes," he'd said, "so they give them lots of room."

But the road had only two lanes and no verge, and despite traffic being light, the cars and trucks that whizzed by seemed perilously close to my handlebars. Just beyond the head of the Fertha Estuary, I escaped onto a quiet road, which climbed a hill before dog-legging back along the north side of the estuary. I was now on the mountainous peninsula known locally as "Over the Water," that separates Dingle Bay from Valentia Harbour.

Along the hedgerows, fresh green shoots of montbretia were poking through old growth, and brambles clung to the slender trunks of *salix*, a white willow tree locally called "sally." Above me rose Knocknadobar Mountain, steep and brooding, its slopes covered with heather and bracken and peppered with rocks. Below, fields of marsh grass hedged with a type of gorse called furze ran gently down to the estuary. The tide was out, and channels of silvery water wound around red sandbanks on their way to the sea. Spanning the estuary were two narrow bridges: one, for vehicles and pedestrians, connected Over the Water with Cahersiveen; the other, constructed of wrought iron, had been for the now defunct railway that once ran between Valentia Harbour and Killorglin.

I stopped to look down at Cahersiveen. It was long and narrow, squeezed between the base of Bentee Mountain and the estuary. Beside the massive church, its terraced, slate-roofed houses looked petite. The old police barracks, a strange folly complete with turrets and towers, lent the town a fabled, fairytale quality.

There was barely any traffic on this high road. So far I had met only one car, a girl on a bicycle and a woman walking two dogs. The woman stopped to chat.

"It was lovely when we had a train," she told me. "You could change in Killorglin and go all the way to Dublin. It's hopeless trying to travel about now. The buses are terrible. Without a car, you're cut off from the world."

The railway opened in 1893, and provided local farmers and fishermen with a faster means of getting their product to market. When the fishing industry foundered, it increasingly lost money, and in the 1950s the government made plans to close the line.

"There was an Iveragh Railway Protection Society set up," said the woman. "They went to Dublin with a petition. The transport minister asked them how they had travelled from Cahersiveen. We drove, they told him. And why didn't you take the train? he asked. Because it was cheaper and quicker to come altogether in a car, they said. He laughed at them, and they lost their case, of course. Can you imagine the stupidity of such people?"

After a mile or so, I turned down into a narrow valley that cut north-south across the peninsula, between the mountains of Knocknadobar and Castlequin. The lane was poorly maintained, and I swerved about on my bike to avoid the numerous potholes. Rough tracks led to traditional, two-storied farmhouses with dormer windows and chimney stacks on the gable ends. Around them, stretching up to the lower slopes of the mountains, were small green pastures bounded by stone walls. In one, a scarecrow dressed in a yellow rainjacket stood with arms outstretched. Cows grazed in another, along with a donkey that raised his head from the grass to watch me cycle by. Hooded crows hunched on telephone lines, the wind ruffling their feathers. Below them, along the sides of the lane, holly trees, scrambling brambles and clumps of montbretia grew in profusion.

Sunlight broke through a gap in the clouds and flooded across Knocknadobar Mountain, turning it to pure gold. By the time I reached the harbour at the end of the lane, half of the mountain was aglow, the light reflecting off the speck-like sheep close to its summit. The harbour was shaped like a key-hole and well protected from wind and waves. Across its crescent beach were pink and purple rocks and long strands of seaweed. On a jetty, green nets lay in tangles, and crab and lobster pots made from blue-green rope tied around black metal frames were heaped high. Across from the jetty, several long, slender boats were upturned. A few brown hens scratched about in the grass between them. I leaned my bike against the jetty wall and stood with my face to the wind, looking across the wide bay, beyond the headlands of Castlequin towards Dingle Peninsula and the Blasket Islands. The hens wandered by, then made a dash for a cottage which stood a few steps away. They stood in a cluster around its front door, which opened suddenly to reveal a young woman. The birds scattered as she strode out, basket in hand, towards a pile of turf. Behind her toddled a small child, who fell backwards onto his bottom and began to wail. Abandoning her basket, the woman scooped him up in her arms and jiggled him around until his crying subsided.

"Look at this lady's nice bike," she told him, wiping away his tears. She smiled at me. "Are you enjoying your holiday?"

I told her that the sight of her hens had brought on a bout of homesickness. In Canada, we kept a few hens; they had become family pets, feeding from our hands and following us around the garden.

"If you lived here in the valley you could keep some more," said the woman. "We don't have many foxes—the O'Shea boys take care of that."

It took several seconds for her casual remark to sink in. I explained I was looking for a place to rent and asked if she knew of any cottages that might be available.

"There's three holiday homes here. They're mostly empty except for the summer."

She pointed to an uninspiring bungalow close by. Then she walked a little way past the jetty, and turned her gaze towards the mountain. It had lost its glow and was steadily being engulfed by lowering cloud. Tucked in at its feet, at the top of a track through fields of reed grass and furze, was a whitewashed cottage.

"That one's rented out to tourists in the summer," the woman said. "The people who own it are over from England right now. You could talk to them—I'm sure they'd be interested. They drove into town this morning, but they'll be back by tonight, so why don't you come again then? Tell them Kathleen sent you."

Wind gusted in from the bay, bringing a shower of fine rain. Kathleen hurried inside the house with her son and I set off up the valley, intent on telling Dag that maybe, just maybe, I'd found us our cottage by the sea.

✦

CHAPTER FIVE

Our welcoming committee to the valley was a lone ewe with long shaggy fleece. It stood resolutely in the middle of the lane, refusing to move until I got out of the car and shooed it away.

Once past the sheep, we turned up a track between stands of large holly trees and fuchsia bushes. It led to the house of Peggy O'Sullivan, who looked after the cottage we had rented and was holding the key for us. The front door was wide open, and when we pulled up Peggy stepped through it. Loose brown curls framed a rosy face with a broad, gap-toothed smile. She was small and strong-looking, and wore a baggy sweater over trousers tucked into Wellingtons.

"Was Chloe directing the traffic again?" she greeted us, referring to the sheep that was now leisurely walking up the track behind us. "Ah, she's a blaggard, always taking a ramble. It's a habit we can't get her to beat. She was our pet lamb last year, and we spoiled her I suppose, we did, we spoiled her."

Peggy's words tumbled out quickly, and she often repeated herself in a lyrical fashion. She had a strong Kerry accent; she added an "h" to words with a "s" in front of a consonant, turning "spoiled" into "shpoiled" and "stop" into "shtop." "Blackguard" she pronounced as "blaggard," and "beat" as "bait."

"Here's the key for you now. But won't you stop for a drink first? Stop for a while now, do."

We were anxious to get settled in, so we turned down her kind offer, but promised to call by again soon.

"And we'll call down to you one evening," she assured us. "We will. We'll call down when you're at home."

Three cows gazed curiously at us over the stone wall surrounding the boggy field that was our garden, and the plaintive cries of sheep drifted down from the higher slopes.

"I have patients right on my doorstep," said Dag happily, as he unlocked the door of our new home.

By holiday home standards, the cottage was poorly appointed. It had no automatic washing machine or dryer, no shower, no television, none of the amenities that went with the other houses we'd been offered. The ceiling beams in the living room were so low that Dag repeatedly banged his head against the light fixture.The only heating source was an open fire, and pinned to the mantelpiece was a note warning that the chimney smoked badly. But there were compensations: the kitchen window looked along the valley and across to the curving ridge of Bentee Mountain; from the living room we could gaze up at the dark, impressive slopes of Knocknadobar; and three small fields away, across a stream and past an old donkey standing implacably beneath a tree, was Dingle Bay, and an ocean that broke unceasingly against the cliffs and rocky ledges.

While I unpacked our bags, Dag got a fire going. Our landlords had kindly left us some turf, cut from nearby peat bogs. As their note warned, however, the chimney was far from cooperative, sucking up most of the heat from the flames and periodically belching great clouds of smoke into the room. We opened all the windows and ate our supper with our overcoats on. Around ten-thirty, we decided the warmest place to be was bed. Just as we were heading up the stairs to the loft bedroom, there was a loud knocking on the door.

"Who the hell is that?" said Dag, looking at his watch.

"Patients?" I suggested.

"No one knows I live here yet."

Peggy O'Sullivan knew, and she was on the step with two teenagers.

"We saw the smoke coming from your chimney, and I said to Nell, I hope that chimney isn't poisoning them, so we came down with Peter to check."

We ushered them into our living room. Nell and Peter sat on a wooden, straight-backed bench that Peggy called a "rack." She accepted an easy chair next to the fire, which promptly coughed out smoke at her.

"When I was a child, this house was only the one small room with a thatch roof on top of it," she told us. "Its chimney was poisonous in the north wind even then, it would never draw. My kitchen stove is the same. When the north wind blows I have to take the fire out of it, I do. I take the fire out of it altogether."

Dag offered the family tea, coffee, wine, whiskey and juice, but Peggy steadfastly refused everything. Taking this at face value, he sat down, but my Irish upbringing had taught me that these refusals were only a polite form of stalling and that Peggy expected the pressure to continue.

"Surely you'll take a drink?" I asked her, mimicking what I'd heard my mother say many times in such circumstances.

"Ah no, I only ever have a drop of sherry once in a while."

"Please, then, you must take a glass," I insisted, ignoring Dag's puzzled stare.

"We've troubled you enough," said Peggy. "We've troubled you enough as it is."

"A small one won't hurt."

"Ah no, it's too much trouble, it is."

"It's not a bit of trouble, really. We were just going to have a drink ourselves."

"Ah, well, I won't let you drink alone, I'll have a drop of sherry then, just a drop."

While the sherry, juice and biscuits I served were being polished off and refurbished, Peggy told us that her husband Michael had suffered a stroke a few years ago, and that since then she and her eldest son John had run the family farm, with Nell and Peter helping in their spare time.

"They're a big help, especially when the lambing starts, for it's madness then. It's madness."

"I'm looking forward to the lambing season," Dag told her. "I really like working with sheep."

"Is that so?" Peggy looked genuinely pleased. "Most vets have no interest in sheep, no interest at all. We'll be down to you before long, for we hope for forty lambs this year."

"If Mr. Fox don't get a half of them first," added Peter shyly.

"The O'Shea boys up the road have Mr. Fox taken care of," said Peggy. "'Tis only Mr. Mink we have to worry about."

The mink, she told us, were a fairly new addition to the predators in the area. Some fifteen years before, a Norwegian man had started a mink farm near Waterville. Some of the animals had escaped and bred, and now they were to be found right across the peninsula.

"One summer, Mr. Mink got into Kathleen's henhouse and left her without a hen, he took them out of temper, sucked the blood and left them. Another year, a swan moved into the harbour. He was a lovely swan, big and grey, and he was a great attraction, people would come all the way from the town to admire him. But one day, he was gone, and we were all asking what had happened to the swan. Then we found him on the riverbank, his head almost hanging off. It was the work of Mr. Mink, of course. Can you imagine the cheek of him, tackling a big strong bird like that?"

"He got our pet drake too, Mam," Nell quietly reminded her.

"He did. He did. He did indeed." Peggy covered her glass with her hand when I offered the sherry bottle again. "We had a lovely drake, we raised him from the egg, and he was a real pet, he ran around with the dogs, pecking at their ears and their necks. He was great company, he'd follow me into up the fields when I was checking the sheep, and he'd come into the kitchen and sit by my feet. By night he slept with the dogs; he lay right down among them, so we thought he was safe from Mr. Mink. But one morning he was gone. I looked everywhere for him, all up and down the fields and in along the ditches, but all I found was a pile of feathers. I was heartbroken, so I was, heartbroken."

The family left just after midnight, and we stepped outside to wave as they drove away down the track. The air smelt of turf smoke, damp grass and salt. In the clear, moonless sky, the stars were startlingly dense and bright. Dag pointed out the Plough, the Northern Cross, glittering Sirius, Orion the Hunter drawing his bow and nebulous Pylades, seemingly deeper in space than the rest. With a pang of sadness I remembered that only two weeks before we had gazed at the same constellations above our house in Canada, a place that already seemed worlds away, as distant from me now as these stars.

✜

CHAPTER SIX

Since our arrival in Cahersiveen, the days had been unseasonably mild and dry. Fluffy buds appeared on the sally trees and yellow flowers unfurled among the prickly arms of the furze. But during our first night in the cottage, we heard a loud crack, and a flash of lightning lit our bedroom. A great booming roll of thunder followed, then the wind came up, blowing harder and harder until it was shrieking around the outside walls and hurling hailstones at the windows. The storm raged for hours. By morning the worst of it had passed, but above Knocknadobar Mountain clouds raced crazily across the sky and within an hour more rain arrived, blown almost horizontal by the gale-force wind that brought it.

For a week, one great frontal system after another swept in from the Atlantic. When I dashed into our garden to collect more turf for the fire, rain hammered against my hood and the wind slapped my scarf against my face. Sometimes, I heard the growl and rattle of tractors further up the valley. Despite the weather, farmers were out spreading fertilizer on their fields, preparing them for the pregnant ewes that would soon be herded down from the mountain. Deciding it was too wet for hiking and too windy for cycling, I holed up inside the cottage, wrapped in sweaters and socks, and tried to fill my days. Each morning, after Dag left for work, I did the dishes, tidied up, raked the fire grate, carried out the ashes, collected more turf and built a fire. I listened to the radio. I hand-washed our laundry in the kitchen sink, left it dripping on a line over the bath and finally hung it in front of the fire to dry. I spent hours reading the history books I'd picked up in the library. I even read *The Kerryman*, cover to cover, including the farming news. I cooked dinner, and waited for Dag to come home again. I wrote long letters to my author friends in Canada, trying to cast a positive spin on my new situation. I knew that most of them would give their back teeth to spend three months in a lonely cottage on the west coast of Ireland—it was a writer's dream, was it not? I was in-between writing projects, however, with no deadlines to focus me, and unaccustomed to dealing with this newfound leisure. I grew bored, and the boredom soon turned to listlessness. In the brief respites between storms, I thought about going to introduce myself to some of our neighbours. But I felt shy about knocking on their doors and had no idea of what we might find in common to talk about. As one day gave way to the next, and rain continued to blur the windows, I felt the tiny cottage's walls closing in on me.

Dag was unsympathetic.

"How can you bear staying indoors?" he cried, bursting through the door one afternoon, wet, muddy and bright-eyed. "The skies are fantastic! If I didn't have a job, I'd be outside, running around with my camera."

He was unremittingly, annoyingly cheerful. He loved his work. He loved the Iveragh Peninsula. He even loved the weather. On his free evenings he sat by the fire, making little watercolour sketches of local landscapes, and telling me stories about the eccentric farmers he'd met.

"They say the weather's due to improve," he told me one night after dinner.

I picked up the phone book and began looking through it for numbers of bicycle shops, vaguely thinking that I should buy some panniers for my bike.

"Maria?" asked Dag, some time later. "Are you alright?"

"Yes," I said, my eyes still on the page. "Why?"

"You've been reading the phone book for the last fifteen minutes, that's why."

"It's quite interesting," I told him. "The Yellow Pages are called Golden Pages here, and there's a whole section on consumer rights and a double-page spread on sporting events. And while I was looking for bike shops I found this entry for convents and it almost fills up an entire page. Convents in the yellow pages—isn't that funny?"

I looked up at him; he was staring at me with an expression of profound concern. As I reached for my glass of wine, the phone book slid off my lap and onto the rug. I left it there, and sat in silence for a while, sipping the wine.

"It's time I got out of this cottage," I finally announced.

Dag nodded in agreement.

"Do you need an assistant?" I asked.

Next morning, the phone rang at eight.

"Did I wake you, Marie?" asked Frank cheerfully.

"No," I lied.

"You might as well get some sleep while you can," he said, "for there will be little enough of it to be had before long. Is Dag there with you?"

I looked around the bathroom door to see my husband on all fours in the tiny tub, his backside in the air, rinsing shampoo out of his hair.

"Can he call you back?"

"Maybe you could give him this message, Marie. Tossy McCarthy from Over the Water just rang in about a calving. The cow's off in a field by the first stone fort, not too far from you. Would you mind asking Dag to go? Tossy says she's stroppy, so make sure he gets a bit of breakfast inside him before he goes."

Dag wouldn't consider breakfast, and ten minutes later we were in the car, driving through blustery rain. The sky was low and unremittingly grey, until a fierce gust of wind suddenly tore it open, revealing great swathes of blue. Sunlight poured though the clouds, double rainbows arched up from wet fields, and in seconds the whole world was agleam. But away over Dingle Peninsula, dark clouds were rebuilding, and soon they raced in from the sea, dragging heavy veils of rain.

"It's a fresh day!" Tossy greeted us, as hail pelted down, stinging our faces. "I'd say you have plenty of this snowball rain in Canada, you must be well used to it."

We had found him with two other men along the track leading to Cahergael, a medieval fort. Its massive, circular drystone walls loomed over the field where the cow stood. She was inside a pen made of old wooden gates and bits of scrap iron. Her ribs were heaving, her eyes were staring, and threads of saliva hung from one corner of her mouth.

"Now sir, this cow isn't my cow at all," Tossy shouted, over the din of the hail. "She belongs to Michael Martin O'Shea, he lives away in Kells. I was on my way to check my own cows when I saw this one. I went straight away to Peter's house and we telephoned Michael Martin but we could get no answer. I'd say he was out in the town last night, and he's suffering the effects. So we telephoned Frank O'Leary and he said you'd be down. How well you found your way so quick. 'Tis easy to get lost in these parts. A stranger here needs a fierce sense of direction."

Peter and another of Tossy's neighbours, John Pat, had come out to help with the calving. None of the three men seemed to resent being out so early in such bad weather to look after the cow of a farmer who was probably sleeping off a hangover. When I commented on this, Peter gave me a quizzical look.

"Ah sure, Martin's an old boy and he's all alone. And wouldn't he'd do the same for us? Where would any of us be without our neighbours?"

Dag had stripped off his shirt and donned his calving gown, a green rubber garmet with short, tight-fitting sleeves. It fastened at the back, reached from his neck to his knees and matched his green over-trousers and Wellingtons. The men filled buckets with warm water from a churn in the back of Tossy's car, and Dag poured disinfectant into them and began scrubbing up, looking worriedly at the cow from beneath his wide-brimmed hat.

"Is there any shed we can get her into?" he asked.

"There's only the fort, and we couldn't get her in there even if we wanted," Tossy told him. "She's fierce bold. It took us long enough to get her into this old haggard."

As the four men went into the pen, the hail stopped abruptly and the sun came out again, turning the grass to glitter. But they were too busy to notice the change; Tossy grappled frantically with the animal's head, trying to get hold of her nose, while Peter grabbed her tail and Martin pushed on her back end. After much wrestling and swearing, they finally managed to tie her up against one of the fences.

"Okay girl, relax, don't worry," said Dag, as he began to examine her.

Far from relaxing, she kicked out repeatedly, catching him once on the shin.

"You'll have a nice bruise there, boy," commented Peter.

Dag sent me off to the boot of the car for a bottle of lubricant, which I squirted up and down his arm before he plunged shoulder deep into the cow. He strained forwards, his rubber boots slipping from under him on the wet grass, his mouth twisted into a grimace.

"No wonder she's having trouble," he said, with his arm still inside the cow. "The calf's big and lying on its back. I can't budge it on my own; I'll need your help, Tossy."

"Alright, so," said Tossy, pushing back his sleeves and spitting on his palms.

"When I tell you, push hard with both your fists into the flank here, and I'll try to swing the calf into an upright position. Are you ready? One, two, three, now!"

Tossy pushed with all his weight, but it didn't work. Again and again he and Dag tried, getting into a rhythm of pushing and swinging, grunting with the effort of it, yet still the calf stayed resolutely on its back.

"One more go, OK?" said Dag, panting heavily. "One, two, three, now!"

This time, Tossy threw himself at the cow, his face clenched with determination. And at last Dag withdrew his arm, shaking it limply and flexing his fingers.

"Great, Tossy, that one worked."

He sent me to the car again for the calving ropes and the wooden blocks, which were soaking in a bucket of disinfectant. One by one, I passed the ropes over, and he put his hand back inside the cow to secure them to the calf's front feet and head. I marvelled at how he could work by feel alone. He'd once told me how much he enjoyed the challenge of calving and lambing: checking for life by gently touching an eyeball or the umbilical cord, sorting out the tangle of limbs, coordinating his efforts with the mother's pressing to bring a new little creature safely into the world. He was, I mused, a man who loved to work with his hands, and who needed to see quick results from his efforts. Early on in our marriage, after completing his doctorate, he had accepted a college teaching post, and I remembered how he had languished within the confines of academic life. Much better this, I concluded, as I gazed at the side of his face, pressed against the rump of the cow and set with the concentration required to correctly attach the ropes. A tough life but a romantic one, I was still thinking, as his slime-covered arm reappeared, as a cloud burst open above us and rain began lashing down. But when he picked up the calving jack, the rosy glow I'd created around him began to fade. It was the first time I'd seen the jack assembled and ready for use. A seven-foot-long metal pole, with a ratchet and a yellow lever at one end and a big brace at the other, it looked like an instrument of torture.

"Will one of you gentlemen hold the end of the jack?" asked Dag, as he fitted the large U-shaped brace over the cow's rump.

"We're going to pull carefully, to see how he comes," he continued, tying the ropes that were dangling out of the cow onto the jack. "He's bloody huge, so there's a chance we might have to do a caesarean."

"Christ in heaven, I hope not," said Peter, who was still holding onto the tail. It was now raining so hard that water was running off the peak of his flat cap and the cuffs of his jacket.

"No kidding," said Dag, as he began to work the ratchet. "These aren't exactly ideal conditions for a major operation."

He pulled back on the lever of the ratchet until the ropes were stretched taunt. Then he stopped and put his hand inside the cow once more to check the position of the calf and to get an indication of whether or not it would fit through the cow's pelvis. The farmers watched intently for his decision. The cow had given up kicking and was straining hard instead; her head was down, and she was lowing pitifully. Dag returned to the ratchet and worked it steadily.

"It'll be tight but we're going for it."

"Thanks be to God," muttered Tossy.

The calf's front legs appeared, their brown and white hair slick with amniotic fluids. Then the head was almost out, the large purple tongue protruding and the eyes glazed and pre-occupied, like someone in a trance. But the cow's vulva was stretched too taunt over the head, and I heard Dag swear yet again.

"She's not open enough, I'll have to do an episiotomy. Run and get me a scalpel, Maria. They're on the left-hand side of the car boot, in a wooden tray."

My hands were so wet and cold that I fumbled uselessly at the sterile wrapping of the blade. Tossy came to my rescue and handed the blade to Dag. Swiftly, he made a clean two-inch incision into the vulva, then returned to the jack. After a few more pulls, the front end of the calf appeared. But just when I thought that the worse was over, Dag stopped hauling on the ratchet and once more stepped forward. Grabbing the calf by its forelimbs and chest in what looked like a strange wrestling hold, he twisted the torso through ninety degrees, onto its side.

"Just to keep it from getting stuck at the hips," he muttered, stepping back to the lever.

I saw him worriedly bite his lip as he pulled the lever again, encountering yet more resistance. The cow gave a long moan, her legs buckled and she fell on her side. Dag kneeled down by the jack and kept pulling. As the clicking of the ratchet slowed, Tossy exchanged nervous glances with his neighbours. If the calf got stuck now, it would have to be killed and cut up inside the mother, who might suffer permanent damage as a result.

Click, click, pause. Click. Pause. Click. Pause. Click . . . The tension was palpable. Everyone seemed to be holding their breath. Then suddenly the calf's hips popped out and a pair of hind legs quickly followed.

"Lord Jesus, he's a fecking monster!" cried Tossy with relief, staring down at the hundred-and-twenty-pound animal.

"Christ, the size of him, what bull did Peter let loose on this poor cow?" added Martin.

Dag released the ropes, cleared mucus from the calf's nose and mouth and hauled the new animal over the grass, out of sight of the mother.

"Once she sees him she could get stroppy again, and I don't want that to happen while I'm stitching her up."

He slapped the cow hard on the ribs to make her stand, inserted his hand inside her and turned to wink at Tossy.

"Just checking to see if there's another one in here."

"Jesus, Mary and Joseph, if there's room for anything else, 'twill be a fecking miracle. Is she badly banged up?"

"She's a bit bruised inside, but she'll be alright."

Although a local anaesthetic injected into the base of her tail numbed the back end of the cow, she still stamped her feet and flailed out at Dag with her back hoof while he stitched her.

"She thinks it was all my fault," he joked.

But he was watching for the danger signs in the cow—the head down, the sidelong glance—and he neatly avoided each kick.

"By god, he's a man who knows his animals," said Tossy admiringly. "It must be all that cowboy stuff they go for in Canada."

After giving the cow a penicillin injection, Dag dragged the calf back to her and left it by her front hooves. He watched in obvious relief and pleasure as she sniffed the newborn and dragged her big tongue over his body, warming and drying him and bringing him properly to life.

While Dag used a stiff brush to scrub the blood off of his rubber boots and gown, I talked to Tossy about the stone fort above us.

"They say it had farms within it," he said. "Archeologists came digging here and they found all manner of things. Iron knives and nails, and animal bones more than a thousand years old. They say they kept sheep and goats and pigs in there, and grew their crops on the land round about. Not so long ago, before the Public Works took the place over, there would still be farmers sheltering their animals in the fort during the winter months. I heard an old man telling of how he used to keep his weak lambs in a little stone hut within."

Dag was rinsing off the ropes and poles he'd used for the birthing.

"I don't suppose the farmers had the use of calving jacks a thousand years ago," I joked.

"And nor did we until recent years," said Tossy. "When the cow was in difficulty we'd put a rope around the calf and five men pulled on it. If the calf wouldn't come we tied the end of the rope to a tractor and drove away."

"There were never any cows in those forts," said John Pat. "Wasn't it only fairies who lived in them?"

"Fairies my arse," laughed Tossy, but John Pat persisted, recounting a story about a cow that grazed in the fields around the nearby fort of Leancanabuile.

"Of a morning she never had a drop of milk in her, and the farmer thought it was his neighbour stealing it by night. So one time he stayed out of bed and hid behind a tree to watch the cow. Around midnight, didn't he see a fairy come creeping out of the fort with a bucket and a stool, sit herself down by the cow and start milking. Your man's too scared to chase the fairy away, so instead he makes a bargain with her. He tells her that if she leaves his cow alone he'll deliver milk to the fort every day himself."

"And what kind of logic was that?" said Tossy. "Wouldn't he have been better off keeping his mouth shut and letting the fairy do the work for him?"

The old belief in "fairy forts" probably originates from Celtic legends chronicled by twelfth-century monks in the *Book of Invasions*. According to these stories, the Tuatha De Danann, a race of gods who ruled Ireland for a time, retreated to the underground forts, or *sidh*, after their defeat by the Milesians and continued to work their magic from there. As with many Irish legends, this may have a link to historical reality. Earthen walled forts, or *raths*, were built as far back as the middle Bronze Age, from 1350 BC to 950 BC, which is approximately the period of the mythical Tuatha De Danann's rule. What mostly remained of the raths in more modern times were mounds and banks of sod-covered earth that some farmers refused to plough over for fear of disturbing "the good people" who were said to still inhabit them.

"Do you believe in fairies?" I asked Martin as we were leaving.

"I can't say I do," he replied. "But I've heard that sometimes on a full moon night you see them playing football down on the White Strand. They say the fairies from Staigue Fort fly over and challenge the Cahergael team to a match. 'Tis nothing but a story, but then again, you can never be sure."

✦

CHAPTER SEVEN

It was the beginning of March and for now the storms had passed. The sea was calm and the air had a fresh smell that held the promise of spring. Down at the harbour, oystercatchers with long red legs and beaks stepped delicately across the rocks. Blue tits fluttered about the stone wall of our garden, and from the fields behind the cottage came the "*tsak tsak tsak*" of stonechats starting to nest in the furze.

Along the valley, sheep were appearing in the fields. The mountain ewes had been brought down to the farms for scanning; those carrying twins were put on rich pasture to fatten them up for birth, while the ones with single lambs had been sent back up to higher ground to fend for themselves a while longer.

Some farms on the peninsula, where lowland sheep were raised, were now in the thick of lambing. Early in the morning or late at night, farmers were regularly turning up outside our cottage with distressed ewes. Often it was twins, and occasionally triplets, that Dag had to untangle, reposition and pull safely into the world.

"The lowland sheep produce plenty of milk," Ted Donnelly explained to me, "so they can manage couplets."

We were sitting with him in the East End Bar, where we'd gone for a pre-prandial drink to celebrate the start of Dag's first weekend off.

"The farmer has to feed and fuss with lowland breeds all winter long," he continued. "Come spring, he wants as much as he can get from them. And usually they produce two strong lambs for him. But it's not like that with mountain sheep, Marie. Oh no! The mountain sheep are smaller, and if the ewe has two lambs, the chances are they'll both be weak. So it's singlets you want from mountain ewes, not couplets. One strong lamb is better than two weak ones. It's better any day."

I stifled a yawn.From behind the counter, Noreen caught my eye and held up a jar of instant coffee, grinning mischievously. She was caught in a sheep conversation, too. Her husband, John, was telling Dag about their problems. That morning, one-half of a set of twins had died, and the ewe was showing no interest in the survivor. They had also found a single lamb wandering about in circles. He appeared to have something wrong with his eyelids as he couldn't see where he was going.

"Sounds like entropion," said Dag.

"We had that in a lamb last year," Ted called over. "What is the cause of it, now?"

Dag drained his glass.

"The eyelids are turned because of a birth defect. So the eyelashes rub against the cornea, and this leads to blindness. It's easy to treat. Injecting paraffin oil into the lid makes it thicker and keeps the edge from curling in towards the eyeball. It's like plastic surgery really."

"My farm's only down the road," said John. "If you think about it next time you're on call—"

"I've got some liquid paraffin in the car," Dag interrupted him. "We might as well go now. Want to come, Maria?"

I hesitated, weighing up which was worse: to go out and look at sheep or to stay in the bar and talk about them.

"Go on with them," Noreen encouraged me. "The lambs are lovely."

We drove over the Carhan Bridge and parked at the side of the road close to some stone sheds. From here, John and Noreen's twenty-acre farm sloped gently down to the banks of the Fertha river estuary. Long shadows of evening fell across smooth green fields, where ewes grazed peacefully while their lambs sucked, their little heads butting against the teats and their woolly tails waggling furiously. One family group stood out from the rest. The mother was anxious and restless, watching a lamb that staggered about in random directions tilting his head skywards. "The ewe's only a year old, she was too young to have a lamb, but the ram got out and caught her," explained John. "She's a good mother, though; she looks out for him all the time."

He looped one end of an aluminum crook under the lamb to catch him. While the ewe hovered about us, bleating nervously, Dag held the black-faced creature in his arms, carefully examining his eyes.

"He's almost completely blind," said Dag. "But this isn't entropion, it's microphthalmia—his eyes are underdeveloped. There's nothing we can do for that, I'm afraid. He looks okay otherwise, though. Can he find the mother's teats without a problem?"

"He can," said John. "He's mad for them, too."

Dag nodded.

"You may as well let her raise him. He might make it until it's time to send him to the market in September."

As we walked up the field I kept glancing back at the sheep and her sightless offspring. When first they were reunited, she followed him about, sniffing his fleece. Then she started nudging him with her nose towards a wall. When I looked for the last time, she had settled down in the shelter of the rocks, her legs tucked beneath her, and was peacefully chewing her cud with the lamb curled up against her chest.

A far less fortunate lamb lay all alone in the corner of a shed. It was a pathetic sight, diminutive, weak and shivering, its tightly curled fleece covered with muck.

"He was born this morning," said John. "His twin died and the mother won't stand still long enough to let him suck."

"Did he get his beestings?" asked Dag.

John nodded.

"He did, alright."

"*Bee* stings?" I asked incredulously.

"Colostrum," said Dag, but this still meant nothing to me. It was only later, in the pub, that I learned that they were talking about a secretion produced in the ewe's mammary glands, which comes with her first milk. It is rich in antibodies, and getting an early and adequate feed of it is the most important factor for a lamb's survival.

"I'd say he got enough of the beestings, alright," continued John, "but he hasn't sucked since, because she won't let him near her. She's got a hurt in her teats, I'd say."

The ewe was in the adjoining shed. While John held her by the horns, Dag knelt and checked her teats, expressing some milk into his palm then sniffing and tasting it.

"The milk's fine," he said. "Let's get her over with the lamb and see what happens."

"She'll kick him away," warned John.

Holding the ewe's horns, they walked her over to the shed where her lamb lay. Dag picked up the tiny figure and held it close to the mother's teats, pushing its nose against them. The ewe stood quietly, then turned her head and sniffed at the lamb.

"She wouldn't do that for me," said John. "You're a better shepherd than I am."

"If you pen them together, she'll take him eventually, but he's too weak to suck right now," said Dag.

He spat on a thermometer and slipped it inside the lamb's rear end. After taking it out and reading it, he shook his head in dismay.

"Ninety-eight degrees. He's hypothermic, John, his temperature should be at least a hundred and two. His blood sugar levels will be down, too; he needs some energy in him, and then we've got to warm him up fast."

Back in the East End Bar, men stood two-deep at the counter, and Noreen was busy pouring out pints of stout.

"We've got a present for you, Noreen," I announced, as Dag appeared behind me with the lamb in his arms.

"Oh, Jesus Christ, no!" She lifted a section of the counter to let us though. "Come on, you'd better bring him into the kitchen."

When Dag carried the lamb past the men, they all had a comment to make.

"That's some gimp you have there, boy."

"You'll have to perform a few miracles to get him standing."

"I'd have let that one go to heaven if it were mine."

Deserting their customers, John and Noreen stood in the kitchen watching Dag stir glucose powder into boiled water. He drew up fifty millilitres of the mixture into a huge syringe, cooled it under cold running water, then asked John to hold up the lamb by its front legs.

"This goes right into his body cavity," he said, inserting the thick needle just below the navel. The lamb offered no resistance, but as Dag slowly pushed down the plunger, Noreen bit her hand and looked away.

"Now he needs a bed and some sort of heat source. Got a hair dryer or anything, Noreen?"

Before long, the lamb was lying on newspapers inside a cardboard box, with a blow fan balanced on a stool and aimed down at him. Noreen brought us each a pint of stout, which we drank standing around the box, gazing down at the patient. By the time we'd drained the glasses, his temperature was up by a degree and he was beginning to look a little brighter.

"He thinks he's at the hairdresser's," laughed Noreen, patting the wispy fleece between his ears.

"His chances are still pretty slim," Dag warned her. "I'll leave the thermometer with you as you'll need to check his temperature every ten minutes. Once it's up to a hundred and two, take him back to the mother and put them together in a pen."

I opened the door to the bar, revealing a dozen sets of elbows planted along the counter, with a crowd of ruddy, impatient faces above them.

"Tell Noreen that we're dying of the thirst," growled one man. "And that if she's not out here soon she'll have more than a lamb to look after."

Soon, pints were being poured again, and the talk was all lambs.

"Wouldn't you like a pet to take home with you tonight, Marie?" asked John. "You could cuddle him by the fire."

"Don't listen to him," a farmer warned me. "Pet lambs are like spoilt little children. They're always a nuisance, even when they're reared. They're afraid of neither man nor beast, so you can't keep them with the flock. And they won't touch the heather, they'll only eat the soft grass, so they never have any muscle on them. They're no good on the dinner table, at all."

By the time we left the pub, the lamb's temperature was up to a hundred degrees.

"Keep a careful watch on him now," Dag reminded Noreen. "You don't want him getting too warm."

After dinner we sat by the fire, drinking wine and reading. I was deep into a William Trevor novel and Dag was immersed in an article entitled "Efficacy of Moxidectin, Ivermectin and Albendazole Oral Drenches for Suppression of Periparturient Rise in Ewe Worm Egg Output and Reduction of Anthelmintic Treatment for Lambs," when we heard the growl of an engine on the track.

"I bet this is a patient," sighed Dag.

"You're not on duty."

"I hadn't reckoned on being on duty when we went for a pint, either," he said wryly, getting to his feet.

On our driveway, a grim-faced Joe Golden opened the boot of his car, revealing a Suffolk ewe.

"She's been trying to gain for five hours."

"Did you put your hand inside her?"

"I tried, but I couldn't feel anything."

A quick examination showed that her cervix hadn't opened, and a caesarean was urgently required. The men hauled the sheep over to the wooden picnic table in front of our cottage, and I flicked on the outside light that illuminated it.

"I hope the tourists who rent this place in the summer don't find out," I told Joe, as the ewe's blood spilled over the table.

"Arra, tourists," said Joe disparagingly. "What they don't see won't hurt them."

The lamb came out alive. Dag laid it on a bed of clipped wool, and put a few drops of dopram on its tongue to stimulate the breathing centre of its brain. I held the womb for Dag as he stitched it. With two incisions to close, and membranes that had become friable and easily torn after such a long labour, it was a difficult job.

"The lamb will be okay, but there's a chance the ewe might not make it," Dag told Joe as he worked.

"Sure I know," he said resignedly. "And it will be me who is to blame, for I should have had her over to you long before now."

While I was making breakfast next morning, I looked out of the window to see a neighbour's dog nosing around the picnic table and eating up the remains of the previous night's operation.

"I wonder if that ewe is still alive," I questioned aloud.

"Probably not," said Dag.

"What will happen to her lamb if she dies?"

"Joe will try to get another ewe to adopt it. And if that doesn't work, he'll bottle-feed it."

"Like a baby? How sweet."

"Lambs raised that way turn out like pets. They're hilarious. They bond with whomever feeds them and they follow them around."

When I carried the teapot over to the table, he was looking quizzically at me.

"Hey, why don't we get a pet lamb?"

"What for?"

"It would be fun. There will be plenty of orphans for the taking soon; the farmers often don't want to go to the trouble of raising them. Maybe Joe Golden's got one for us already. There's a little haggard in the garden we could keep it in."

I considered the idea for a few moments, then shook my head.

"No. I don't want a lamb. What would I do with it?"

"It would be good company."

"It sounds like it would be a nuisance. And anyway, I'd get too attached, and then we'd leave and it would end up in someone's freezer."

"I'll give Joe a call," said Dag. "Just to find out about the ewe."

Joe Golden's ewe had survived, and her lamb was thriving. But the news from the East End Bar wasn't so good.

"How's the little guy making out?" Dag asked, when we called in there at lunchtime.

"He's dead," said John bluntly.

Dag's face fell.

"We got so busy in here, we forget all about him," admitted Noreen, "and his temperature went up to a hundred and five."

"Jesus, you practically roasted the little bastard," said Dag.

"But he was alright still," she insisted. "After we closed the bar we took him back to his mother, and before long he was doing grand, feeding away. Then when John checked this morning, he found him squashed."

"*Squashed*?" we chorused.

"She must have forgotten he was there; she turned over in her sleep and lay on top of him."

I sat in silence, feeling stricken with guilt that I hadn't taken the lamb when John had offered it to me. But Dag just shrugged in resignation.

"And after all that effort. Ah well, you can't win them all."

✤

CHAPTER EIGHT

Government regulations demanded that every herd of cows in Ireland, no matter how small, had to be tested annually for tuberculosis. It was routine, monotonous work, and the part of Dag's job that he liked least. After injecting each cow on a farm with a shot of tuberculin, he returned two days later to check for any reactions. A slight swelling called for a retest; a significant swelling indicated the animal had tuberculosis and therefore, according to regulations, had to be slaughtered.

"Sometimes it's heartbreaking," he told me over breakfast one morning. "I've got to check old Paudie Falvey's cows first thing today. He's only got a few and he knows them all by name, so I dread any of them being positive."

He was testing all morning on several farms, and had asked me to come along to help. All I had to do, he assured me, was to fill in a record book as he called out the tag number of each cow and the size of the lumps on their necks where he had injected the tuberculin. It sounded straightforward, so I was surprised when he suggested we should stop on our way through Cahersiveen to buy me some protective clothing.

"What kind of clothing?" I asked.

"The sort of stuff that I wear. You can get pretty dirty in farmyards, and you never know what other calls I might get during the day."

I stirred my tea for a minute, thinking of Dag's rubber overtrousers and jackets, and how he scrubbed them down with a stiff brush and a bucket of water after mucky examinations or bloody operations. Dressing like he did, I suspected, might take me deeper into this veterinary business than I cared to go.

"I don't want any protective clothing," I said firmly. "My waxed jacket will do fine."

Over his teacup, he flashed me a bemused look.

"Suit yourself," he said.

In the car, I looked at the list of Dag's calls that morning.

"Paudie Falvey, Fasagh.

John Joe O'Conner, Eanach.

Bridie Flathery, Letterbrick.

Pat Golden, Gurteen."

The small farms scattered over the peninsula were identified by their owners' name and the townland they were situated in, and this information, when added to "County Kerry, Ireland," constituted internationally acceptable mailing addresses. Ireland is divided up into the four old Gaelic provinces of Ulster, Munster, Connaught and Leinster. These are subdivided into thirty-two counties, into baronies and parishes and finally into the townlands, sixty thousand of them in all, that constitute the smallest official land units. Each townland covers somewhere between fifty and five hundred acres and encompasses several farms whose original owners were related to each other. The Irish names of these townlands date back centuries and usually reflect a feature of the surrounding topography, the animal or plant life, or some man-made addition to the natural landscape. Letterbrick translates to Badger Hillside, Eanach to Watery Place, Gurteen to Little Tilled Field and Fasagh, where we were now headed, to Wild, Uncultivated Place.

All the townlands were shown on our 1:50,000 *Ordnance Survey* map, and to find them was straightforward enough, but locating each individual farm within them was another matter altogether.

"It's easy enough to get to Paudie's," Frank O'Leary had said, when we'd stopped off in the surgery. "After you leave the main road, follow along the lane through the bog until you reach a T-junction, turn right, carry on along the bog road that runs down to the sea and take the next track on the left. The house is away up behind a few trees. You can't miss it."

We drove for miles, past lonely fields where sheep sat on rocks placidly chewing their cud, and into an area of bogland striped with long brown furrows, the scars left by mechanized turf cutters. There were no houses in sight, yet a blue and white sign at the side of the road announced we had just entered a "Community Alert Area."

"I think we're lost," I said.

"According to Frank O'Leary," Dag told me, "just when you think you're lost you should keep going, because that's when you're bound to find your way."

This logic obviously worked in Ireland, for presently the trees came into view. We approached the farm along a track riddled with so many potholes that we were forced to drive through them, wincing each time the bottom of our car scraped against the ground. A black and white sheepdog dashed out from behind a wall and raced alongside us, barking furiously and snapping at the wheels. We parked in a muddy yard, between a two-storey house with smoke curling from its chimney and a few low stone sheds with rusty tin roofs. Six or seven scrawny cats skittered fearfully from sight when we stepped out of the car, but the sheepdog ran joyfully towards us, jumping up at me and covering my jeans with muddy pawprints.

"Go to bed!" came a voice from the direction of the house. "Go to BED!"

The dog dropped to the ground and snaked away, casting furtive glances at the small man limping across the yard. Paudie Falvey scrutinized me through greasy black-framed spectacles.

"Christ, that dog has you destroyed. But it's not often we see a woman here and your bright colours have him excited."

A grubby shirt collar stuck up above the neck of his thin sweater, and wide braces held up a pair of woollen trousers.

"Now, sir." He turned to Dag. "You've come again for the testing. I have the cows all ready for you."

The shed was about thirty feet by ten, with a low doorway and a small casement window. Its walls were of drystone construction, large rocks carefully laid one on top of another. Stonecrop and pennywort grew from between the cracks. Paudie pushed open the door and flicked on a switch, illuminating a single bulb hanging from a rafter. There was one room inside. Five cows and a calf were tethered along the opposite wall. The floor had been recently swept, and dirty straw was heaped in an old inglenook at the far end of the room. Paudie used this shed to house his animals over the winter, he told us, but until he was a young man it was his family home.

"There would be seven of us kids knocking about in here, and my mother boiling the spuds over the open fire. In 1929 my father built the new house, and I'm in it since. I never left the ashes, you might say. I looked about for a wife, but most of the girls went away to the city, and those that stayed had no interest in the farming life. So I'm here alone."

Dag was standing alongside a heavily pregnant, brown and white cow. She was crossly shaking her head, making it hard for him to read her tag.

"Agnes there, she's a grandmother," said Paudie. "And here's her daughter Mona next to her and her new son Fintan. Kitty, Roisin and Mary are cousins of sorts to Mona."

"OK, Agnes." Dag grabbed her by the nostrils and twisted her head to one side to restrain her. "We'll have to do it this way."

I stood close by, my pen poised over the open book.

"Watch the plops, missus," Paudie warned me. "These cows always make their plops as soon as the vet comes. It must be his smell."

"HUV, 875, 032," Dag read from the cow's tag.

I was running my pencil down the page in search of this number, when from the corner of my eye, I noticed Kitty lifting her tail. As a brown stream began issuing from beneath it, I took a couple of steps backwards, promptly losing my place in the book.

"Nine at the top, eight at the bottom," called Dag, reading from the calipers he had used to measure her skin. "Okay, Maria?"

The brown stream hit the concrete floor with such force that it splattered my boots, my jeans, my jacket and the testing book.

"Ah, Christ, the plops got you!" cried Paudie in dismay. "Watch out, now, missus, there's more on the way."

Dag had already moved on to Mona.

"HAN, 67401, 3. Twelve at the top, nine at the bottom. Have you got that, Maria?"

"Not exactly," I said lamely. "What was the first one again?"

Four tests later, I was liberally covered with dung and Roisin had tested inconclusively. Dag broke the news to Paudie while we all stood in a stream outside the shed, washing off our boots.

"I'm afraid you'll have to separate her from the rest of the herd until she's retested, Paudie."

"Sure, that's the way it goes, and I don't blame you, for you're only doing your job."

Paudie looked up from rubbing the soles of his boots in the gravel bed of the stream, and regarded me with pity. "Isn't it a queer thing now, that if there are city people about, it's always them the cows get?"

"Don't worry about the shit, it dries quickly," said Dag, as we drove towards John Joe Daly's farm. "But you've got to keep up with me while I'm reading tests; sometimes we have at least fifty cows at a time and it gets pretty hectic."

Soon we were standing inside another old stone shed. It was dim and stuffy, and thick skeins of cobwebs hung from the wooden rafters. Chickens scratched about at the far end, and a sheep lay in a wooden pen with its legs tucked out of sight. When the testing work was finished, John Joe asked for advice on a cow that was limping badly.

"There's a good chance she's got an abscess in the hoof," said Dag. "We'll have to hoist it up so I can have a look. Do you have a crush, John Joe?"

Over the past decade, most farmers in Ireland had built narrow corrals of bars and gates alongside their sheds. The advent of these crushes had been a boon for vets, as animals could now be more easily and effectively restrained for examination and treatment. Unfortunately, however, John Joe still hadn't got round to installing one.

"My neighbour put one in, and it cost him several hundred pounds," he said grumpily. "I can do without one for that money."

"Do you have a rope?" Dag asked him.

"I can find one of those for you, sure enough."

Dag tied a loop in one end of the rope and slipped it around the cow's lame fetlock. He threw the other end over a rafter, pulled it to lift the leg backwards, wrapped the rope once more around the leg and gave it to John Joe to hold. It was the best he could do in the circumstances, but it wasn't good enough for this cow. As soon as Dag touched her sore hoof, she tried to kick back with it. On her other three feet, she banged about in the stall.

"Can you go to the far side of the stall and hold her nose, Maria?" asked Dag.

"Me?" My eyes widened in disbelief.

"Yes. Or should I ask that sheep over there to do it?"

"I'm not putting my fingers up her nostrils!" I protested.

"You don't have to. You'll find some nose tongs in the back of the car."

The tongs were made of rounded steel and shaped like an hourglass. Dag slipped them inside the cow's nostrils, clamped them shut and showed me how to hold the handles.

"Keep her head up and hang on tight."

She was fairly relaxed while Dag scrubbed her hoof clean with a stiff brush, and only jerked her head a little when he worked a length of baling twine between the two cloves, pulling it to and fro like dental floss. He sniffed the twine to check for foot rot, then began paring the hoof to see if he could find an abscess. The cow didn't take happily to his paring knife. She groaned, drooled, twisted her head and let fly with her hoof. Each time she kicked, Dag jumped out of the way.

"I think I've found something," he called. "Put your weight into it, Maria!"

I clamped hard on the tongs and braced my feet against the bottom of the wooden stall, leaning away from the cow.

"Sorry girl," I muttered, but the apology wasn't enough. She stared wildly at me, showing the whites of her eyes. She snorted, blowing big bubbles of snot that broke over my hands and the ends of my sleeves. We strained against each other in a battle of will and strength that she was steadily winning; inch by inch, she dragged my arms over the top edge of the stall.

"Not long now, Maria," called Dag encouragingly.

My arms ached and my hands were wet, sticky and beginning to cramp. I was about to give in when Dag at last reached the abscess.

"Got it! OK, you can let her go."

The cow and I parted from each other with mutual relief. When I heard Dag say, "You'll start to feel better now, girl," I wasn't sure which of us he was talking to.

During the afternoon, Dag's work was fairly routine—more testing, a cow with milk fever, some calves with coughs. Around five o'clock we pulled up outside a small petrol station and corner shop on the main road, a few miles south of Cahersiveen. Evening had drawn in, fields and stone walls lay in shadow and the mountains were dark lines etched against the sky. Inside the shop, however, fluorescent lights burned so brightly that we blinked against them.

"Isn't it a lovely night?" the woman behind the counter greeted us. "It's grand weather altogether."

Dag introduced himself as the new vet and asked if he could phone the surgery.

"Dial away," she told him, indicating a white telephone next to a display of chocolate bars.

While Dag talked to Ann, I wandered around the small shop, filling a wire shopping basket with milk, bread, biscuits and a newspaper.

"Bernard O'Shea, Aghort? Yes, I know where he is," I heard Dag say. "I'll be there as soon as I can. Can you phone him back and tell him to round up a couple of strong men? And I'll need lots of hot water, ropes, some clean towels and an empty whiskey bottle."

I wasn't the only one listening in.

"What manner of a problem has Bernard O'Shea?" the shopkeeper asked Dag, when he replaced the receiver.

"One of his cows has a prolapsed uterus."

"She's put out her vessel, now, has she? God save and preserve us all. Tell Bernard you were just in Eileen's shop, and that I'm saying a prayer for his cow." As we drove away, I questioned Dag as to why he needed some strong men for this job.

"The cow has to be lying down for me to get her uterus back in place. If she's standing up we'll have to wrestle her to the ground and into position."

"And what's the whiskey bottle for?"

We were stuck behind a tractor—Dag was craning his neck to watch for the lights of oncoming cars.

"You'll see," he said, accelerating sharply to overtake. "I'm glad you're along, because I'll probably need your help."

I didn't like the sound of this. For the rest of the journey I was very quiet, picking abstractedly at the patches of dried dung on my jacket. O'Shea's farm was two miles on the far side of the town. A car was parked in darkness by a large, corrugated iron shed. When we pulled up, three men in overalls and rubber boots appeared, wielding flashlights.

"You were quick," one of them said. "We have everything you asked for and more."

Inside the shed were buckets, towels, sheets, ropes and several milk churns filled with water. Along the far wall, in the concrete aisle between two rows of slatted pens, a cow lay sprawled on her side, next to a newly born calf. The cow's rear end was an alarming mess. Her uterus, a fleshy sack covered with ribbons of pink, purple and white afterbirth, was hanging out of her and lay on the floor among pools of blood.

"I pulled the calf myself," said Bernard worriedly. "It came with no trouble, but the next time I looked this had happened."

There was no electric light in the shed, and the men's flashlights were insufficient for Dag to work by. Bernard's cousin Dermot pulled opened the high double doors and Brendan, his neighbour, drove his car right inside and turned the headlamps to full beam.

"Thank goodness she's already down and we don't have to wrestle with her," said Dag, as he changed into a calving gown. "She's in shock, though, so we have to work quickly."

He hurried about the shed, getting everything organized. A rope halter was slipped over the cow's head and attached to a ring on the end wall. More ropes went around each of her back fetlocks. While Dag and Brendan heaved the cow onto her stomach, the other men pulled on the ropes and secured them to the metal bars of the pens, so that she lay frog-like with her legs stretched out behind her.

"We're just about ready to go," Dag told the men, as he gave the cow an epidural injection into the base of her tail. "If she tries to stand up, pull hard on the ropes."

I leaned against one of the pens, enjoying the atmosphere of drama and expectancy. The men's figures cast long shadows across the smooth concrete. Hot water steamed from buckets, escaping the bright pools of light made by the car's headlamps and rising into the darkness among the rafters above. A wind had blown up, and one of the metal doors was banging about against the wall.

Dag was scrubbing his hands and arms; he glanced at me over his shoulder.

"Maria. I want you to sit on the cow."

For the second time that day, I stared at him in disbelief.

"Sit on her," I repeated stupidly.

"Yes, do you mind? I'll need everyone else on the ropes. Straddle her so you're facing her back end, then grab her tail."

As I hesitated, all eyes turned on me. Dermot stepped forward with a towel and laid it on the cow's back.

"There, that'll help keep you tidy," he said kindly.

Tentatively, I swung one leg over the cow and eased myself onto her backbone, resting a hand either side of it for balance. Beneath me, her rib cage rose and fell as she sighed deeply.

"Grab her tail near the base with both hands and hold it up and to one side," instructed Dag, who was now squatting at her rear end. "That will help keep the muck off the uterus."

The tail was thick, and more solid than I'd expected. Dung caked its underside; the rest was slick with fresh blood and slime. Grimly, I hung onto it, watching Dag pull bits of afterbirth from the uterus. This was a big, flaccid organ, deep pink in colour and covered with knobbles the size of golf balls. Gently, he lifted it onto the calving gown stretched between his knees, and washed it with his hands while Bernard slowly poured water from a bucket. Using his fists, he began pushing the uterus back inside the cow's body. Its flaccidity made this a slow procedure, for as soon as he got one part in, another part popped out.

"Keep hanging on to the tail, Maria," he reminded me.

"Is this the first time you've had this experience, Marie?" asked Bernard. "It's my first time, too. Christ, it's amazing what can be done."

When at last the uterus was back inside the cow, she began to strain as if consciously trying to rid herself of it again. Her ribs heaved violently, rocking me about as if I was astride a racing camel. To brace myself, I stretched one leg to the ground, but my boot landed on some of the afterbirth, slipped from under me, and I began to fall. Brendan quickly came to the rescue, grabbing my arm and pulling me upright. The towel, rucked up beneath me, had offered little in the way of protection, and my jeans were thickly covered with brown hair.

"There's not many women would do this," said Bernard admiringly. "You'd make a great farmer's wife, by God you would. If you're ever in need a new husband, remember there's plenty to be had around here."

Dag's arms were deep inside the cow as he tried to keep the uterus in place.

"Did you bring that whiskey bottle?" he asked Brendan. "Give it to me, would you?"

"Surely you're not . . . ?" My voice trailed off as Brendan handed him the bottle.

"It might look weird," Dag said, shoving it end first into the cow, "but it works."

"And which kind of whiskey do you find works the best?" joked Brendan. "Powers or Paddy's?"

The bottle came out and was replaced by a large funnel. Dag poured a whole bucketful of water through it, hoping to keep the uterus in place until it had contracted to normal size.

"It's injection time now, Maria," he warned. "Hold on tight."

The instant she felt the needle in her neck, the cow tried to struggle to her feet. Bernard took her head, Dermot and Brendan grabbed the ropes and I grappled with her tail, squeezing her sides with my legs while she bucked beneath me.

"Whoa, there, cowboy!" called Dag, mirthfully.

"Your wife needs more weight on her for this job," chimed in Bernard. "You'd better feed her up with stout and spuds."

Dag waited for the cow to calm, then began sewing up her vulva to prevent another prolapse. The suture material was like twine, and each time he jabbed the foot-long needle into the flabby flesh I braced myself for another ride, but thanks to the epidural the cow didn't feel a thing. He completed the stitching with a bow tie that Brendan could easily remove. At last I was able to dismount. I felt terrible: my legs were trembling, my back was stiff and my hands ached. The cow, on the other hand, seemed fine. Within minutes she was on her feet, happily licking her calf.

"Now, sir, I think it's your wife who needs some help next," suggested Brendan. "Take her to the pub and buy her a glass or two of stout. There's nothing like it for bringing the strength back."

On our way through Cahersiveen, we stopped off at O'Donaghue's, which was a pub, estate agency and haberdashery. In one of its front windows, rubber boots, rainjackets and socks were on display. In the other, notices in spidery handwriting about land and houses for sale were pinned to a board. Between them was a narrow red door that led into a dimly lit room. Its low ceiling was panelled in white-painted wood yellowed by smoke. On the small bar, the electric signs on two beer pumps glowed in the gloom. Propped on a shelf behind them, between the spirit optics and a mirror with Dunville's Whiskey inscribed in gold lettering across the glass, a red vigil lamp burned beneath a large, framed painting of the Sacred Heart of Jesus.

Across the room was the haberdashery. Many shoeboxes and plastic-wrapped clothes spilled from shelves reaching from floor to ceiling. Separating the two areas was a low counter topped with red formica. In front of this, an elderly man sat on a bench, holding an empty pint glass.

"Hello, Michael," Dag greeted him. "How are you this evening?"

We had called into O'Donaghue's three times before. Michael had always been in residence on the bench, yet he never appeared to remember us.

"I'm still alive and afraid to die," he said, sucking in his cheeks. "Just like yourselves, I suppose."

There was no one behind the bar, but from the back kitchen came the rattle of pots and pans.

"Mary!" Michael called in a quavering voice. "Come in here. There's people looking for you."

Mary bustled into the room, wiping her hands on an apron. She was a bird-like woman, with a long nose, darting eyes and metallic red hair held back from her face with a large, ornate pin. Catching sight of me, she stopped and stared in horror.

"What in God's name has happened to you, girl?"

"I've been out helping Dag all day."

"And which of you is it that's been doing the work? Himself there is all fine and clean, while you're completely destroyed!"

"I suggested she buy some protective clothing this morning, Mary," Dag explained defensively, "but she wouldn't listen."

"Well, I have all you need and more, girl," Mary told me. "But if you want it tonight you'll have to be quick, for a neighbour of mine has died and they're soon to remove his body to the church. What size are you?"

She came round the bar and looked me up and down.

"God save you, you're no size at all. How well you've kept your figure. How many children have you? None? Ah, well, it's easy then for you to stay so slim, it's the childbirth that ruins you."

Behind us, Michael had been slowly easing himself off the bench. He took two unsteady steps towards the door.

"I'll be off to the church now, Mary."

"You're in no state to walk, Michael," said Mary. "Wait there and I'll take you. I won't be five minutes, now."

"Ah, there's no need, Mary."

"Sit yourself down again, Michael. It's no trouble at all."

"Ah well, that's very kind of you, Mary." He turned back towards the bench. "I'll have another drink while I'm waiting."

Though Mary pursed her lips disapprovingly, she went back behind the bar to one of the pumps.

"You two look perished with the cold," she observed, as she waited for Michael's stout to settle. "Won't you have a toddy each?"

While we sipped hot whiskeys, Mary rummaged around in the heaps of merchandise and found the jacket and over-trousers I needed. Then she took off her apron, donned a coat and hat, and began dropping hints that we should all drink up quickly.

"It would be terrible to miss the removal, now, Michael. And you two must be mad to get home, after the long hard day you've had."

Soon she had ushered us all through the door and was locking it behind her.

"Thanks a million times for coming in," she said effusively, as she steered Michael towards her car. "I'll be open tomorrow after the Requiem Mass, so I'll see you again soon, please God!"

❖

CHAPTER NINE

I was in no hurry to climb onto a cow's back again, so the following morning I let Dag go off to work alone. While I was tidying up our living room, I kept glancing out of the window at Knocknadobar Mountain, considering the fact that although we had lived here for almost three weeks, I'd yet to set foot on its slopes. At ten o'clock I listened to the radio weather report. A fine day was forecast, with only the occasional shower. I pulled on boots and a sweater, wrapped my newly purchased jacket around my waist and set off.

In the fields behind our cottage, the ground began to slope towards the mountain. Once I had scrambled over a couple of drystone walls and a stile, I was already climbing steeply. Startlingly lush, green moss grew in soft, waterlogged places, where I hopped between rocks to avoid sinking into the bog. Rust-red bracken lay dried and broken on earth that was firm and springy. Silver-grey heather crackled as I waded through it. Curlews with grey bodies and long curved beaks fluttered up from hiding places in the furze and skimmed away close to the ground, piping their protest. On the higher slopes, I heard the deep and sonorous croaking of ravens, and red-billed choughs treated me to their stunning acrobatic displays, turning over on their backs as they soared with updraughts of air from the cliffs.

I was following a stream that had carved a gully though the Old Red Sandstone of the mountain. Rocks and boulders were heaped along its bed, and the water tumbled and twisted through them, making urgent, rushing sounds. Blackfaced mountain sheep with curling horns looked up from grazing as I passed by, staring at me fixedly for a few moments before turning to run away. Their long, shaggy fleece was daubed with big, bright splashes of blue, orange or red paint, the farmers' method of identifying one flock from another in these wide open spaces.

Twenty minutes of brisk walking brought me to a place where the stream descended a small bluff to form a round, deep pool. I stopped here for a short break. High above me, the topmost ridge of the mountain stretched darkly against the sky. Once beyond the bluff, I anticipated a long steep haul towards the summit, but when I set off again my feet headed unexpectedly downwards, into a hidden bowl with a flat, grassy floor. Protected from the wind, this was a warm, still place, with no view of the ocean or the valley, only heather-clad slopes all around and sky and clouds above. My perspective was skewed here: the sheep looked too small, until I realized they were actually quite far away, and the stone ruins I set off towards turned out to be much closer than I'd estimated. These ruins in themselves were puzzling; with their round design and corbelled stones, they looked like "beehive huts" of early Christian monks, yet my *Ordnance Survey* map showed no such sites on this side of Knocknadobar Mountain.

My feet crunched over heather and rocks as I walked towards the huts. The stillness was unnerving. In this strangely silent amphitheatre I felt utterly cut off from the outside world. A cloud passed across the sun; I glanced up to see mist creeping purposefully over the mountain ridge and down the steep slopes towards me. My first impulse was to flee, but I forced myself to carry on.

"There's no one here!" I yelled out, startling a nearby ewe. "There's nothing to be afraid of!"

Only one of the huts was still intact. It was set apart from the others, higher up and built against the steep slope. Flat stones were piled on top of each other, to a height of about four feet. There was a low doorway, only big enough to crawl through. Dropping to my knees, I peered into the dark interior. A pair of eyes met mine. Lying on the floor of the hut, its head facing the opening, was a dead sheep. A few flies buzzed around its face. I backed away, turned and then ran, imagining the lifeless, glazed eyes following my retreat.

As I descended Knocknadobar, the wind picked up and squalls began moving from the west. A fluid sky cast shifting pools of light onto the ocean. Behind transparent curtains of rain, the slopes of Dingle Peninsula and the Great Blasket Islands shone in bright sunlight. After one squall had passed, a full rainbow exploded into life on the slopes beneath me, its spectrum of colours growing more intense and glowing by the second, until more rain moved through, washing it away.

Halfway down, I cut past the ruins of two old stone houses. Although marked on my map as farms, they were obviously long abandoned, with caved-in roofs and sheep grazing among the rubble of their small rooms. In the fields in front of them, even-spaced ridges were clearly visible beneath a covering of rushes and bracken. These were the remains of "lazy beds," dug long ago for growing potatoes. Using a spade called a *loy*, the farmer sliced through the sods, inverted them and piled more soil on top, creating drainage channels and raising the seedbed above surface water. These beds, and the potato's adaptability to a wet climate and poor acidic soil, meant that marginal land was able to be inhabited during the population boom of the early nineteenth century. The people who lived on this high, windswept hillside found all the materials for building a house close by: stones and mud for walls, shipwrecked timber for rafters, grass and reeds for thatch. They dug turf in the Fertha Valley and transported it up the mountainside in creels on the back of a donkey. And in their lazy beds they grew enough potatoes to keep their children alive.

As I walked across the hard ridges of one of the fields, I imagined a woman digging here, heaping up fresh sods in preparation for planting potatoes on a fine day in early March, a century and a half ago. Maybe she paused from her work for a moment; like me, she pushed a strand of hair from her face as she watched the wind stir the deep blue waters of Dingle Bay. Her life was desperately hard, a meagre, tenuous existence in this unforgiving place. But it became immeasurably harder when the potato blight struck, and her crop failed again and again. During the Great Hunger of the 1840s, famine, disease epidemics and mass starvation left at least a million people dead in Ireland, and drove a million more away. As I hiked down the mountain, I wondered what had happened to my imaginary woman. And I thought of all the other old lazy beds, pleating the hillsides and bog land all across the Iveragh Peninsula. When the light was clear, they were visible for miles, standing out like ghosts of terrible times long gone.

Just below a small copse of trees, three white moorland ponies with long, windblown manes were standing in the furze and heather.

"Come on lads!"

A bandy-legged man was slowly climbing the slope towards the ponies. He carried a sack over one shoulder. His trousers were patched and one pocket of his tweed jacket was ripped off, revealing the lining. Hearing his call, the ponies whinnied and shook their heads, then began picking their way to him across the rough ground. As they gathered around him, he eased the sack from his shoulder, working slowly at the knot in its neck.

I stood by the trees. The bare branches made filigree patterns against the sky, and coal-back jackdaws hopped among them, regarding me with steely eyes. I was sure the old man had seen me, but was choosing to pay me no heed. Only when he had emptied a pile of horse feed onto the ground, and the ponies were happily munching, did he glance in my direction. Beneath a flat cap, his face was weather-dark and mapped with deep wrinkles.

"'Tis a fine day again," he said. "But they say storms are due."

He spoke slowly and deliberately—his thick bottom lip hung open and trembled during the long dramatic pauses between his sentences.

"I haven't seen you on my land before. Are you a stranger?"

It hadn't occurred to me that I might be trespassing.

"I'm sorry," I said, stepping towards him. "I'm the wife of the new vet. I was just out for a walk."

"And where are you living?"

I pointed down to our cottage.

"I knew the man who lived there once. He was a fisherman and a turf cutter. He had no land, only that house. It was a hard life he had."

From his trouser pocket he took a packet of Sweet Afton cigarettes and a box of matches. His knuckles were badly swollen with arthritis, and the ends of his fingers were stained a deep, nicotine brown. He fumbled with the matches, lit a cigarette and inhaled deeply.

"I heard them tell about your husband. O'Leary has a new man from Canada, they said. Canada must be a fine country."

"It is."

A thrush sang insistently from among the trees; I heard cows lowing in the distance. Next to us, the ponies ate contentedly, their soft lips puckering around the nuts.

"I've had these ponies for well on twenty years," he said at length, turning his blue, rheumy eyes on me. "Last year, some tinkers stole the old one."

I remembered Mary Coffey's comments about tinkers, and hoped he wouldn't ask my name.

"The *gardaí* found the man who took her. The judge gave him four months in prison."

"Four months!" I said. "That seems a harsh sentence."

In the long pause that followed, ash fell from the end of his cigarette.

"Horse stealing is a serious thing. Horses are important to a man."

He folded the empty sack and tucked it under one arm.

"Is it up the mountain you've been?"

I told him about finding the round huts in the hidden bowl, and the ruins of the old cottages.

"Those round huts were for booleying. The people took their cows up to that place in the summer to feed them on the good pasture there. They made butter, and they carried it down the mountain on their backs to sell it."

"And the cottages? Who lived there?"

He flicked away the cigarette end and reached into his pocket again for the packet.

"I heard my father say that he heard his father before him talk of some of the people who lived there. They were O'Conners, as I recall. They had animals. Cattle and sheep and a donkey. Their children used to walk to the school that was down where the turf-burning station is now. They left for America, a hundred years ago or more. They weren't heard from again."

He paused to light the cigarette. When he spoke, smoke flowed out with his words.

"I heard my father tell of another man. He lived around the mountain, in a flat place along the cliffs. Did you walk there?"

I shook my head.

"Ah, it's a good step. That man, he was evicted from his land on the Dingle. He came to that place on the mountain and lived there all alone. Every Saturday he walked to Cahersiveen for Confession. He walked there again on Sunday for Mass. He had a cow and he kept geese. One day the geese flew away. It was a sign. The geese left and he left after them. He wasn't seen again."

"What happened to the cow?"

The old man pondered this question.

"That I don't know. If she was a good cow, I'd say he took her with him. There would be no sense in leaving behind a good cow."

The ponies had finished the feed and were gathered around him, nuzzling at the sack under his arm.

"I'll take my leave of you now. I have other animals to see to. I'd say you'll be rambling here again."

"Maybe I'll bring some carrots for the ponies. Would they take them from me?"

"Indeed they would. I'd be glad for anything you give them, for 'tis a hungry time of year."

He began walking away with the ponies ambling along beside him. Then he stopped, turned around and pointed up the mountain in the direction of the stone cottages.

"They say a German man wants to put a road up there. He'll repair the houses, they say, and rent them to tourists in the summer. But I've seen many a summer when the mist never rises from above that place. Maybe no one has told the German that. And I'm not about to. Goodbye now."

✤

CHAPTER TEN

Early next morning, we woke to shouts and whistles drifting down from Knocknadobar. High on its slopes, shepherds and their dogs were rounding up the pregnant ewes and moving them down towards the valley. Patches of white streamed in a fluid motion across the dark heather and bracken, disintegrating at the edges from time to time as errant sheep broke away. Well-trained dogs quickly corralled the flocks, moving fast and low as they guided them steadily downhill.

Just after eleven, I was hanging out washing in the garden when our neighbour Patrick walked by, carrying a heavy sack. He was on his way to feed the pregnant ewes he had recently brought down from the mountain. During a session in the East End Bar, Ted Donnelly had told me that ewes used to come down in the spring from Knocknadobar fattened up and in good shape for lambing. But now, with close to five thousand sheep grazing on the mountain, there was little left for them to eat and farmers had to buy expensive feed to get them strong enough for lambing. As usual, Patrick just raised his stick and nodded to me shyly, then carried on without exchanging a word.

Later in the day, Dag arrived home with a roll of fox wire, and set about making a roof and a door on the haggard, the small stone enclosure in our garden. He begged some hay from Patrick, and spread it over the floor of the haggard, creating a comfortable, predator-proof home for any young animal.

According to Dag, a lamb was soon to enter our lives. He said he'd prefer a mountain ewe, but would take a Suffolk if it were offered. I had no preference, and very little enthusiasm. I was sure our neighbours would think me ridiculous and frivolous, having a lamb as a pet. And the idea of mothering anything, least of all a helpless baby sheep, left me somewhat perplexed.

The following night Dag was on call, so I prepared a hearty stew that could simmer in the oven until he had time to eat. Its comforting aroma filled the cottage as I waited for him to come home. In the living room a cozy fire burned, obligingly sending most of its smoke up the chimney. It was close to seven-thirty when Dag hurried through the door.

"Any calls?"

"No," I told him. "Let's have dinner before you get one."

"We need to run down to Ballinskelligs first. I met John Joe O'Sullivan earlier on. He told me he's got an orphan ewe lamb, a Suffolk Cheviot cross, and he wants to know if we'll take her. I said that if I was free we'd meet him at eight in Rosie's Bar."

"You agreed to take the lamb already?" I said in alarm.

"Not exactly. Only if you like her. I'll turn on the telephone answering machine and we'll go."

Rosie's Bar was a twenty-minute drive away. We arrived there before John Joe, and had a drink while we waited for him. I asked Roisin Sigerson, John Joe's wife and the owner of the pub, how an Irish woman had ended up with such a Nordic surname.

"The Sigersons have been in Ballinskelligs for generations," she told me, as she pulled our pints of Guinness. "They once owned all the land around here. Have you not heard of Sigerson Clifford, the poet? He was my father's second cousin."

While she waited for the stout to settle, she darted into a back room and returned with a scrapbook filled with family history stretching back over three hundred years. The story began at the end of the sixteenth century, when the area now known as Kerry was practically an independent state. It was under the rule of the rebellious Desmonds, an Anglo-Norman family who refused to bow to the changes of the Reformation. Queen Elizabeth I of England decided to crush the Desmonds; she confiscated their estates and granted them to English colonizers, known as "planters." Richard Harding, a merchant from Bristol, became the beneficiary of the Ballinskelligs lands. In turn, he bequeathed them to Christopher Sigerson, a British army officer with a Nordic background who was engaged to his daughter Dora. Sadly, before her wedding day Dora succumbed to illness and died. Christopher only learned of the tragedy as he was riding towards the Harding family home to visit Dora and encountered her funeral procession. Though Robert Harding had lost his daughter, he honoured his agreement with Christopher, who became lord of the manor in Ballinskelligs in 1626. He went on to marry and have children. Though he was never to know it, he played an important part in the course of Irish history, in time becoming the great-great-great-grandfather of the famous Daniel "The Liberator" O'Connell, who in 1829 secured emancipation for the Catholics of Ireland.

"There's only my sister and myself left of the Sigersons now," said Rosie, "so the name could die out soon."

When John Joe arrived he was in a great hurry, anxious to return to his farm and check on some gaining ewes. The lamb was in the boot of his car, inside a cardboard box tied shut with twine. She was the weaker of a set of couplets, he told us. The mother had rejected her at birth, and though he'd tried to foster her with other ewes, they'd shown no interest. She was four days old, she was bottle feeding, and she was scouring. No, he wouldn't take any payment, she was ours, and good luck.

With that, John Joe got into his car and drove away, leaving Dag standing in the road holding the box.

We put the box on the back seat. Apart from a few shuffles, there was no noise and hardly any movement from inside it, but as we drove home the car filled with the smells of wet wool and damp earth. Dag carried the box into the cottage. He laid it on the hearth, cut through the twine and opened the lid. A tiny head with hugely oversized ears popped out, wobbling about on a comically skinny neck. The lamb's eyes were small and dark, and when her mouth opened, a grey tongue appeared, trembling on the bottom lip.

"MEH!" she bleated, in a startlingly loud voice. "MEH!"

In a scramble of muddy hooves, she leapt out of the box and onto the hearth. She had tightly curled fleece, dirty white in colour, with splotches of dark brown. Around her neck, her skin was wrinkled into deep folds, as if she still had to grow into it. Her knees were big and knobby, and her gangly legs were disproportionate in size to her little body. Dag held the lamb under his arm while I spread newspapers all over the living room floor.

"She's been scouring, alright," he said, surveying the dried brown paste caked over her back end. "Here, hold her a minute while I get her feed from the car."

I struggled with the wriggling, complaining lamb until Dag returned with a bag of milk replacer and what looked like a baby's bottle. On seeing the bottle the lamb began bleating louder than ever. Her hooves clacked over the linoleum as she followed us into the kitchen and up to the sink.

"MEH, MEH, MEEEEH!" she yelled, as Dag whisked the powder into warm water and poured the mixture into the bottle.

"It should be blood temperature, just like for human babies." He squirted a little onto his wrist to test it. "Why don't you feed her, then she'll start bonding with you."

When I lowered the teat towards the lamb's mouth she butted against it, and the solution sprayed out over her nose. Holding her tight, I guided her mouth towards the bottle. After a couple of failed attempts she clamped onto it and sucked hungrily, her nose squashed up against the teat and her eyes glazed in concentration.

After the feed, I wiped splashes of milk off the lamb's nose and carried her to a chair by the fire. She promptly fell asleep in my arms, making soft grunting sounds as she breathed. I liked her smell; it reminded me of parched earth after rain. Opposite me, Dag was working his way through a bowl of stew. When he'd finished, he took the lamb so that I could eat. As I passed her across to him, she woke up and began wriggling, but after Dag scratched her head for a while her eyelids drooped and her body relaxed once more.

"Well, Maria," he said a little later. "What do you think of our lamb?"

Her large ears twitched as she dreamed.

"I'm still not sure this is a good idea," I said, suppressing a smile. "But we should think of a name for her."

I fancied something from Irish mythology. I suggested Cessair, Noah's granddaughter, who according to the *Book of Invasions* was banished from the ark, built her own ship to escape the Great Flood and ended up shipwrecked on Ballinskelligs Bay.

"Cessair sounds like an airline," commented Dag.

My next suggestion was Amergin, the bard to the Milesians when they landed in Ballinskelligs Bay after defeating the Tuatha De Danann. Setting foot on Irish soil, Amergin was so overcome by the beauty around him that he composed a poem then and there.

"I am an estuary into the sea," it began. "I am a wave of the ocean. I am the sound of the sea. I am as powerful as an ox. I am a hawk on a cliff. I am a dewdrop in the sun."

"That's nice," said Dag, "but we can't call her after a man. What about one of those women in Irish mythology?"

We ran through a few of them: Anu, Brigit, Dana, Niamh, Finola, Maeve. None seemed right.

"There should be some connection with Ballinskelligs," I insisted, "because that's where we got her."

Then I remembered Christopher Sigerson's intended bride, who had died so tragically young.

"We'll call her Dora," I said decisively.

"Dora?" Dag pulled a face. "That's a stupid name for an Irish lamb."

Before we could argue about it, the phone rang. It was an overwrought farmer asking for help with a calving.

"I've got to go," said Dag. "See you later."

I looked down at the lamb he had deposited in my arms. "But what about—?"

"You can put her inside the haggard for the night. There's lots of hay to keep her warm. Give her half a bottle of feed to settle her down first. The directions are on the packet. Bye!"

Still clutching Dora, I followed him to the door.

"Dag, how do I—"

"Blood temperature," he called as he left. "Don't forget."

His car was barely through the gate when the phone rang. I shut Dora into the kitchen, trying to screen out her bleats while I took down a message. When I joined her again she ran for my legs, pushing her nose against them while I wiped up the pool of urine and the tracks of muddy hoofprints she'd left across the floor. Scooping her under one arm, I wrapped her in a warm towel from the airing cupboard and laid her in the box by the fire. I dug the ends of my fingers into her tightly curled fleece, scratching her head until she fell asleep.

Five minutes later, the next round of phone calls started. Gerald O'Sullivan had several sheep walking in circles, Mike O'Donaghue's calf had eaten a length of baling twine, Deidre Baker's poodle had a fish hook in its nose, Paddy Riley had a cow calving down with two legs showing and the head back. Where was the vet, they all wanted to know, and how soon could he get out to help them?

Between calls, I sat and stared at the sleeping lamb. She had been lying in her own liquid scours, and patches of dried dung were caked on her snout and along her sides. I stroked her, thinking that in the morning I should clean her up, though I had no idea of how to go about it. Put her in the bath? Stand her in the sink? Neither seemed feasible. Then I started wondering about this bonding business, and what it would involve. I was dreading taking the poor little mite out into the haggard—a sure sign, I decided ruefully, that I had started to bond with her, never mind the other way round.

Around ten, I went into the kitchen to mix up her final feed. Just as I was testing it on my wrist, Dora woke up and began bleating at high pitch.

"It's alright, Dora," I called.

She made a mad dash towards the sound of my voice, her hooves skidding wildly across the kitchen floor and her rear end erupting once more. I was on my knees wiping up the mess, with Dora pushing her nose against me in search of a teat, when the phone began to ring yet again. I ran to answer it, forgetting to shut the kitchen door.

"I have a very sick cow," was all I heard, before Dora drowned out the voice at the other end with her bleating.

"Can you speak up?" I shouted.

"MY COW IS DOWN," repeated the farmer. "Is that a pet lamb you have there with you? Ah, Jesus, those things can drive you wild if you let them."

After I'd fed Dora, I took her outside. She lay quietly in my arms until we reached the haggard, but when I gently pushed her inside it and secured the wire door, she burst into terrified bleats. For a while I stood in the garden, helplessly listening to her. Then I forced myself back into the house. Her voice carried clearly up to our bedroom, where I lay with a pillow around my ears, stricken with guilt.

Dag came home four times in the night, only to find a farmer waiting for him or another call to attend to. Each time Dora heard his car, she began bleating at full volume. He finally returned around eight-thirty next morning, lay down on the bed beside me with all his clothes on, and fell fast asleep. I was exhausted, too, but the pitiful cries from the haggard brought me down to the kitchen. While I was blearily mixing up some feed, Mike O'Leary rang to ask how Dag's night had gone.

"Christ, he's done a marathon," he said, when I recounted the events of the past hours. "I'll cover him until mid-morning. Leave him where he is until then and make sure he has a good breakfast before he comes into the surgery. I hope you got some sleep last night, Maria."

"Not really. Our pet lamb kept me awake."

"A lamb?" cried Mike in horror. "Whatever possessed you to get one of those? You'll have no peace at all from now on!"

CHAPTER ELEVEN

When Dora saw me coming with her morning feed, she began frantically throwing herself against the fox wire, her wails reaching a new level of desperation. Once I'd let her out, however, she showed no interest in the bottle. Instead, she ran around me as I crouched on the damp grass, sniffing me and butting her nose against the crook of my knees. When I finally managed to push the teat into her mouth, she sucked hungrily, her sides visibly ballooning as the half pint of liquid went down. She seemed dazed after the feed, and made no protest when I put her back into the haggard and closed the door.

Before Dag went to work, we cleaned up Dora. I held her on the kitchen floor as he cut away the dirty, matted fleece from around her tail and rubbed her with a damp cloth. To warm her after the wash, we laid her in her box by the living room fire.

"She needs to be fed every four hours," said Dag. "But she'll remind you of that."

After he'd gone I did some laundry in the kitchen, peeking around the door from time to time to check on my sleeping lamb. Shortly before noon, she woke up. Her next feed wasn't due for an hour, so I decided to see what she'd make of a walk. When I called her, she jumped out of her box and followed me into the garden like a well-trained dog. A strong wind was blowing in from the sea, and massive cumulonimbus clouds were building up to the west. As we walked through the fields, Dora kept right on my heels, but when I stopped she circled me, curiously checking out her new surroundings. She stared at stones and sniffed at dried bracken and the tiny dog violets that had just begun to bloom. She put her face into a clump of furze, recoiling in shock when she felt the prickles on her nose. What intrigued her most, however, were the six brown hens scratching around in the grass outside Kathleen's house. Dora stood stock still, so utterly mesmerized by them that I was able to walk on alone. When at last she realized I'd deserted her, she raced to catch up, her front legs meeting the back ones in a tangle.

The front door of the house opened, and Kathleen appeared. It was the first time I'd seen her since our first meeting on the jetty.

"Is that your pet lamb?" she called. "Ah, she's lovely. We used to have pet lambs when we were kids, but they got to be an awful nuisance. They followed us to the school bus every morning and stood there screeching while we went up the steps. I wish my little lad was here to see this lamb. He's away with his father right now. Will you come again with her?"

On the beach, Dora left a set of neat little hoofprints across a stretch of wet sand. She sniffed at the long, ribbony strands of seaweed, then took a run at a pink boulder. Losing her grip, she skidded into a tide pool, where the purple, velvety anemones closed up tightly in defence. Deciding that she'd had enough adventures for the day, I called her and we headed back across the lane. We were just about to go through our gate when a car pulled up. A rangy, weather-browned man wound down the window.

"That's a fine lamb. Is she a pet? What breed is she?"

"Suffolk and Cheviot cross, I think," I said.

"That's not a cross you'd see much around here. It's all mountainy sheep in this valley. Where did you get her?"

"Ballinskelligs. From John Joe O'Sullivan."

"I know him. Aren't you the wife of the new Canadian vet? I saw you up the mountain yesterday. You had a good old chat with Dennis McCarthy."

"Do you live around here?" I asked.

He pushed his cap back from his forehead.

"Indeed I do. I'm Jer O'Donaghue, I'm a neighbour of yours and I have a hundred ewes on this mountain above us. What do you call this lamb?"

"Dora," I told him, feeling rather silly.

"Dora," he repeated seriously. "We had a pet lamb. A ram lamb, he was. We named him George. He was a fine big lamb. When the time came we put him out with the ewes. The very next day, we were in the house when we heard a clatter at the door, and when we opened it, didn't George come running in among us. Those ewes had terrified him, the poor man. So I sold him to a neighbour, and I hear he got the hang of things in time."

Piled up on the back seat of his car were several crab and lobster pots, made of brightly coloured plastic and netting.

"I only do a bit of fishing now," Jer told me. "There isn't much to catch in Dingle Bay these days. When I was a young man, rising up, I would fill my seine boat with fish several times of a spring morning."

He pointed to the long sleek boats lying upturned on the grass close by. They were seiners, he told me, first brought to Kerry in the seventeenth century by an Englishman named William Petty who set up a fish-curing station in Ballinskelligs Bay.

"You find them nowhere else in Ireland," he said, "only in this part of Kerry. They don't fish with them anymore. They use them for rowing races and regattas."

In his younger days, Jer worked on the seine boats. He was one of ten men on the oars. There was a spier, a captain and two men to cast the net, which was held on the surface with cork floats and weighted below with lead. They only fished on dark nights. The spier's job was to look out for the *Barr Iasc*, a silvery phosphorescence made by shoals of fish passing through the water. At his signal, the net men threw a rope attached to one end of the net to a smaller boat following in the seiner's wake. The two boats manoeuvred the net so that it encircled the shoal of fish, then pulled the rope to form a purse and entrap it. Millions of fish were caught like this. In the 1920s, Cahersiveen sent thirty thousand barrels of fish every year by train to Dublin, and by ship further afield. On a single day in September 1928, a local man witnessed fifty-two thousand mackerel being pulled aboard a seine boat.

I'd seen old photos of the harbour, displayed in a pub in town. They showed it bustling with people: barefoot women dressed in long black skirts and shawls, dousing the fish in boxes of salt while the men rowed out to sea for another catch.

"That's right," said John. "The place would be black with fishermen in the spring. They'd sit on the wall, saying the rosary before heading out. If the captain of the seine boat heard one of them whistling while they pulled in the nets, he'd be raging. Ah, but it didn't last. The fish went away. You only get the odd school of mackerel now. Do you like brown crab? I'll bring some claws to you once we have some."

I was about to say goodbye, when John asked, "How are you people liking it round here?"

"We love it."

"Will you stay here with us?"

I paused.

"I don't think so. But you never know."

"Ah, I'd say you will. I'd say you'll buy a plantation and build a house and settle. A lot of the foreigners do that."

Dora's pace slowed as we walked up the track, and one of her ears began to droop. When I fed her, she drank only half of the bottle of milk, and I noticed that her scouring was getting worse. I spent the afternoon worrying about her. When Dag came home, he found me paging through his veterinary books. We both pored over the lamb, discussing in great detail her diarrhea, the way she was moving, what her eyes looked like, and all the little changes in her that I had observed during the day.

"I'd be embarrassed if anyone overheard this conversation," admitted Dag.

He diagnosed a mix of things, including cryptosporidosis.

"We'll put her on oral fluid replacement therapy and start a course of antibiotics against bacterial infection."

Cryptosporidosis, he told me, was a parasite for which there was no specific cure, and which lasted longer than other forms of diarrhea. We could only treat the symptoms of the disease and nurse her back to health.

It was Dag's evening off and we planned to go into town for a drink later. After dinner, he sat with Dora on his lap by the fire, bottle-feeding her. Before long they were both asleep. Dag's head rested on the back of the chair; Dora's head lay in the crook of his elbow, and one hoof dangled over his arm. I hadn't the heart to wake them, and they only roused when I was heaping more turf onto the fire.

"I think we'd missed last orders," I told Dag.

"I don't care," he said sleepily. "Why would anyone want to go to the pub when they have a lamb in their arms?"

✦

CHAPTER TWELVE

Oral fluid replacement therapy involved taking Dora off milk replacer for two days and substituting a product with the ominous name of Vet Scour. It came in a powder form and when whisked into warm water produced a murky drink with a sickly sweet smell. As it was less filling than milk replacer, by the following morning Dora was complaining about this new diet. A good hour or so before each feed, she began to call from the haggard, at first pitifully, then angrily, and finally with a cracked, anguished, "YOU'RE STARVING ME!" tone that wrenched me apart. It was unbearable to listen to. By three o'clock the first day I could stand no more; I jumped onto my bike, intent on escape.

On the lane I met Peggy. She was pushing a bike with a large plastic bottle strapped to the rack over the rear wheel.

"We have frogs in our well! I cleaned it out but they came back. Their jelly comes through the tap and I can see the little frogs inside it. I use it for the washing but I can't boil it for the tea. No, I can't do that. So I come down here to get water for the tea from my neighbour."

She seemed to be aware of everything that Dag and I had been doing recently .

"We saw you out for a ramble the other day. How well you met Dennis McCarthy, he's not one to talk to strangers in the ordinary way of things. And how's himself? It's getting busy for him now, indeed it is. He's driving up and down the lane all through the night until the morning. I hear you have a pet lamb. Why don't you bring her up to me? Bring her up to me, do, bring her up for a visit."

"She's sick," I said.

"Sick?" Peggy took a step back in alarm. "With what?"

"Cryptosporidosis," I told her, stumbling over the word.

"Oh Jesus, that's a terrible thing. The poor lambs, they fade away to nothing in no time with that. Oh Christ, it's terrible. But your man's a vet, now, so surely he can do something for her?"

"It's hard to treat, apparently," I said, feeling a wave of guilt wash over me.

"Ah it is, it is, by Christ it is. We've lost several fine lambs to that ailment."

I turned my bike around.

"Are you heading home? Look after that lamb now. And bring her up to me when she's better."

Within a few days, Dora was back to full strength, gulping down her bottles of milk replacer and gaining weight by the hour. When we set off one morning for Peggy's house she skipped along beside me, leaping into the air with mad twists of her body, all four hooves leaving the ground at once. But when we reached the lane, her progress slowed, until eventually she stopped altogether. She stood staring into a field, where nine stern rams with impressive curling horns stared defiantly back at her. Waddling about on the grass among them were two large glossy ravens, collecting sheep's wool to line their nests.

"Come on!" I encouraged Dora, hoping no shepherds were in earshot to hear me. "You can do it!"

A little further along the lane we met Chloe, who was too engrossed in eating the hedgerow to take any notice of us. By now Dora was dragging herself along and her ears were hanging down, as if she were encumbered by a heavy weight. She stopped again. I was standing over her, arms akimbo, when the green postal van drove down the lane at its usual breakneck speed and juddered to a halt beside us. The postman wound down his window and leaned out to scrutinize Dora.

"Is that a pet lamb?" he asked. "She has great condition."

"I can't get her to walk any further," I complained.

"Ah, she's young yet and the tarmac is rough on her. Sheep never get used to it at all. Their hooves were made for the fields, not for hard roads. Goodbye now."

He drove off towards the harbour. I hoisted the fifteen-pound lamb into my arms and carried her the rest of the way. In the fuchsia bushes along Peggy's track, fresh scarlet shoots and tightly curled buds showed among the brown remains of last year's growth. Between the stones of a wall, yellow petals of celandine were opening up among cushions of glossy green leaves. A lapwing landed on the wall, briefly flashing its black and white tail feathers before resuming its jerky flight across the fields.

"Hello!" called Peggy. She was standing in the doorway, wearing a heavy jacket. "You carried your lamb a long way! Did the postman have any news for you?"

Two black cats sat on the windowsill. In the yard a donkey was eating white bread crusts scattered on the ground. Slinking around Peggy's legs were three sheepdogs. When they barked at Dora, she fled beneath the donkey.

"Go to bed, boys, go to bed!" Peggy commanded the dogs. She reached for Dora and tucked her under one arm. "If you stay there you'll get a kick from Bess, so you will."

"Your donkey's in good shape," I said, admiring its healthy grey coat and neatly trimmed hooves.

"Ah, Bess is doing great for nearly twelve years of age. She worked hard for me all her life, chasing the cows down the field and carrying the sheep nuts up the hill on her back. She's retired now. She's retired, she is, she's taking a rest and God knows she deserves it."

She set Dora down on the bare concrete floor of the living room. A boxed-in staircase ran up one wall. Opposite it was a large fireplace, where a pile of turf burned between two low stone stoops. A third wall was dominated by a rack, where I sat. From here there was a good view through the window and the open doorway, right across the valley.

"We can't see your place when we're sitting there," Peggy told me. "But we only have to take two steps outside and we know if you have a fire going or not."

Despite my protestations about my not being hungry, she brought me buttered cream crackers, sandwiches and sponge cake with my tea. For a while Dora huddled next to me, chewing on my wax jacket for comfort and reassurance in this strange new world. Eventually mustering some courage, she started to explore the room. She had her head stuck into the turf bucket when I noticed a puddle of urine forming beneath her on the floor. Waving away my apologies, Peggy took a mop from the corner and cleaned up the mess.

"Sure it happens all the time; I haven't swept out the ashes today anyway."

Apart from her elderly mother, who was asleep upstairs, Peggy was alone in the house. Her husband, Michael, was in town with their daughter, Nell. Peter was at school, and John, the eldest boy, was up in one of the fields with the cows.

"A man came by just now with a week-old calf to replace one that had died," Peggy explained. "We put him in the shed away up. Now we have to move a mother that lost her calf to be with him. We hope she'll take him on and that he'll suck from her."

It struck me that she must have been on her way out to join her son in the fields when I arrived, but had been too polite to say so. Though John was doubtless hanging about in the cold, wondering where his mother was, I knew that if I expressed concern Peggy would insist it didn't matter. To prove her point she would force more tea and cream crackers on me. There was only one way out of this dilemma.

"I'd like to see the new calf," I said. "Can I go there with you?"

"You can, of course! And Dora can come too. Let's away."

Dora had no problem walking on grass and earth. She happily followed us along a track through some abandoned farm buildings to a field where about fifteen cows and a few calves were grazing. We found John leaning against a wall. He had a shy and guarded air, and watched our approach through narrowed eyes.

"There's the mother." Peggy pointed to a brown cow. "Will you look, she has no milk left again. She was full of it yesterday, but when John came down in the evening to milk her, hadn't Creamy gone and done the job already."

Creamy was a black and white cow quietly grazing nearby.

"Ten years old, and still acts like a calf," grumbled Peggy. "Going round to all the cows and stealing their milk from under our noses."

She and John went to the field with the dogs. They skirted round the cows, gradually moving in towards the bereaved mother and working her closer to the gate.

"Yosh, yosh, yosh!" shouted Peggy.

Spreading her arms wide and brandishing a stick, she jumped nimbly to and fro each time the skittish animal tried to get past her. The cow had its head down and was watching her from the corner of one eye. Suddenly, it made a dash for freedom and raced across to the far side of the field with the dogs bark-ing frantically at its hooves.

"The fecking bitch!" shouted John.

I found it shocking that he'd use such language in front of his mother, until Peggy echoed him.

"She's a bold fecker, she is, a bold, bold fecker!"

After twenty minutes of hard work, the cow was through the gate and ambling down the track in front of us. I looked admiringly at Peggy; her face was flushed, but her breathing was steady.

"You must be very fit," I said.

She laughed, and tossed her head.

"Ah, it's the way of life, I suppose."

The track led to a derelict house. Its front door was boarded up, and bushes grew wild through upstairs windows that com-manded fine views over Dingle Bay.

"This was Patsy's mother's house," said Peggy. "It's a lovely place alright. We have foreigners coming every summer and wanting to buy it, but it will be Nell's home in time. 'Tis best to keep the land in the family."

The spindly calf was in a stone shed alongside the house. John herded the cow in there and tethered her to the wall in reach of a basket of silage and a bucket of water. She turned to look at the calf and strained her head to sniff at him, but he showed no interest in his new mother.

"He's been bucket-fed so far, and getting him to suck could be mighty hard," said Peggy. She slapped the cow's rump. "Now, girl, here's your new child, and we'll go home and pray you get used to each other."

As we retraced our steps, Peggy pointed to the houses in the valley, explaining who lived where and how they were related to each other. It was an account made confusing not only by an intricate web of intermarriage, inheritance and feuds over land access and water rights, but also by people's names. Almost everyone in the valley was called O'Sullivan or O'Donaghue or O'Shea, after the old Gaelic clans that once ruled this part of Kerry. To help distinguish between them, men were often called by their fathers' first names as well as their own. Among our neighbours there was a John Joe O'Sullivan, a Michael Pat O'Sullivan and a John Pat O'Sullivan. Nicknames were used for the same purpose, and these usually had some reference to family history. John Smith O'Shea's father had been a blacksmith, Johnny the Horse's grandfather kept horses and Micky Wireless's father had also been known as Wireless, for reasons no one could remember. Sometimes the nicknames reflected personal attributes. Texas had so many sheep and so much land he was considered to be a big rancher, Paddy Fox had bushy red hair, Michael the Mouth never stopped talking and John Batty was said to be as eccentric as they come. My favourite was Gerald Cassure, who had phoned up one night when Dag was on call.

"It's Gerald O'Sullivan and I have a cow with a hole in her udder," he said. "Your husband's been to see me before. Tell him it's Gerald Cassure, that's how he knows me."

When I asked him what cassure meant, he explained it was Irish for hammer. "And how did you get that name?"

He paused, then began to laugh. "Because I'm a bold boy I suppose!"

Back at Peggy's house, Chloe was lying across the front step, chewing her cud. She had to be shooed off so we could get inside.

"She's peaceful now, but sometimes she has the devil in her, and starts battering on the door wanting to get inside," said Peggy. "Once we had a cousin visiting, and he woke up in the middle of the night to hear this awful clattering. So he came running down in his nightclothes and took up the shot gun to fight off the madman at the door. But when he ran outside, there was Chloe asking to be let in, and didn't he fall over her and nearly break his head in two pieces!"

Nell had returned with her father, a portly man with a kind face. He was sitting on the rack, keeping a keen eye on the lane.

"Your husband drove by not long ago," he told me. "He's home early for his lunch today."

Dora jumped up onto the cushion next to Michael. I rushed over to remove her, but he just laughed, and patted her with his good hand.

"She likes it here. She's a fine lamb."

More tea was offered, as well as sherry, whiskey, ham sandwiches and cake. I declined everything, insisting I had to get home to feed Dag and Dora.

"Call again," said Peggy when I left. "Bring himself along next time, and bring Dora. She knows her way round here, she does, she's used to us now, she feels at home here."

"I feel at home here, too," I shyly told her.

Her face lit up.

"You do of course. And why shouldn't you? You're very welcome. Call again!"

✛

CHAPTER THIRTEEN

One Saturday evening we called into Rourke's Bar. It was quieter than usual, as most of the regular customers were at Mass. John Joe Rourke sat on a bench with his back to a radiator, smoking a pipe and with the day's newspapers spread out on the table in front of him. Next to him was his wife, May, wearing a bulky hand-knitted sweater buttoned up over her apron and dress. Close by, two men hunched over a table, nursing bottles of Guinness. They were all watching the news on a television balanced on a high shelf. Only May dragged her eyes away to greet us when we walked in.

"Here's the new vet and his wife," she told her husband, who slid along the bench to make room for us.

She walked heavily across the linoleum floor towards the counter. "Is it two pints of Murphy's you're having again?"

The news was followed by a weather report. A pretty young meteorologist pointed to a map of Ireland festooned with puffy black rain clouds.

"There's poisonous weather due," said John Joe, his pipe clenched between his teeth. "'Twill be no good for the lambs."

May carried our drinks to the table, cleared the newspapers out of the way and sat down next to us.

"The lottery is on next," she told us in a confidential tone, "then we'll switch over for *The Winning Streak*."

The two men kept glancing over, but whenever we looked back they quickly averted their eyes. Eventually Dag asked the younger of them why he preferred to drink bottled rather than draught Guinness. The man leaned forwards to answer.

"The draught beer is softer." His elbow slipped off the table and his head jerked sharply. "The bottled beer is stronger. You need drink only two bottles to three pints of the draught."

On the television screen, coloured balls were bouncing around inside a clear plastic dome.

"Have you got our lottery ticket?" John Joe asked May.

She fished around in a pocket of her apron, and pulled out a slip of paper. "I have. Let's pray to God we're lucky at last."

The balls began randomly dropping through a spout at the bottom of the plastic dome. A man in a suit collected each one and read off the number on it.

"By God, we have two already" cried May excitedly.

The drunk man's companion was staring at me. His eyes had a wicked twinkle, and he wore his cap at a rakish angle.

"Are you single?" he suddenly shouted.

"Timmy O'Driscoll, enough of your rudeness," snapped May. "John Joe, did we get another number?"

"We did not. It'll be another week at least before we retire to Florida."

"Ah, I wouldn't want to live there anyway," May told me. "I went there once to see a cousin we have in Orlando. Her house was lovely. It had a swimming pool in the garden. In the kitchen there was the biggest refrigerator you ever saw; it was taller than me and had two doors; I could have set up home in it with no trouble. The people in America were very friendly, they really were, but I wouldn't leave South Kerry for them. I've lived here all my life, I know everyone and they know me. Who would I know in America? I'd be awful lonely there."

Dag and the man at the next table had moved on from discussing beer.

"Do you play the lottery?"

"No, I have no interest in it."

"Do you bet on horses?"

"I do indeed. I have a great interest in that."

He began to tell Dag about his ponies, and how he entered them into the local road races.

"Sure, Danny, didn't you buy your ponies from Dennis McCarthy?" said May. "This is the new vet; this girlie is his wife. She feeds Dennis's ponies with carrots."

I was silent, wondering how May could have known this.

"Dennis told me he had a nice new neighbour," said Timmy O'Driscoll, with a wink. "You have to watch him. He's mad for the women. He'll be in after Mass."

"One of my mares is about to foal," Danny was telling Dag. "We crossed her with a spotted horse. If it's a spotted mare that's born, she'll be worth four hundred pounds. If it's a stallion it'll be worth less than two hundred. 'Tis a gamble, alright, and that's part of the interest."

"Don't forget *The Winning Streak* now, May!" cried John Joe suddenly.

"Oh God, that's right, it's on the other channel."

From behind the counter she collected a long branch. Her heels left her furry slippers as she reached up to poke the branch against a button on the television set.

"We can settle in for a while," she said, sitting next to me again as the program's opening credits rolled. "I'm serving no-one until this is over."

A studio audience appeared, clapping enthusiastically. Then the compere's smiling face filled the screen. Thick make-up had turned his skin a startling shade of orange.

"You can be sure that fucker didn't get his suntan in old Ireland," cackled Timmy.

"Timmy O'Driscoll, watch your language!" May scolded him. "If I hear another word like that from you, out of this bar you go!"

The game was an electronic form of Scratch and Win. Four contestants sat at little desks and selected numbers that caused various sums of money to appear on a big screen. Although this required no skill or intuition, the crowd hooted and whistled when large sums flashed up. Between games, the compere interviewed the contestants about themselves.

"Here we have Michael Malloy of Killala in County Mayo."

A huge cheer arose from the audience. The camera panned to a group of people holding aloft banners saying, "Good luck Michael" and "Killala Forever."

"Now, Michael, I understand you have a fascinating story about a tree that fell on you," said the compere.

Michael ran a finger inside his collar, which appeared to be far too tight for him.

"Didn't it happen while you were out ploughing?" the compere prompted.

"Ah, well, it did, it happened while I was on the tractor."

The door of the bar opened. Dennis hobbled in. He hoisted himself up on a stool, then took a packet of cigarettes from the inside pocket of his jacket.

"Dennis McCarthy!" screeched Timmy gleefully. "Did you know this girl is feeding your ponies with carrots?"

Dennis turned to look in our direction, frowned, and looked away.

"Dennis!" Timmy carried on relentlessly. "Aren't you worried one of your ponies might choke on a carrot? Come here now, Dennis, and sit next to your neighbours."

May patted my knee. "Take no notice of Timmy O'Driscoll. He's only in it for the fun."

The door opened again. Two couples occupied the stools along from Dennis. The men nodded to May; their wives stared at the television set. With a sigh, May got to her feet.

"They'll all start charging now. I wish the priest would wait until *The Winning Streak* was over before finishing Mass."

A man in a smart leather jacket had joined Danny and Timmy. He leaned over to shake Dag's hand, and told him that he had recently retired from farming.

"He's a bachelor, but he's got women all over this peninsula," Timmy interjected.

"You're a scoundrel, Timmy," said the man.

The bar was rapidly filling, and a haze of smoke had formed at head level. On the television, *The Winning Streak* was reaching its finale. The compere stood on one side of a giant wheel. Its neon-lit rim was divided into sections and marked with different sums of money. On the other side was the leading contestant, Catherine from Longford, whose hobbies included power walking and rug making.

"Now, Catherine," said the compere. "Spin the wheel as hard as you can, and may luck be with you!"

Catherine's supporters roared when she grasped the wheel and gave it a strong, sharp pull. It spun into a blur. Gradually, it slowed, and first the spokes reappeared, and then the ball that was dropping from section to section. All eyes were focused on this ball; where it finally landed would decide Catherine's main prize. The tension grew as it bounced from twenty thousand pounds, to fifty-five thousand pounds, to five thousand pounds to thirty thousand pounds. The wheel began turning slower and slower. It had almost stopped moving when the ball landed in the section marked two hundred and fifty thousand pounds. A great gasp arose from audience. The ball rolled very slightly, wobbled on the edge, then dropped away.

"NO!" groaned the gathered occupants of Rourke's Bar in unison.

With the ball firmly lodged in a section marked seven thousand pounds, the wheel finally stilled.

"Jesus, that was bad luck!" said the man in the leather jacket.

"Congratulations, Catherine!" cried the compere, ignoring her obvious disappointment. "Seven thousand pounds as well as the four thousand three hundred and twenty pounds you've won already. It's your winning streak!"

"Ah, the girl should be thankful," said John Joe. "Wouldn't most of us be delighted with seven thousand pounds?"

Dennis was leaning over the bar and whispering in May's ear. She came over and stood in front of our table, her hands clasped in front of her.

"Dennis McCarthy wants to stand you and your wife a drink."

"Oh, that's very kind of him," said Dag. "We'll join him at the bar."

"Don't be leaving your husband for Dennis, now!" yelled Timmy after me.

Perched on his stool, Dennis gazed at Dag through drifts of blue cigarette smoke.

"Now sir, I am pleased to meet you. I didn't recognize your wife when I came in. I didn't know it was you until May told me. How well you found this pub. It is a good place. There's good people and good drink here. 'Tis no use having bad people and good drink or bad drink and good people."

Timmy continued to roar at us from the corner about the ponies. Dennis turned and scowled at him.

"What do you think of that man?"

"He's a bit of a clown," I said.

"He's that alright. He's banned from every pub but this. One Saturday evening, I was sitting next to him at Mass. He kept picking at me and pushing me with his elbow. There was a woman in front of us with her stick on the ground by the kneeler. What does Timmy O'Driscoll do but take the stick and hold it over my head, making like he's going to crack me with it. Then he dropped it and it fell on the floor with an awful clatter. The man behind us said that with the two of us carrying on it was like watching a circus. I'll never sit by Timmy at Mass again."

"Any lambs yet, Dennis?" May asked him.

"One! When more start coming, I don't intend to have to call upon this man to help me."

He lit another cigarette, and looked searchingly at Dag.

"I know enough about the animals myself. There's those that don't know, but I do. I have two donkeys as well as the ponies. One of them I paid fifty pound for. Some donkeys they cost more. I saw a piebald donkey at the fair, and I thought she was worth a hundred pound. I asked the man who had her and he wanted five hundred. People are mad for donkeys in this country nowadays. They've become very fashionable. They put them in with the cattle. There's a disease cattle get. It goes by the name of red water. It's ticks that cause it, but you know all about that I suppose. I nearly lost a cow from it. I had to get the vet up to look at her. So now I put the donkeys in with my cattle; and I don't lose them from the red water. Did they teach you that at university?"

"Not that I remember."

"Why do the donkeys stop the cattle getting red water disease?" I asked Dennis.

He smoked in silence for a minute.

"Because they eat the grass that has the ticks that carry it," he said at last, looking pleased with himself. "I'm as good as a vet, you know."

"Are you ready, Dennis?" called the man in the leather jacket. "If you are, I'll drive you home."

Dennis climbed stiffly from his stool.

"One of these evenings, when I see smoke coming from your chimney, I'll be over to you. Then we'll talk some more."

As the evening Mass crowd drifted away, it was replaced by a new batch of customers. The noise level rose steadily. May calmly poured pint after pint of stout, leaving each one to stand and settle, then smoothing off the creamy head with a knife before handing it over.

"Francis, here's one on the house, in lovin' memory of your mother, God rest her soul, she was a fine woman. Michael, I'll be with you right away."

People clutching musical instruments began arriving and gathered at a table by the end wall. Before long there was a fair-sized band: an accordion, a bodhran, a tin whistle, spoons, a fiddle and a guitar. May carried a tray of pints over to the table. As the musicians chatted to her I thought I detected American and German accents.

"They're mostly foreigners who live around here. We call them blow-ins," explained a young woman who had occupied the stool next to mine. A pretty redhead, she sported a delicate nose stud. A blond three-year-old sat on her lap. He took a sip from his mother's pint of stout, which left a moustache of froth on his top lip.

"The girl with the accordion is the only Irish one among them, she runs the taxi service. The fellow on the bodhran and the one on the fiddle, they're from England. They live here now and they teach traditional Irish music to the kids. Isn't that a funny thing? When I was a teenager, none of us could sing an Irish tune. Now it's all the rage, and the old stuff is coming back."

"I wish I could sing," I said.

"It's a great thing, it is. My mother talks about the sessions they used to have in the bar on a Sunday after Mass. The place would be full and they'd go around and each person would sing a song or tell a story. No matter how bad a person was, even if they couldn't hold a note, everyone would listen and be respectful. Isn't that how it should be, instead of all the criticism you get today?"

The musicians had started to play a lively reel. Delighted by the music, the blond child clapped his hands and chortled with glee. His mother introduced herself as Theresa. She was married to the man on the tin whistle; he had a long ponytail down his back and several rings in each earlobe.

"Achim's from Berlin," she said, bouncing her son up and down in time to the music. "We met when he was here on holiday. I was mad to move to Germany, but he won't go back. He loves the west of Ireland. All the blow-ins do."

I was glad to have found Theresa. For the previous half-hour Dag had been engaged in a discussion with several farmers about breeding sheep, a subject on which I had nothing to offer. May set down pints of beer between us.

"Pat Casey stood these for you. And here's a treat for little Eamon."

"Ah, May, you know we don't like to give him too many sweets," Theresa protested, but the child was already reaching a hand towards the foil-wrapped chocolate.

I now had two pints of stout waiting to be drunk, as well as the one I was presently working one. If I drank them all, my intake would amount to five pints, and I doubted I'd be able to get off my bar stool, never mind drive home. Neither Dag nor I had ordered the drinks. They just kept appearing, stood for us by various farmers in the bar. As she delivered them,

May told Dag who had bought them. According to local tradition, he then ordered a round for that person and his companions, and without fail, one of them felt obliged to buy drinks for us and whomever we were talking to. So it went on, in a spiral that threatened to go out of control if we didn't escape the pub soon.

"Your husband's a vet?" said Theresa. "I must have a chat with him, so. One of my ewes is forever getting sick."

"Are you a farmer?" I was surprised, for she certainly did not look like one.

"Not at all, I keep a few sheep just for the fun of it. I have a ram and thirteen ewes that I raised myself from the bottle. The farmers around us knew I wanted a little flock, so when they got a weak lamb, instead of slamming it against the wall they brought it to me. Emma's my favourite; she's the one that's sick. Last year she had bloat, then she aborted and now she's losing her fleece."

I was going to tell her about my pet lamb, when Dag and his companions butted into our conversation.

"Losing her fleece, you say?" asked Dag.

"Ah, wool drop, that's a nasty thing," said a farmer.

"Could be a skin infection," suggested another.

Eamon had fallen asleep on Theresa's lap. She rocked him as she talked.

"The vet was over to us several times last year, and I had her into the surgery as well. She's cost me a fortune. I could have bought another flock for what I've spent, but she's a real pet."

The session was in full flood now with the band belting out one jig after another. The windows of the bar had steamed up, and the pace of drinking and talking was fast and furious. I'd lost Theresa to Dag and the farmers, so I began listening to a couple of men on the other side of me. They were discussing the crossword in that day's *Irish Independent*.

"I have only the one left to do, four letters beginning with r and ending with l, and the clue is 'a small stream.' Do you have an idea?"

"Christ, for the life of me I can't think what that would be."

The word "rill" popped into my head, though I no had idea from where I'd trawled it up.

"What in God's name is a rill?" asked one of the men.

"I think it's a stream of some kind," I said uncertainly.

"Jesus, she's right," said his friend excitedly. "It's an old word, from Elizabethan times, I've read it in Shakespeare. Look now, we'll check. Pass over that dictionary, would you, May?"

A *Concise Oxford Dictionary* was pulled out from behind a case of cigarettes, "rill" was found and agreed upon, and the crossword was completed.

"There's another one done. Let's drink to it. May, we'll have two pints, and a drink for this young lady here."

My new friends turned out to be a local bank manager and a pharmacist. They shared a keen interest in literature, and over several more rounds lectured me entertainingly on the merits of new Irish poetry. Some indeterminate time later, Dag and I left the pub with the accordion lady. Neither of us was capable of driving, and she had agreed to run us home in her taxi while the band had a break between sessions.

As it was past the official closing time, May had drawn the curtains and locked us all in. She put her head around the door and checked up and down the street to make sure no *garda* were about.

"Sure, it's early you're leaving?" she said in puzzlement, as we slipped past her. "They're all just getting warmed up in here."

CHAPTER FOURTEEN

On the Iveragh Peninsula, the lambing season for mountain ewes begins in earnest after St. Patrick's Day, as soon as hangovers have subsided. Kevin O'Shea, who never touched alcohol, obviously paid little heed to this, and neither did his sheep. By the time St. Patrick's Day dawned, Kevin had thirty lambs in his fields, and at eight o'clock that morning he was knocking on our door, asking for help with a ewe who was having trouble producing the thirty-first.

"This is the real beginning of it," he admitted, as I stood with him in our garden, watching Dag examine the ewe on top of the picnic table. "There's madness ahead for the sheep farmer, alright. But the weather should improve; St. Patrick promised every day fine after his Feast."

For days we'd had wet, blustery weather, but the morning of March 17th was bright and sunny with a fresh breeze from the south. This was good news for the festivities due to take place in most of the towns across the country, and for the million people, a third of the entire population, who would attend them. The bigger centres had already begun their celebrations. In Dublin they spanned four days and included an extravagant fireworks display, a street carnival and a huge outdoor ceilidh. Marching bands, musicians and performers from all over the world were taking part in a huge St. Patrick's Day parade, led though the streets of the city by a young Irish pop star.

These celebrations were a copy of the showy events put on every year by Irish-Americans in New York and Boston, and had little to do with local traditions. For over a week, newspapers and television and radio shows covered plans for the big day. In the midst of all the hype, only a few lonely voices spoke up for St. Patrick. *The Kerryman* printed a letter complaining about references to "St. Paddy's Day."

"Sir—I would make a very special appeal to those who appear on radio and television, to please refer to the Feast Day of our Patron St. as St. Patrick's Day and not as Paddy's Day. The printed press is also guilty of this insult to the Irish people in showing disrespect for our Patron Saint, St. Patrick. Out in the commercial world, the term Paddy's Day is also used quite frequently. To me this is an appalling situation where people show disrespect for our Patron Saint.

Sincerely,
Paddy O'Brien,
Cork."

A member of Our Lady of the Rosary National Crusade phoned into Pat Kenny's radio show, expressing concern about the pagan nature of the festivities.

"There's an event in Dublin where people are asked to get dressed up as earth or fire or water," she said. "What has that to do with St. Patrick? Wasn't he against all manner of warlocks and wizards?"

Kevin O'Shea had a pragmatic approach to the celebrations.

"It's a time when we can be proud to be Irish," he said. "And it reminds us of St. Patrick, of course. He was a great man. Did you know he was a shepherd for a time? A king of old Ireland took him from England as a slave and put him to work for years in the mountains up north. It was a terrible experience for a young boy of sixteen. They say it's what turned him to God. He escaped and became a priest. But he never forgot us. He came back here as a bishop and converted the Celts."

"Are you celebrating today?" I asked him.

"I might go to Mass. It depends on the lambs."

Like most of the sheep kept on the hills of Iveragh Peninsula, his ewe was a Scotch Blackface mountain sheep. She was smaller than the lowland breeds, with longer, shaggier fleece, a more delicate face and very slender legs. Two hooves were showing from her back end, but she wasn't dilating properly. Her lamb was stuck. Dag gave her an injection of calcium into the jugular vein, and an epidural into the tail. Then he massaged her cervix for ten minutes to help open it up.

"It's going to be tight," he said finally, as he manoeuvred a wire loop into the ewe's vagina and around the back of the lamb's head. One gentle tug brought it into the birth canal. Quickly, Dag grasped the front hooves, stretched out the legs, and pushed back the vulva as the lamb's head began to slip through it.

"That's it!" cried Kevin, as the rest of the tiny body slithered out. "Good man!"

The ewe wasn't too impressed with her newborn daughter; when Kevin put the lamb by her she tried to butt it away.

"Ah, she'll take her yet," he said, holding the lamb under the mother's nose.

"You should call her Patricia," I told him.

"I should indeed, considering the day she was born."

That afternoon, on my way to see the St. Patrick's Day parade in Cahersiveen, I looked for Patricia. Kevin O'Shea kept his postpartum ewes and lambs in some fields on either side of the lane. Careful tending and fertilizing had made the grass so long and thick that when newborn lambs lay down they practically disappeared from view. A single lamb—Patricia, perhaps—was cuddled up to its mother, who sat chewing her cud. Nearby, sets of twins chased each other around, leaping up and down as if they were on springs. When I dismounted my bicycle, a lamb trailing a bloody umbilical cord took a few wobbly steps in my direction, while its protective mother stared at me defiantly, stamping her hoof in warning. Sunlight gleamed on the damp grass, the first yellow buttercups were opening up and the air was filled with the reedy cries of new lambs. It was a scene of simple gladness that made me laugh and sing outloud. As I cycled up the lane I thought about St. Patrick, certain that, despite the hardships, he must have experienced many such moments during his days as a shepherd.

The shops and pubs along Cahersiveen's Main Street were emblazoned with green, white and gold paraphernalia: leprechauns and goblins, harps and shamrocks, bunting and balloons and hats and badges saying "Kiss Me, I'm Irish" or "Have A Nice St. Patrick's Day." The procession, due to start at two, was already an hour late. Families sat inside cars parked with the front ends facing to the road. Along the pavements, smartly dressed women sporting bunches of shamrock on their lapels held the hands of small children eating green ice cream. Old men sat on benches outside the library; younger men leaned against the walls. Police stood in the middle of the road, diverting traffic. Everyone commented on the weather: weren't we fortunate to have it so fine, thanks be to God, and may it last now through the spring and summer.

The parade finally appeared, led by a group of teenaged soldiers in green fatigues. They marched in strict formation, trying not to grin at people they knew in the crowd. Behind them, flanked by watchful teachers, came the school bands, nine in all, playing traditional tunes on drums, accordions and tin whistles. Most of the bands had mascots: little girls dressed as shamrocks, their faces framed in large, green cardboard leaves; miniature St. Patricks, with paper mitres crayoned in green and gold; American-style majorettes in short skirts and cowboy boots twirling pompoms and sticks in front of a large, fluttering tricolour.

Four shire horses pulled the lead float, which featured a miniature pony and a blacksmith in a leather apron banging on an anvil.

"It's ridiculous having that one first," said Mary Margaret O'Connell, whom I'd met while helping Dag with TB tests on her farm. "Now everyone behind it will be stepping in the horse's shite."

Accompanying the dancing girls on the second float was a small dog, supine on a stool and wrapped in a tricolour. Mary Margeret snorted derisively.

"Will you look at Batty McCarthy's dog? Isn't he usually yapping and jumping up over everyone? They must have drugged the poor creature."

On the Keating's Bar float, a dozen or so obviously inebriated people milled around a bar drinking glasses of champagne. Mary Margaret, who had joined the Pioneer Total Abstinence Association when she was twelve and had not touched a drop of drink since, made disapproving noises. Six more floats went by. My favourite had a group of men dressed as mountainy farmers, ripped coats tied shut with baling twine and trousers tucked into woolly socks, cycling rusty bikes on the spot.

"I think the vet surgery should have a float next year," I told Mary Margaret. "My husband could be on the back, delivering lambs."

"That's a good idea, now. If Frank O'Leary agrees to it, tell him my husband and I will play the part of the poverty-stricken farmers, for we know all our lines already."

The parade went as far as the east end of Main Street, where eleven judges sat inside a trailer, conferring about the prizes. Mary Margaret pointed to the only female judge.

"That woman up there, she's from England. She came here no more than ten months ago, and already she's in everything and joined up to every club and committee. Yesterday, I heard that she's been chosen to give out communion at Mass, over some of us that have lived here all our lives."

"That's social climbing for you."

"It is," she agreed. "It is indeed!"

There were cheers and applause as the winners were announced and prizes handed out. But already the crowds were dispersing, sucked back into the pubs, where the serious business of the day continued.

The old tradition of drinking *pota Phadraic*, "St. Patrick's Pot," on March 17th was religiously observed in Cahersiveen. That evening, Main Street had a party atmosphere, with music spilling from doorways and people flowing in and out of pubs, advising each other on where to find the best "craic." In Keating's Bar, the party begun on the float had been growing for the past five hours. A small band competed with the hubbub of voices and laughter. We joined the people standing three-deep at the bar, trying to attract the attention of the bar maids.

"Brilliant here, innit?" a man kept yelling at us. "I moved here from Souf London last year and I wouldn't go back there for nuffin. Innit brilliant?"

Things were quieter in the Scellig Rock. A pretty check-out clerk I recognized from the supermarket sat alone at the bar, looking tragic and refusing to talk to the series of drunken young men who periodically lurched over to her.

On the way to the Daniel O'Connell, we passed a group of people in their twenties staggering around the bank machine, which had not only refused to spit out money for them, but had also swallowed up the plastic card they'd inserted.

"You whoore!" the owner of the card yelled at the machine, while his friends screeched with laughter. "You fecking bastard of a whoore!"

Next to the pub entrance, teenaged couples stood against the wall, locked in passionate embraces. The door to the lounge swung open; more teenagers streamed out clutching bottles of lager. The girls' midriffs were fashionably exposed despite the cold, the boys' hair was stiff with gel. Inside, an enormous sing-song was underway. At least a hundred drunks tunelessly yelled out the lyrics of "Foggy Dew," "The Leaving of Liverpool," "Dirty Old Town" and "Home on the Range."

"I think we've arrived a bit too late," said Dag ruefully.

After two hours spent watching masses of people getting very inebriated, we decided to go home. On the way to the car, we passed a pub called Bowlers. I had never seen it open before, but now a light shone through the frosted glass of its window. From within we heard the sound of a lone accordion playing a traditional Irish air. For a minute we stood on the pavement, listening, then poked our heads round the door. There, to our great surprise, was Ted Donnelly, sitting up on a high stool and performing to a crowd of eight people. The publican and his wife stood behind the bar. Three men wearing tweed jackets and caps leaned against it. Next to Ted, a woman clutched a large plastic handbag. A couple with a Jack Russell terrier occupied the bench running along one wall of the room.

"Dougeen!" cried Ted, pausing in his rendition. "I'm delighted to see you. Delighted! Your wife's keeping well. Come in and sit down. What will you have? Whiskey, is it?"

Everyone in the room was glassy-eyed, including the sheep whose head was mounted on one of the walls. It was a long-haired sheep with large, impressive horns.

"What's the story of that sheep?" I asked John.

"It is stuffed, Marie," he said solemnly. "Preserved, you might say."

The woman next to him had begun to wobble about on her stool. "Play on, Ted," she implored him.

He shook his head. "I've played enough, Eileen."

"Play on, do! Give us the 'Ewe Song,' Ted."

"Ah no."

"I'd like to hear the ewe song," Dag chipped in.

"You would of course!" she agreed. "It is a true story and Ted wrote it himself."

After much cajoling he was persuaded. His song, to the tune of a waltz, told of some local farmers who gambled on a ewe lamb during a card game.

"*Four tables were played for to make up the prize,*" went the third verse,

"*Two in Coors, one in Bahaghs, one in Carhan likewise.*
Fol Dew and Stack were the winners in town
And they came up to Bahaghs for to bring this ewe down."

A man next to John asked the publican's wife to dance. She was as well-padded as he was skinny, but he swung her confidently around the linoleum-covered floor, keeping perfect step. Perturbed by the sudden movement across his line of vision, the Jack Russell terrier grew agitated. Crouching in an attack position on the bench, it barked incessantly at the two pairs of feet.

The publican, a portly man in his sixties, came out from behind the counter with a wooden hoop and a stool. He set the stool on the floor in front of the Jack Russell, which promptly jumped onto it. When he held out the hoop, a foot away from the stool, the dog leapt through it without hesitation. Time and time again, the terrier repeated this performance: up onto the stool and then through the hoop, which the publican held further and further away, until the little animal was having to launch himself horizontally through the air to reach it. The dog became so engrossed in this trick that he didn't notice two extra pairs of feet on the floor: the woman sitting next to John was now being partnered by another of the farmers for the last few verses of the song.

> "Patty Moriarty got vexed and he threw up his cards,
> Saying, 'To hell with it all, I won't play with blaggards.'
> They soon calmed him down and then resumed play,
> And the final was over without much delay.

> "So God bless all the boys now who this lamb did play,
> I hope she'll be successful for many a day.
> Whatever butcher will buy her, will you please let me know,
> For I'm awfully anxious for a piece of this ewe."

"I played my neighbour for a calf last week," one of the farmers told Dag. "I won him, too. He's a fine red calf."

Ted winked at me.

"Sure it's a common thing, Marie. If your husband doesn't take more care of you, he'll find you gambled away one of these days."

It was after twelve when we left Bowlers, but the publican didn't go through the usual routine of checking up and down the street for *garda* before letting us through the door.

"They turn a blind eye tonight," he assured us.

I drove home, aware of the fact that I was probably the only relatively sober person behind a wheel for miles around. Halfway down the lane, we saw a couple of flashlights in a field.

"It's the O'Sheas, I'll bet," said Dag, as I slowed down. "They're out here every night now. Frank says they get punch drunk from lack of sleep as the lambing season wears on."

He rolled down his window.

"Is that you Kevin?"

"Hello there, Dag!" rang out a voice.

"Checking the ewes?"

"Ay, and checking for the fox, the bastard. He took two new lambs last night, but he'll not be around to take any more if we catch him, and that is a fact, boy."

"I smell him," another voice boomed from the darkness. "He's close by, the fecker. Are you busy?"

"No, it's my night off, so don't call me out, okay?"

"I hope we don't have to boy, I hope we don't. Good luck now, good luck!"

✤

CHAPTER FIFTEEN

Just before seven each morning our neighbour Patrick headed up the fields with a sack of sheep nuts slung over his shoulder, to feed his pregnant ewes. On catching sight of him, the ewes broke into a cacophony of desperate bleating, which continued for half an hour as they manoeuvred for position around the feed troughs. Until Dora's arrival I'd slept through this racket without a problem, but now she was roused by the sound, and her first demanding cry had me wide awake and stumbling downstairs to prepare her bottle.

As Patrick trudged back down the hill towards his house, he often glanced in my direction. I must have been a strange sight: tousle-haired, in a long nightdress with a sweater or rainjacket over top, and crouching down in the wet grass to bottle-feed a lamb. I often wondered what went through his mind as he waved his stick to me in greeting.

"Ah, we've had pets ourselves," he said tactfully, when I finally plucked up the courage to talk to him. "You get very attached to them, and it's hard to send them to the butcher come September. One year we lost seven ewes to listeriosis, and we had nine pets then."

"It was madness," added his wife Margaret. "It was like a nursery round here. You'd be feeding three of them, with a bottle in each hand and one between your knees, with the other six lambs pucking at you from all sides."

We were standing in hazy sunshine outside their house. Their daughters had spied me walking by with Dora, and come running out to play with her. I felt less shy about meeting my neighbours when I was walking with the lamb, as she gave us something in common to discuss.

"Ah, she's a dote," said Margaret, watching her daughters race Dora around their turf rick. "Hasn't she got a lovely face? She looks so different to our lambs."

"They turn into problems when they grow up," warned Patrick. "When our lambs were bigger, they'd go after the tourists staying in your house, and they'd hang around their door all day expecting food."

While most people hadn't objected to the sheep, one set of tourists took great umbrage over Patrick and Margaret's donkey, Neddy. An ancient ragged creature with overgrown hooves that curled up at the ends, he spent his life moving very slowly about the surrounding fields.

"The kids are mad to feed him," Patrick told me. "They give him bread and cake and crisps, and a boiled potato now and then. Sometimes the little one shares her sweets with him, but he has great trouble with them, on account of them getting stuck on his teeth. So whenever he sets eyes on a child now, he thinks it's come to feed him. Last summer some English tourists rented your cottage. They had a little lad with them, about five years old, I'd say. One morning the three of them were walking down the track when Neddy set off towards them. When your man caught sight of the donkey, he let out such a screech of fright, and he grabbed hold of the child and ran like his life depended on it, with the wife panting along behind him. The donkey thought this was great fun, of course, and carried on slowly after them, but didn't they get behind the gate and yell at him like he was some wild animal that might eat their child. They never walked down the track after that, but went a big long way around the fields to the lane."

"Ridiculous," said Margaret with a shake of her head. "And Neddy so old it takes him half a minute to blink his eyes once."

During the daytime we let Dora wander around outside, where she was starting to sniff at clumps of grass with great interest, and suck at the long, flat leaves of the montbretia growing wild all over the garden. Whenever I appeared from the cottage she rushed at me with joyful bleats, nudging her nose against my legs and following me faithfully wherever I went. The only time I could escape her attentions was between her noon and four o'clock feeds, when she usually took herself off to the haggard for a nap. I'd creep away then, and cycle into Cahersiveen for some shopping.

On my way to town I usually passed the same people, taking their daily exercise: a woman power-walking up the lane, a man running his dog on the high road, a nun holding a set of rosary beads and praying as she crossed the bridge. Like them, I was a creature of habit, and on Main Street I always followed the same pattern: into the post office, across to Sheehan's for free-range eggs, along to the bank, over to the supermarket, into Quirke's newsagents, down to Jim Curran the butcher, and then back to Johnny Apple's fruit and vegetable stand in front of the library before setting off again for home. By now it was all very familiar, and the shopkeepers no longer took me for a holiday-maker, but recognized me as one of their regular housewives.

"How's himself?" they'd greet me. "Is he busy? Ah, it's a busy time of the year for the farmers and vets, alright."

The Easter holiday season was almost upon us, and the first tourist buses of the year had begun to appear in Cahersiveen.

They came through as part of their day-tour of the Ring of Kerry, squeezing between the cars parked on either side of Main Street and usually causing a gridlock of traffic. They were monstrous vehicles, two-storied and garishly painted, with over-aggressive drivers who forced smaller vehicles out of the way while keeping up running commentaries through microphones to their flocks of passengers. No one in Cahersiveen was fond of these buses. They contributed little to the place, making only one quick stop for lunch at the Park Hotel, on the western end of town.

Such tours were a far cry from those described in a 1897 guidebook, offered by the GS and WR railway company. In those days, tourists went by train from Killarney to Cahersiveen, where they enjoyed "a good luncheon" at Leslie's Railway Hotel, now the Daniel O'Connell. Then they boarded a "line of well-horsed first-class four-in-hand coaches built expressly for Mr. Leslie," and set out for Waterville and a night in the Butler Arms Hotel. At ten o'clock next morning they continued in their horse-drawn coaches to Sneem and lunch in the splendid Parknasilla Hotel. By four o'clock that day they had reached Kenmare, where they boarded a train once more for their return to Killarney.

Groups of cyclists, looking like aliens in big helmets, wrap-around sunglasses and skin-tight, luridly coloured lycra outfits, risked their lives with the buses on the Ring of Kerry. Smoke curled from the chimneys of holiday cottages, and new faces appeared in the shops, people wearing brand new Arran sweaters, waxed jackets and caps, and carrying copies of Fodor's Guide to Ireland. Overnight, the supermarket began stocking products I'd never seen there before: crème fraîche, Greek olives, poppadoms, Balti paste and good Australian wine. But still there were no salad greens, save for elderly, browning heads of lettuce. I continued to look in vain for any more interesting vegetables than potatoes, carrots, turnips and onions, or fruits more exotic than the grapefruits, oranges and bananas that Johnny Apple always had on offer.

One fine afternoon towards the end of March, I found a new, smaller stall set up in front of Johnny's regular trestle table. In astonishment, I stared at boxes of shiitake and oyster mushrooms, at endives, red romaine lettuce and corn salad, at tomatillos, shallots, corn on the cob, jalapeno peppers, snow peas, at bean sprouts, star fruits, kiwi fruits, even coconuts—a whole host of produce I'd never dreamed I'd see in Cahersiveen.

"It's all queer stuff!" Johnny called to me. "I thought I'd try it out to see how it goes."

It seemed to be going well. A smartly dressed young woman had pulled up in a car and was buying up the queer vegetables fast.

"What will you do with it?" Johnny asked her.

"Sure, it's wonderful for stir-fries," she told him.

A old man with whiskery cheeks had stopped to watch me make my selection.

"These mushrooms, now," he observed, "aren't they the type they pick in the woods? And this lettuce here, is it the sort they blanche? And these little things, are they a type of tomato? How should you eat them?"

"I'm not sure about the tomatillos," I confessed. "I think they're used in Mexican cooking"

"Maybe I should buy some to try," he said. "It wouldn't hurt me now, would it?"

Johnny went though my bags and estimated by eye what everything weighed, making a quick calculation in his head. The total was fifteen pounds, a record amount for me to spend at his stall.

"You're mad for this queer stuff," he said happily.

I set off home, cycling across the bridge and looking forward to the salad I'd make that evening. A fresh breeze blew against the tide, rippling the surface of the river. To my right, the sharp ridge of Knocknadobar Mountain curved down into the valley. On the river bank to my left, the ruins of Ballycarbery Castle, once a stronghold of the McCarthy clan, stood in clear profile against the sky. I laboured up the hill past Kilavarnogue Cemetery, then turned onto the high road. In the topmost branches of some high trees, crows were busily building their nests. One flew down and alighted on the wall, holding a sizable stick in its beak. As I cycled by it flew off; almost immediately a mistle thrush replaced it, holding a beakful of grass.

Whizzing down the lane towards the harbour, I passed a field where a young calf lay alongside its mother. A magpie stood on the cow's back, picking through her coat. By Kevin O'Shea's field, I stopped to admire his latest batch of lambs, prancing about on carpets of yellow primroses. Across the lane stood a small shrine. It was built from whitewashed stones, shaped like a grotto, its front covered with a pane of glass set in a rough wooden frame. Inside it was a statue of the Virgin Mary and a jar of daffodils and freshly cut sally branches, complete with fat, downy catkins. This grotto marked a nearby holy well, dedicated to Saint Fursa, a sixth-century Irish missionary who was famous for a scar on his neck caused when an evil spirit hurled a lost soul at him. Fursa had regularly gone into trances so deep and long that his fellow monks sometimes thought he had died, and they prepared for his burial. During these trances he had visions of heaven and hell, which he wrote about in vivid poetry that is said to have profoundly influenced Dante.

Just beyond the shrine, a white stone cross indicated the start of a pilgrimage route up to the peak of Knocknadobar. It was the first of fourteen Stations of the Cross erected in 1888 by Canon Brosnan, while he was overseeing the building of the Daniel O'Connell Memorial Church in Cahersiveen. Since that time there has been an annual pilgrimage up Knocknadobar in late spring. This is a quiet echo of Lughnasa, a Celtic festival marking the start of harvest, once celebrated on mountain tops all over Ireland with bonfires, sumptuous feasting and the sacrifice of bulls.

While I was peering into the shrine, Peggy pulled up in her car.

"Hello! Are you praying? How's your pet lamb? Why don't you bring her up to us? We have a pet now, a little ram lamb. Bring Dora up to us, and the two of them can run around together."

Later that afternoon, I set off for Peggy's house with Dora, carrying the lamb half the way. In the fields below our cottage, the first tiny Teesdale violets had bloomed, their delicate purple flowers nodding atop fragile bowed stems. Clumps of pale primroses clung to stone walls, and along the centre of the lane was a line of new grass and buttercups. Chloe stood at the bottom of the track, chewing on the new shoots of fuchsia bushes, and other sheep and lambs were nosing around by the turf rick outside Peggy's door. Peggy leaned against the jamb of her doorway, watching our approach.

"Here you are with Dora." She gazed around the yard, then called into the living room, to her son Peter.

"Where's Mikey?"

"He's in bed. Shall I get him?"

"Do so, get him out."

Beneath a tree was a tiny shed tacked together from scrap wood and corrugated iron. Peter lifted away the plank securing its door, and seconds later a lamb came hurtling out. Mikey was a week-old, pure-bred Scotch Blackface ram. He had clean white curly fleece, a black nose and socks, neat little ears and budding horns, and was pretty enough to be a model for a stuffed toy lamb. Dora, by comparison, with her muddy colouring, scrawny neck and huge ears, looked homely and unkempt, but this only endeared her to me all the more. Mikey took great interest in Dora, and ran around her in circles, but she completely ignored him, paying more attention to the dogs lying close by.

"She doesn't know she's a sheep," observed Peggy. "Sometimes they never seem to find out. Come in now, do, and have a drink."

A posse of lambs and dogs followed us into the living room. Michael was in his usual place on the rack opposite the window, and Peggy's elderly mother sat in an armchair pulled close to the fire. A stick lay across her lap, her chin rested on her chest, and she appeared to be deeply asleep. But when the lambs skittered past her she woke up abruptly, grabbed the stick and whacked Mikey hard with it.

"Lambs," she growled bad-temperedly. "Inside the home is *no* place for them."

Unperturbed, Mikey settled down in the hearth just out of her range, lying perilously close to the glowing turf sods.

"All our pet lambs lie there," said Peggy. "They like the warmth. You can always pick out our pets in the field, for they are the ones with their fleece all singed down one side."

I sat next to Michael on the rack. Peggy produced a small folding table and set it in front of us. Quickly, she covered it with a plate of buttered cream crackers and glasses of sherry and whiskey. Then she prepared bottles of milk for Dora and

Mikey. Both lambs pulled so hard at the teats that they slipped out of their grasp, and milk sprayed over their noses. As soon as the feed was over, the dogs moved in to clean up the lambs, licking their faces.

"You've been rambling on the mountain again," Michael said. "I've seen you."

"Aren't you afraid to be up there, all on your own?" asked Peggy.

"Afraid of what?" I asked warily.

The mountain often looked ominous to me, with its dark slopes and its swirling mists, and I clearly remembered how spooked I had been finding a dead sheep inside a beehive hut.

"They say there are evil spirits up there," she told me.

"Arra, nonsense," Michael injected.

"Have you not heard Tom Batty talk? He says he's had to fight off devils with a crucifix up there."

"Tom Batty's off his head, Mam," said Peter, who was leaning against the kitchen door.

"He is so!" agreed Michael.

"What about *Sagart*?" insisted Peggy. "There's lots more than Tom Batty afraid of *Sagart*, and I'd be scared to walk past it myself. I've heard Albie in the UN Bar tell terrible stories of it."

Sagart, the Irish word for priest, was the name given to a Mass rock high on Knocknabodar. Such rocks dated from 1695, when the English imposed the Penal Laws on Irish Catholics to punish them for their support of King James II. These laws, which lasted until 1829, barred Catholics from civil life, the vote, attending school or practising their religion. But the Irish would not be bowed, and continued to regularly celebrate Mass in remote places, where priests used flat rocks as altars. Knowledge of these Mass rocks was passed down from one generation to another; to this day they usually command great respect.

According to Peggy, however, supernatural forces long ago invaded the Mass rock on Knocknabodar, and many people have suffered bad experiences close to it. At the turn of the century, a man was sent up Knocknadobar by the last Knight of Kerry, who resided on Valentia Island but had land scattered about the Iveragh Peninsula. The man's job was to spend the night on the mountain, flushing out suspected poachers. Up by *Sagart*, however, something terrible happened to him. He fled down the mountain in the dark, running all the way to Kells, where he took the first train back to Valentia Island. Like all the other victims of *Sagart*, he refused to give details of the horror he'd suffered, but warned that no one else should go near the rock.

Peggy often climbed the mountain behind her house in search of sheep, but she only set foot on Knocknadobar once a year, toiling up there with a large group of people to say the Stations of the Cross.

"'Tis a pity you'll miss the pilgrimage. It's a good day out. Though sometimes we have poisonous weather, and then it's miserable."

In 1929, she told me, some nuns got lost on the mountain. Sister Attracta, Sister Stanislaus, Mother Joseph, Mother Bridie and Sister Bernadette of the Cahersiveen Presentation Convent had been given permission by their Reverend Mother to make the pilgrimage on their own. In terms of piety the five nuns were well-matched, but when it came to physical fitness they were a mixed bunch. Two nuns reached the summit first, and on their way down passed the other three who were still labouring uphill. As the slower nuns finally got to the last station, close to the top of the mountain, clouds moved in, obscuring their route home. They attempted to descend, but quickly became hopelessly lost. Darkness fell; when the nuns failed to return to the convent, an alarm was raised. Two search parties spent all night looking for the three women. As hopes for them faded, the searchers heard faint singing in the distance. Drawing closer, they recognized it as a hymn: "Hail Queen of Heaven, pray for the wanderer, pray for me!"

After stumbling around in the mist and dark for almost nine hours, the exhausted nuns had simply sat down to wait for dawn. It was a lucky decision; the rescuers' lamps revealed the cold, frightened group perilously close to the edge of a high, sheer cliff. A few steps more and they most certainly would have fallen to their deaths.

"There must be some good spirits up on Knocknadobar, too," I said, when Peggy concluded this story.

"There must be, I suppose," she agreed, refilling my sherry glass.

Dora was lying on the floor next to me, her legs tucked beneath her. Mikey, happily singed by the fire, and the dogs sat in the open doorway, their eyes watchful and their tails swishing the ground. For the past few days, since our neighbour Patrick had told me how he hated to see his pet lambs go off to slaughter, I'd been worrying about the fate of Dora. Now I had an idea.

"Is there any chance," I asked Peggy uncertainly, "that you could take Dora when we leave?"

"We could of course!" she cried, in obvious delight. "She'll be company for Mikey. And she'll make a fine ewe in time. You'll come back and she'll have lambs of her own, she will, she'll have lambs of her own."

❖

CHAPTER SIXTEEN

As March turned into April, we had fine, breezy days, with the occasional shower passing through and rainbows rising from the earth in their wake. Dora was spending most of her time in our garden. She had progressed from sucking montbretia leaves to tearing off the heads of daisies and ribwort plantain and swallowing them whole. This new dietary supplement didn't affect her appetite for milk replacer; she sucked down each feed at an astonishing rate, with her sides visibly ballooning. When the bottle was empty, she would wander off to a protected corner of the garden and turn round and round in the long grass until she'd made a hollow, where she sat happily for a couple of hours, her nose turned to the wind and the sun.

As Dora steadily became more independent, I grew restless at home and began to miss driving around the peninsula with Dag. Our neighbour Margaret and her daughters had volunteered to feed the lamb at any time, so one afternoon I took them up on this offer. After lunch I set off with Dag for the Inny Valley, to assist him on his calls there.

The valley stretches for twelve miles, from the high mountains at the head of the Iveragh Peninsula, to the great curving sweep of Ballinskelligs Bay. We drove its length on a narrow and badly maintained road, crossing the Inny River several times via old, hump-backed stone bridges. At its far end, we followed a track that skirted a dark lake, scooped out a million years ago by ice. From this high vantage point, the whole landscape was like a lesson in geology spread out before us. We could see across the east-west ridges of the peninsula, pushed up two hundred million years ago during the great Amorican upheaval and since weathered to their present heights by ice and the elements. Between them were the valleys the sea had flooded into, forming the bays and peninsulas along the coast. And in the fields on either side of the track were whale-backed, striated rocks, left behind when the glaciers finally melted away from the Iveragh Peninsula twenty thousand years ago, and on which Michael Whooley's sheep now sat, impassively chewing their cud.

Michael's small house was painted bright yellow, with blue doors and window frames. In front of it, a vegetable patch was protected by a hedge of *phormium*, a large succulent plant with sword-like, fleshy leaves that shivered in the wind.

"'Tis an east wind," Michael greeted us gloomily. "Nothing good but the three wise men ever came from the east."

His eyes were the colour of the Mediterranean, and filled with sadness. While Dag worked on his sick animals, a scouring calf and a sheep with foot rot, Michael talked to me about his wife, who had died two years before.

"She was a great gardener. She kept us in vegetables all the year. She was a young girl still when we married, not thirty yet, and the widow of one of my neighbours. After he died I put the question to her and in time she accepted. There was talk around here, of course, for I was twice her age and she was twice the size of me. But we were both lonesome and so where was the harm in it? She was easy to get along with and that was a blessing, for I was an old bachelor, set in my ways like bachelors are. One Sunday after Mass, she put a roast of beef into the oven for our dinner then came out here to pick a cabbage. When she didn't come back I went looking for her. She was lying in the dirt, with the cabbage she'd picked beside her. It was a heart attack that killed her, a terrible thing in one so young and fresh. By rights it should have been her burying me, not the other way round."

There were no children to cheer him. During their ten years of marriage they'd tried for them, but she'd twice lost a baby.

"'Tis all misery now. My old friends are dying and there's no one to replace them. The foreigners come and they buy their houses. The forestry people come and they buy their land and plant it with trees."

He stared down the valley for a few moments.

"It's forestry and foreigners," he added bitterly. "They're what's ruining old Ireland."

I followed his gaze, past the lake and along the sweep of the Inny Valley. Across its moorland and bog were a few small farms and some isolated holiday homes, left empty until the summer season. Crawling up the slopes were plantations of Sitka spruce trees, their straight lines and uniform colour striking a note of discord with the bare, rocky terrain around them. The handsome subsidies farmers received to plant trees on their land were the cause of much controversy. Already we'd heard stories of local arson attacks, with whole plantations burned to the ground and the *gardaí* never able to find a culprit.

Michael pointed to several different houses.

"There's Germans own that one, British there, Canadians there. They come here in the summer and they love it. I don't know why."

"It's very beautiful around here," I said quietly.

"Is it? We don't see that, I suppose. It's hard country, that's what it is."

On our way back through the valley, I picked some heather and sedge grass and tied it into a twist which I laid on the dashboard.

"What's that for?" asked Pat O'Brien, a cheerful young farmer who lived near Ballinskelligs Bay.

"Decoration," I told him. "Maybe I'll put it in a letter and send it to Canada."

"I saw a program on the television about the Canadians cutting down all their trees. Give it a few thousand years, and you'll have plenty of peat bogs there, I'd say."

Pat Casey's farmyard was clean and orderly. A new Land Rover stood outside his large, modern cattle shed.

"I have a bull in here who's usually bright," he told Dag. "But this morning he was slow on his feet, and now he's down."

A bull that to me looked the size of a rhino lay on the concrete floor of a roomy pen, while another, smaller bull wandered listlessly around him.

"How long has he been down like this?" asked Dag.

"I found him so at noon."

"Is the other bull quiet?"

"He can be stroppy, alright, but he's wore out from running around after the cows yesterday. He'll not bother you."

Dag swung his legs over the gate. He ran his hands along the prone bull's massive flanks. He checked his eyes, nostrils and mouth, placed a stethoscope on several places along his body and took a rectal temperature. The bull's pink ears twitched during this examination, but otherwise he didn't move. His companion, however, became restless, and started pacing back and forth.

"His abdomen is taunt, Pat," said Dag. "And there's not much happening in his rumen. Could he have got at any feed recently without you noticing? Sugar beets, or nuts, perhaps?"

Pat leaned on the gate, considering this question.

"Now you mention it, he did. These lads got away from me this morning while I was moving them in here, and by the time I got hold of the big boy he had his nose in a pile of beets that I'd left in the yard."

"How much did he eat?"

"That I can't say. It couldn't have been a whole lot, for I got to him quick enough."

From his pocket Dag pulled out one of the plastic disposable gloves he used for rectal examinations. This was no ordinary glove: it reached right up to his armpit. Kneeling down, he pushed his hand, elbow and upper arm inside the bull. Luckily the animal seemed too dozy to care about such an indignity. The smelly scours Dag found confirmed his suspicion. An overdose of sugar beet had caused the rumen, a delicate fermentation chamber, to become acidic, and the acid was being absorbed into the bloodstream, poisoning the bull.

"It's quite serious," said Dag, climbing out of the pen. "I'll treat him intravenously to try and counteract the acidosis, and we'll give him a drench to help sort out the rumen."

While he went to the car for medicines, I stood with Pat, breathing in the warm, sweet odours of the shed and listening to the cows in the other pens munch on silage. I felt sorry for them, cooped up indoors all winter.

"When will you put these cows out to pasture?" I asked Pat.

"Not until June. I don't like keeping them in so long, but there won't be the grass for them until then. The EU says we have to allow two acres per cow. Good land costs fifty pounds an acre to lease; I can't afford any more."

Dag was soon back with needles, bottles and tubes.

"Take his nose ring for me, will you, Pat?"

Pat seemed perfectly at ease handling the bull, but he kept his eyes averted while Dag searched for the creature's jugular vein with a needle. Once he hit it, blood flowed out in a steady stream, pooling on the brown dung and changing from dark red to brilliant scarlet. Quickly, Dag attached a tube to the needle and fixed a bottle onto the tube.

"Maria, can you come here and hold the bottle?" he called.

I didn't move. The idea of setting foot inside that pen, with those two large bulls, had turned me to stone.

"Maria?"

"Are you sure it's really necessary?"

Noticing Dag's exasperated look, Pat tried to reassure me. "These lads won't hurt you. They're in no mood for a stampede."

Gingerly, I tiptoed across the pen, never once taking my eyes off the upright bull.

"Stand here and hold the bottle high," instructed Dag. "I've got to make sure the needle stays in place."

Close up, the bull seemed more massive than ever. Only his eyes were of a relatively normal size. To calm myself I focused on them, watching the pale lashes move up and down as the animal blinked. Some cows in the adjoining pen had gathered by the fence and were gazing curiously at the scene. One stretched her neck towards Pat, who still had the bull by the nose, and began licking the back of his sweater. We were on the third bottle of fluid when the other bull wandered over to sniff at his friend, brushing against my back as he passed.

"Go away now!" barked Pat.

The bull ambled off, but for the rest of the procedure I stood stock still, not daring to move.

"I think we should be able to get by without operating on him," said Dag, withdrawing the stomach tube he'd inserted to administer the drench. "But he'll need some more fluids tomorrow morning, so I'll come back then."

"Would you have time for another visit now?" asked Pat hesitantly.

Dag gave him a knowing look. Farmers often tried to way-lay him when he was passing their farms, hoping to avoid a call-out fee.

"My cousin Finbarr has a scouring cow. It's in a field away down the road. I'll drive on and show you the way."

We followed his Land Rover for a couple of miles, then parked by a gateway. In the adjacent field was a windowless stone shed with a low tin roof. Leaning against it, smoking a cigarette, was Finbarr.

"The cow's within," he greeted us, flicking his cigarette into the grass.

She lay in the corner, looking drawn and dull. Dag knelt down, examining her in the light of the open door.

"How long has she been scouring?"

Absent-mindedly, Finbarr searched the walls with his eyes, as if looking for an answer there.

"Some days I'd say."

"She doesn't have a temperature, but she's badly dehydrated," Dag told him. "I'll give her some intravenous fluids and some powders."

He was ducking through the shed door on his way to the car when Pat piped up, "What about those powders you were to give her yesterday, Finbarr? The ones the other vet left with you?"

Dag stopped, and turned round slowly.

"The other vet?"

Finbarr's eyes searched the shed roof.

"Ah well, yes, Mike O'Leary was over to me. But wasn't she due for those powders today, Pat, and not yesterday?"

Pat sighed and shook his head. "Where are they, Finbarr? The powders?"

"Well now," said his cousin vaguely. "That I couldn't say for sure."

Dag returned from the car with three bottles of fluid. He was administering the last one when the light spilling through the doorway was suddenly blocked.

"Ah, Christ, my mother," muttered Finbarr, shrinking away into the far corner of the shed.

Mrs. Casey was a wiry little woman with hard, glittering eyes and a strong handshake.

"Are you this man's wife?" she asked me. "You're a fine looking girl! How do you like it around here? You're very welcome, we're glad to have you."

When she discovered the state of the cow, however, her charm quickly dissolved and she began haranguing Finbarr.

"Whose fault is it that she's sick, now? You sitting there last night, away with the moon, smoking those cigarettes, and the poor cow needing a drink! You're a useless article!"

Drawing breath, she turned back to me.

"Seven children I brought into this world, and each one turned out worst than the last, and Finbarr is the most useless of the lot!"

"By God, Finbarr," chuckled Pat, who was safely positioned behind the cow, holding her nose, "you have a quiet life alright."

"Is it any wonder I have no woman?" Finbarr muttered back.

Unfortunately, his mother overheard this.

"What about Philomena?" she exploded, grabbing one of his ears and yanking it hard. "Whose fault was it that she dropped you? Was it my fault? Tell me that? Four years you were courting her, and she was a lovely girl, too. But there she'd be, waiting for you, and where would you be? Down in the pub with your friends, that's where! Ah, my lad, you missed your chance. You're twenty-eight years old now and never will you find another woman like Philomena, you mark my words."

"He's got plenty of time, Mrs. Casey," said Dag placatingly, removing the tube and needle from the cow's neck.

"Dag was twenty-eight when I met him," I added.

"Well, let's pray to God there's hope yet," she sighed. "And for you, too, Pat. Maybe you'll marry that girl of yours, now that you have the child and all."

Dag and I both stared at Pat, who blushed.

"You've had a child with your girlfriend, Pat?" Dag asked him.

"The Church speaks sternly against it," said Mrs. Casey, "but surely to God it's better to live with someone and find out if you like them first. My daughter's in Wales, living with her boyfriend. He's a lovely man, and so are his people."

"You didn't say that at first," ventured Finbarr, rubbing his ear. "You as good as scared him away when he first came here."

"Well," she said defensively, smoothing her hands on the apron she wore under her overcoat. "I didn't like the Welsh then, on account of that Welshman over the way beating the Jesus out of his wife. I thought they might all be the same."

Dag stood up, and patted the cow.

"That's all I can do for her now. Just remember to give her the powders twice a day. The prognosis isn't good, I'm afraid. She's not a strong animal."

Mrs. Casey whirled round on Finbarr once more.

"That's your doing, Finbarr, buying her in the first place, I told you back then she was no good, can you not do anything right!"

"Whisht now, mammy, you're embarrassing these people," said Finbarr, ducking past her and out of the shed.

"You bring them back to me for a cup of tea," she yelled after him as we headed up to the cars. "And it's time you settled your bill! I had a call from the vet's office, you're after owing them over two hundred pounds. And don't you be forgetting about this poor cow again, or you'll have me to talk to about it!"

"Does your mother get onto you so?" Finbarr wistfully asked me, watching Mrs. Casey stride across the fields towards her cottage.

"You'd be lost without her," I teased him.

"I would so. She's a great woman, but Christ, she can be desperate at times."

At Pat and Finbarr's insistence, we went ahead of them on the short drive to Mrs. Casey's house. When we turned into her gate, their Land Rover roared off, with the two men waving cheerfully at us through the window.

A goat with a long beard was tethered in front of the white cottage, and pots of pink plastic geraniums stood on the windowsills. Mrs. Casey ushered us into her kitchen. She had cakes and biscuits arranged on her best plates, a kettle steaming on the range, and a tray laid with mugs, milk, sugar and a jar of instant coffee.

"On my way down here I remembered you're from Canada, so I said to myself, it's coffee those people will be drinking, not tea, and thanks be to God my neighbour had some I could borrow. But you'll have to make your own, now, as I've no idea about it."

We sat on either side of the range, under a line of men's shirts hanging to dry. Mrs. Casey leaned her back against the sink and talked, barely pausing for breath between a steady streams of words.

"This was a council cottage when my husband was alive, God rest his soul. Before we lived here we were years in rented places, me with six children then and him working nights, coming home in the morning as I was getting the children ready for school. It was a hard old life all round, so sometimes I went to stay with my mother in the week, but I could never get on with her, she was forever telling me what to do. So later when we had the last child we got this house, and then he got sick, and after that he was no good, for years he sat in that chair where you sit now, it was terrible to see, and three years ago he died, and I'm still heartbroken—"

Tears spilled from her eyes and ran down her cheeks. She wiped them away with a corner of her apron, drew breath and carried on.

"I still had three children living at home but they weren't bringing anything in, just a bit of food now and then, so I told the council there were only two of us and that way the rent was just eighteen pounds a week. Take some more cake there, now, and don't leave those biscuits, they'll only go to waste. Then one day there's a knock at the door and a woman from the council is standing on the step, and she tells me she's heard there are four of us here not two, so the rent is going up to sixty pounds a week. I tell her the three aren't bringing any-thing in, but she says those are the rules, and then she asks me why I don't buy the house, that it would be cheaper in the long run, and that's what I did and now I only have two thousand pounds to pay off. I heat the place with turf, I've rented the same piece of bog for thirty years, I have a man come in to cut it and then I lay it out and turn it myself, and a friend of mine helps me to put it in the trailer and pile it up in the rick, and isn't that a thing, a son living with me and I'm turning my own turf? Finbarr's away with the moon, sitting here smoking of an evening, puffing on those evil sticks, it's no wonder my ceiling's black. He only goes out on a Saturday night, he's down in the town then with his friends and I'm lonely when he's gone but I can't keep him tied up all the time now, can I?"

We stayed as long as we could. When we eventually left she took both my hands and pressed them between hers.

"It's grand that you like it round here and I hope you decide to stay," she whispered to me. "But it's a hard life alright. God made this part of Ireland last, and he forgot to bless it."

✦

CHAPTER SEVENTEEN

During the first week of April, just as the first bluebells appeared in the hedgerows, the weather turned cold and blustery. Standing on the slopes of Knocknadobar Mountain with Dora one morning, I watched monstrous clouds roll in from the west, causing the light to shift and slide over the waters of Dingle Bay. Within minutes a squall hit, pelting us with stinging rain. As we raced down the hill towards shelter, we flushed out a pair of curlews from their new nest among the gorse and they flew ahead of us in a dipping pattern, letting out mournful whistles.

By now I'd grown used to the weather, and found its sudden changes invigorating. That afternoon I cheerfully cycled to town against the wind and rain, enjoying the thought that on the way back I'd be blown downhill at twice the speed. As I was labouring up the lane, I met Dennis. He was dragging a branch wrapped in ivy behind him, and he looked exhausted.

"Ivy is good for the ewes after they've lambed," he explained. "It gives them strength."

"Any new lambs this morning?" I asked.

"Four. And one calf."

"Dag was busy last night."

"I know. I heard his car."

"You must come over and see us one evening, Dennis."

"I will. But I'll not come until the sheep have finished gaining. I can't rest until then."

For a minute he stood and watched me slowly crank the pedals. Then he called out after me, "Only a fool would cycle up a hill!"

The lambing season was in full swing. In the fields along the valley, flocks were literally multiplying before our eyes. Each morning, more tiny Blackface Mountain lambs appeared. For the first few hours of life they tottered uncertainly alongside their mothers, but before long they were bouncing gaily among the yellow primroses and furze.

Everyone in the farming community was working flat-out. Throughout the day and night, shepherds were in the fields, checking on newborn lambs and ewes in difficulty with labour. Unbroken sleep and regular meals became past luxuries for Dag, and he rarely sat down to eat before the phone rang or someone banged at the door. Our kitchen looked like an operation prep room, littered with buckets, shears, ropes, syringes and bottles of antiseptic solution. On some nights, cars and trailers queued up in our garden and along the track, and an assembly line of birthings took place on top of the picnic table. Mostly these were happy events, with a healthy lamb, a relieved ewe and a satisfied farmer the result of Dag's work. But the lambing season also had its grim side, to which I was slowly becoming inured.

While I was getting dressed one morning, I glanced at my reflection in the wardrobe mirror and noticed something attached to my left breast. In horror, I stared down at a red spot on my skin, and the small, round crab-like creature hanging off it.

"Dag?" I called to the still form in the bed behind me.

He didn't stir.

"Dag, wake up!"

My urgent tone caused a flurry of bedclothes, and Dag was at my side, rubbing his eyes.

"It's a sheep tick," he said with great interest. "It must have crawled onto you from Dora."

The tick, he cheerfully explained, had legs and a head that were now firmly attached to my skin. The scabby part was its abdomen, which was filled with the blood it was sucking from my body.

"Get if off me," I said tersely. "*Quickly.*"

He shook his head.

"We can't just pull it off, because then it would break and you'd be left with its head still stuck in you. Have we got any Vaseline? A good smearing of grease will suffocate the tick, and the whole thing will eventually fall off."

"How long will that take?"

"A day, maybe."

I decided I didn't want to spend a day sitting at home obsessing about the tick suffocating beneath my sweater. After breakfast I went next door to ask Margaret if she'd feed Dora again while I was out with Dag.

"Sure, I'd love to," Emily said. "She's such a pet."

"I thought so too, until she gave me a tick."

"You have a *sciortain*? Ah, we get them all the time, they're nothing to be worried about. But they leave you with a terrible itch."

Dag's first call was to Mary Clifford, who lived north of Caherdaniel. She was a delicate looking woman, with grey curls escaping from around her headscarf. The farm she owned was in the shadow of a mountain, and exposed to the westerlies blowing in from the sea. Rising behind it, forming a natural amphitheatre, was a curve of steep slopes, blanketed with bracken turned a rich rust-red by the rain. Towards the base of the mountain, where the land began to flatten out, lay a patchwork of small fields, startlingly green and lush. They bore testimony to many years of back-breaking effort, of clearing rocks, of heaping them into stone walls, of hauling seaweed from the coast and of mixing it with farmyard dung to fertilize the soil. The farm had been in Mary's family for five generations, she told us, which was unusual round here: most people had only got their land around the turn of the century when the foreign landlords were finally ousted, or in the 1920s, after the partition of Ireland. She was a widow now and ran the farm alone. Her three children, all girls, had married and moved away, to Killarney, to Trimoleague in County Cork, and to Norfolk in England.

"The one across the water," said Mary, referring to her daughter in England, "she wants to come home, but the houses here have got too expensive for her. She can't believe what's happened to the prices. They've gone sky-high."

"That's because of all the foreigners coming in," I said knowledgeably.

"It is indeed," she agreed, without a trace of irony.

"Why doesn't your daughter move here with you?"

Mary paused a moment, looking pained; I was sorry I'd asked.

"She has no interest in farming, and neither does her husband. The young people these days, they want to be in town with their friends of an evening, not stuck away in mountainy places."

Her new, corrugated iron shed was airy and dry. Mary had transformed it into a maternity ward and the sounds of bleating and of hooves clacking on wooden slats echoed around its high walls. Most of the roomy pens were occupied by ewes that she had brought inside for birthing. They gazed up at us as we passed by, their eyes serious and gently questioning. The sick ewe lay on a deep bed of straw, separated from her lamb by a wooden pallet standing on its side against one corner of the pen. Mary had noticed the ewe early that morning, when she was out doing her first round of the day.

"I thought she had a hurt in her back leg, the way she was limping," she told Dag. "But she was kicking the lamb away, and when I caught her I saw her teat. I'd say it's mastitis."

As Dag gently examined the swollen udder, the ewe groaned in pain.

"I know girl, this isn't nice," he said soothingly.

He took her temperature, wiping the thermometer on her fleece after removing it from her back end. Mary had been correct in her diagnosis: the ewe had an inflammation of the mammary gland, and was running a fever. The only effective treatment was a course of antibiotics. Dag warned Mary that, while he could most likely save the ewe, her udder was now useless and she would not be able to raise her lamb.

"Ah, I know." She glanced across to a lone sheep in a pen at the far end of the shed. "I'm thinking I could get that ewe over there to foster her. Only this morning, the crows killed her ram lamb."

"The crows?" I repeated incredulously.

"They pecked the eyes right out of him, the bastards, Sometimes they kill them by pulling out their tongues. I've even seen them attack a lamb while it's being born, when it's halfway out of its mother. 'Tis a horrible thing to see, I tell you."

Mink preyed on her flock, and foxes, too.

"Foxes are the real blaggards," said Mary. "Jimmy Murphy, now, over on Bolus Head, he has a terrible time with them. His fields run down to the sea cliffs and they hide in caves beneath the edge so that Jimmy can't catch them. Last year he lost over forty lambs to the foxes. One got a lamb that was almost two months old, a fine big lamb it was, and the bastard ate the face and half the neck right off of it. His ewes have no sense at all; they start gaining at the edge of the cliff and when the poor lambs come out they go tumbling down and there's nothing to stop them falling to their deaths."

As we walked back to the car, I noticed a dead crow hanging from a fuchsia hedge, its wings outstretched.

"That's to scare off its friends," Mary explained.

"So why don't you string up foxes, too?" I asked.

"Arra, Mr. Fox is too clever by far for that trick," she said.

On our way to Paddy Curran's farm, near Waterville, we tailed a tourist bus crawling behind a flock of sheep. The bus driver kept blaring his horn, but the two shepherds calmly ignored him, obviously in no mind to hurry along their sheep for the sake of some traffic.

Paddy lived in a small cottage built low to the ground. His mother answered the door. She led us across the yard to a stone wall topped with barbed wire on which scraps of sheep's wool and remnants of black plastic silage bags fluttered in the wind. She pointed over the wall, to a field that rose up into a hillock.

"You'll find Paddy away over."

He was standing with his dog along the bank of a small stream. His hands were in his pockets, a cigarette hung from his bottom lip, and he was staring at some sheep on the grass. The animals were in a pitiful state. Three of them were staggering around in circles. Others lay curled on the grass like commas, their heads facing backwards.

"I might as well shoot the feckers, I suppose," said Paddy, when we reached him.

He was a loose-limbed man in his early thirties, with a feckless air about him.

"They've been getting worse all morning. I was in half a mind to call in and tell you not to come, and save myself the money."

"Well, I'm here now, so let's see what we can do," said Dag. "Have you ever had louping ill on this farm?"

Paddy nodded. "I have indeed. I lost seventy sheep to it last year. Mike O'Leary came out to see them time and time again. He said it was ticks. So I treated the flock for ticks and still they got the sickness. Then Mike sent off some animals to Tralee for testing. The people in Tralee said it was ticks. So I burned all my fields. And now here I am, with more sick sheep. I don't believe it's ticks. None of you have a fecking clue what's wrong and you're all making up stories."

"Do you ever feed the sheep with silage?"

"I do not, for Mike warned me against that last year. I've been feeding them on hay and nuts instead, and it's costing me a fortune. Do you think it could be the ticks, after all?"

I listened to their exchange with a growing sense of disquiet, trying to resist the urge to scratch frantically at my chest.

"If you've a history of louping ill on your land, there's a good chance it could be ticks," said Dag. "These animals are in a bad way, Paddy. There's not much we can do for them at this stage, I'm afraid."

"They'd be better off under the ground, you'd say?"

"I think so. They'll only die a horrible death otherwise."

"I have more sheep up by my other house. There's one there with the same thing. Will we go over and have a look?"

Paddy and his dog climbed into the back seat of our car and directed us for half a mile, towards a small, solitary bungalow with a view across desolate bogland. The plaster on its outside walls was painted a garish orange colour, and the garden surrounding it had been completely cleared and covered with loose gravel. Paddy was proud of the place; he'd only recently finished it, he told us, and planned to rent it out to tourists in the summer.

"I can get two hundred pounds a week in the high season," he said confidently. "If you know of any Canadians who are after a holiday here, would you give them my name?"

Apart from his dog, there wasn't an animal in sight.

"Where's this sick sheep, Paddy?" asked Dag.

"Ah, it's just over the hill. Wait there while I get it."

He set off with the sheepdog, leaving us leaning against a windowsill of his house.

"I guess he might find someone who'd like to stay here," said Dag doubtfully, peering through the dirty window pane into an empty room. "It's peaceful at least."

I leaned down to pull at a weed bravely sprouting between the gravel.

"What exactly is louping ill, Dag?"

"It's a type of encephalitis and causes paralysis and convulsions. Most sheep that get it die. Other animals can get it as well."

"Humans, too?"

"Sure."

"And what exactly do ticks have to do with it?"

"They carry the virus that causes it," said Dag, standing up at the sound of some whistling. "Look, here they come."

Paddy and his dog were running down the hill behind at least fifty sheep. They herded them over a wall and into the yard of the house, where the dog raced to and fro, barking wildly and penning them between us and the car.

"I had to catch the lot to get at the one," shouted Paddy over the bleating and barking.

Lunging into the flock, he hauled out a sheep, straddled it and walked it over to Dag. It had the symptoms of louping ill: the trembling legs, the head twisting back, the tendency to run to one side.

"She's not quite so bad as the others," said Dag. "I'll give her a special cocktail into the vein and see if that helps. But her chances aren't good."

"I might as well shoot the fecking lot," said Paddy glumly. "I'll give up the farming altogether. I'll buy a boat, fish a bit in the summer and collect the dole all winter."

"Do you really want to be a fisherman?" Dag asked him, as he began treating the sheep.

"Ah no, I get seasick. But maybe I'll sell the farm and buy a pub. Publicans have it easy. Staying inside all day in the warm, and making good money on every pint they pull."

"A lot of publicans become alcoholics."

"Sure, I'm an alcoholic already," said Paddy. "So what difference would it make?"

Back in the car, I looked under my sweater and saw that the tick had fallen off, leaving a red weal on my skin. By fishing around among my clothes I found the creature, a disgusting red-black sack, and flicked it out of the window.

"How are you feeling?" Dag asked me, as we drove down the track.

"What do you mean?"

"You look a bit flushed." He took a hand from the steering wheel and laid it against my forehead. "I think you've got a temperature. It's the first sign."

"Of what?"

"Louping ill. Now listen, if you notice some trembling in your lips, or if you start walking around in a circle, tell me *immediately*. As long as we treat the virus straight away, you'll have a chance."

I stared at him, wide-eyed.

"Because once you start convulsing," he continued, "and your legs become paralyzed, there's nothing we can do."

He glanced slyly at me from the corner of his eyes. As his laughter bubbled up, I began pummelling him with my fists.

"You bastard!" I yelled, as he swerved under the assault, narrowly missing Paddy's new drystone wall.

✦

CHAPTER EIGHTEEN

It was the Saturday before Easter, and there was a sombre mood in the East End Bar. A funeral had taken place earlier in the day. People were drinking to the memory of the deceased, the young wife of a local farmer. The men held glasses of stout, the women sipped on ginger ales or sherry, and they spoke in quiet, dramatic tones, rehashing to each other everything they already knew about the tragedy.

"It's a terrible thing altogether, to have to bury one so young."

"The poor girl, only thirty-three years of age and with those two lovely children. You couldn't find a nicer girl, or a better mother."

"Ah you couldn't. She was a lovely mother, she was. The children will be lost without her, poor creatures. Wasn't it terrible the way she was so quickly riddled with the cancer?"

"Riddled with it! Riddled! Only six weeks ago she fell sick, and by then it had eaten right through her. There was nothing the doctors could do."

We stood off to one side, not taking part in the conversation, until Ted Donnelly sidled up to us with a couple of drinks.

"Call in on me one day soon when you're free," he told Dag, "and I'll take you up the mountain to see my sheep."

As Dag was presently deluged with sheep and lambs, I thought it unlikely that he would want to be around them during his precious free time. Yet he responded eagerly.

"I've got next Saturday off, Ted."

"Come early then and we'll go up together and Mary will cook us a breakfast afterwards." Ted paused, and thought for a few seconds. "Unless there's another funeral, of course. If there's a funeral on, you better come another day."

Funerals were important events on the Iveragh Peninsula; each death was regarded as a personal sorrow. People listened with great interest to the death notices broadcast twice daily on a local radio station.

"Radio Kerry has been informed of the following deaths," the announcer solemnly began. "The death of Joe McCarthy of Foilmore. Removal will take place this evening at six-thirty from Creen's Funeral Home to Daniel O'Connell Memorial Church, Cahersiveen. Requiem Mass will take place tomorrow at eleven o'clock. Burial afterwards at Kilvonargue Cemetery, Cahersiveen." After a respectful pause, she continued, "The death of Mary Fitzgerald of Knocknagoshal. Waking at her residence. Removal will take place from her residence this evening at five o'clock to Saint Mary's Church, Knocknagoshal . . ." and so on.

In shops and pubs, I overheard people spreading the news of local deaths. On handwritten cards, trimmed with black ribbon and lace and pinned to doorways along Main Street, I read the times of removals and Requiem Mass. In Quirke's newsagents I queued up behind people buying Mass Cards, which pledged payment for a Mass for the soul of a deceased person.

When the young mother died, crowds gathered for a wake in the funeral home. Two days later a crowd attended the removal service, when the body arrived in the church to spend the night there. The following morning, businesses along Main Street closed so that everyone could attend the Requiem Mass. Cars parked two and three deep; there was standing room only inside the church. After the Mass, the mourners walked in slow procession behind the hearse to the cemetery. With the coffin lowered into its grave and the last prayers said, everyone headed to the pubs to remember and praise the dead woman, and to swap stories about fatal illnesses, accidents and the misfortunes of others.

Soon after we arrived in the bar, talk turned from the young woman just buried, to the case of an old fisherman and his wife, who had recently drowned in the harbour close to our cottage. I had met the couple once, very briefly, while walking by the pier with Dora. They had driven up in an old blue van to fish. The man had admired my lamb.

"I can't believe he was seventy-nine," I told Ted Donnelly. "He looked much younger than that."

"Ah yes, he was still fresh for his age."

"Why did they drown?"

"No one knows, Marie, no one knows, and that's the real tragedy of it. The day was so calm they could have seen their own faces in the sea. It makes no sense, no sense at all."

"I'd say they pulled in too many fish and the boat sank under the weight of them," a man chipped in.

"Or maybe it was just the time they were due to go," said another.

"It is a blessing really, for them to go together, and not one to be left behind, mourning for the other," mused Ted.

"But terrible for the families, to lose both the father and the mother together," someone else said.

"Terrible!" came a chorus of voices. "Terrible altogether!"

The following Friday, I tuned in to the death announcements. A Cahersiveen man had died; his funeral was to be held the following morning. Instead of visiting Ted on Saturday, we had a relaxed morning at home, then went into town for lunch. There was a strange, unfamiliar atmosphere along Main Street. Tight knots of people huddled in shop doorways, their collars turned up against the keen wind, their eyes averted from passersby.

"The Requiem Mass must still be going on," I said, as we looked for a parking spot. "I suppose these people are waiting to follow the funeral procession to the graveyard."

"So why aren't they inside the church?" asked Dag. "Surely it can't be that full."

We stopped off first in Craneen's Pub for a quick drink. Dag knew a couple of the farmers sitting at the bar, and asked after their animals, but their replies were curt, inviting no further conversation. We ordered beer and peanuts. Garth Brooks was warbling from a tape-recorder on a high shelf, and the barmaid hummed along with the tune as she poured out two glasses of stout. She was placing the glasses on beer mats in front of us when, above the country and western song, I heard the reedy, mournful sound of bagpipes.

"Turn off that music," one of the men snapped. She silently obeyed.

The piping came from the direction of the church. It grew steadily closer and louder. The men stood up, removed their hats and faced the window, which was opaque save for a clear strip at the top. I slid off my stool, nudging Dag.

"What's going on?" he asked.

"The funeral procession," I whispered. "Stand up. It's a sign of respect."

On tiptoes, I peered through the clear glass. A lone piper walked slowly past the pub. Marching behind him were two ranks of men, wearing black berets, black sweaters and dark glasses. Then came the coffin. It was draped in the tricolour of the Irish Republic, heaped with flowers and borne on the shoulders of six men. Following it was a procession, at least two hundred strong and steadily swelling as the knots of people left the doorways to join its ranks.

Stony silence was maintained in the pub until the last stragglers had passed by and disappeared from view, and the piping had faded into the distance. Then the men replaced their hats and returned to their drinks.

"What was all that about?" Dag asked me.

I was unwilling to explain, in my unmistakably British tones, that what we'd just witnessed was the funeral procession of a member of the illegal Irish Republican Army. Or that on the outskirts of town the procession would halt, and hooded men would emerge from a parked car with rifles to fire off several rounds over the coffin in a honorary salute. Instead, I said nothing, and concentrated on my drink. One of the farmers leaned forward on his elbow.

"That cow you came to me about," he said to Dag, "she's doing grand now, she really is. But I have a calf that's coughing badly. Is there anything you can suggest for that?"

The young woman reached up to the tape-recorder, Garth Brooks began warbling once more and the tension in the bar eased.

After lunch, we wound up our afternoon in the East End Bar. It was filled with people dressed in dark, smart clothes, but no one seemed to be talking about the man whose funeral they had just attended. When we asked about him, the question was shrugged off. Eventually, one farmer took us into his confidence.

"He was one of the *old boys*," he whispered meaningfully. "They still give them the full honours around here, and the *gardaí* look the other way. It's nothing to worry yourselves about."

"Why was everyone so uneasy?" I asked.

"It's the *old wounds*," he whispered. "They still hurt. It's hard for people to forget them."

I thought back to the Civil War, to the five local Republicans from Cahersiveen who were tied to a landmine by fellow Irishmen and blown up.

"You mean, like the Bahaghs Martyrs?"

The farmer's face closed, and he moved away.

I'd run into this time and again. Most people we met in pubs or on farms were happy to talk endlessly on all manner of subjects, with the exception of Irish political history, and particularly the Civil War, over which they drew a veil of silence.

That evening, I rang my mother in Manchester and told her about the funeral. She listened in silence. She had always refused to enter into discussions on Irish history; now, I asked her why this was.

"Terrible things happened in Ireland," she said. "People don't want to think about them anymore. What point is there in stirring up the past? Wasn't it bad enough to have to suffer it at the time?"

"But hundreds of people attended that funeral," I argued, "so they must want to remember."

"Ah, well, there's always some who do," she commented, and would say no more on the subject.

Several days later, on the way home from town, I turned up the track leading to Kilvarnogue Cemetery. Its entrance was blocked by old wrought-iron gates with a chain and padlock wrapped around them, but the stone wall had a gap wide enough for me to step through it. The cemetery was small, the graves tightly packed together, and long grasses, bluebells, ivy and brambles grew between them. Most of the headstones faced the fine view, along the river estuary, towards Knocknadobar Mountain and the pools of sunlight on its steep slopes. As I walked, my feet kept knocking against stones in the undergrowth. Small stubby stones, barely sticking out of the earth, the markings of old, old graves. There were many family graves, some of them long and narrow, as if the bodies had been buried head to toe. One was the resting place of Sigerson Clifford, the celebrated local poet.

Jars of faded silk flowers and clear plastic globes containing statues of Our Lady decorated some of the newer graves. Lying on one was a lobster pot, a plastic dolphin and a large wreath of dead flowers fashioned into the shape of a boat. I wondered if this was the resting place of the fisherman and his wife who had drowned in the harbour. It occurred to me that their parents must have been born just after the famine, and that they had been small children during the Civil War. Had they lived longer, perhaps we would have chatted often down by the pier. There was much I could have asked them about the past, I mused, and much more, perhaps, on which they would have chosen to keep their silence.

✤

CHAPTER NINETEEN

The days leading up to Easter brought cataclysmic weather. After storm-battered nights, we woke to see snow dusting the mountains and little drifts of hailstones piled up on our windowsills. Rain fell in torrents. The streams on Knocknadobar swelled, turned brown in colour with washed-away peat and raged noisily over stones and boulders. The fields below our cottage flooded, becoming shallow lakes with reeds and yellow furze blossoms showing above the surface of the water. Ewes that had been grazing in those fields with their offspring headed for higher ground, many seeking shelter in our relatively dry garden. Soaked and shivering, the lambs huddled against the stone walls, trying to escape the biting wind. One lamb, its umbilical cord still trailing from its belly, looked so pathetically weak that I ran out and scooped it up, meaning to warm it by the fire. But the mother was having none of this, charging me with her head down and bleating harshly in protest until I returned the baby to her.

Towards noon on Easter Thursday, the rain stopped at last. A widening band of blue sky appeared on the western horizon and the light became astonishingly clear, picking out contours and ridges on Knocknadobar that I had never noticed. The lambs ventured a few steps away from the stone walls, shaking themselves like little dogs. Then, as sunlight broke through the clouds and warmed their bodies, they came alive with energy, leaping and gambolling around their mothers, epitomizing pure and simple joy.

It was only a brief respite; by early afternoon, yet another frontal system had blown in, rattling the roof slates and moaning down the chimney.

"I've got a couple of calls over the Glen," said Dag, back for a quick lunch. "Why don't you come along? St. Finian's Bay looks fantastic in this weather."

Outside, the wind was so strong I had to fight against it to open the car door. It whipped out some of Dag's notes and receipts from the passenger seat, and sent them spiralling away across the fields.

From Cahersiveen we drove south for a few miles before turning westwards towards the little fishing village of Portmagee, named after a famous eighteen-century smuggler who conducted business here. The terraced houses along the village's one short street were brightly painted in shades of blue, yellow and mint green. They looked over the fishing boats tied to the pier, across a channel of white-capped water, to the velvety fields of Valentia Island.

Beyond the village, the road climbed a mountain pass. Below us, blanket bog stretched across the plain, a brown canvas awash with subtle, earthy colours. Above, a smooth shoulder of land clothed in yellow sedge grasses rose to meet high cliffs that dropped dizzyingly to the boiling ocean.

"There's a story about a farmer's daughter committing suicide somewhere along here," Dag told me. "She ran to the edge of the cliff, and just kept going. Her father tried to stop her, but he didn't catch her in time."

The car shuddered from the wind as we crested the shoulder. Abruptly, the view changed. The Glen was a steep, green bowl of rolling fields and stone walls, edged by headlands and beaches and open Atlantic Ocean. Eight miles offshore, two dramatic pyramids of rock thrust skywards, with waves breaking against them on all sides. These were the Skellig Rocks. On such a day it was almost inconceivable to think that for six centuries a community of early Christian monks lived there, with fragile, skin-covered boats their only means of access.

By the time we reached Dan Golden's farm, a dense shroud of clouds had rolled in from the west, completely obscuring the Skelligs.

"You get a grand view of the rocks on a fine day," Dan assured us. "This is fierce weather, alright, but there's no cold in it."

Seemingly oblivious to the wind and driving rain, he stood with us outside the little bungalow, painstakingly recounting to Dag every detail of his lame cow's long medical history. While they talked, I examined the old Mini Van that lay close by on its axles, rotting into the grass. Abandoned cars were a common sight on the farms across the peninsula, but this one was unusual in that it seemed to be providing useful storage space. It was filled with tools, calving equipment and odds and ends of ropes, as well as empty plastic milk jugs, sodden cardboard boxes and bulging black plastic rubbish bags.

"Shall we go away to the cow?" Dan suggested. "You'll have no bother with her, she's a good, quiet cow."

His farmyard sloped down the hill. A thick layer of mud and dung sucked us in up to our ankles as we waded through it. At the bottom of the yard several cows roamed around some stone sheds. One of them was limping badly.

"She's severely lame," said Dag, his brow furrowing. "It could be an abscess. We'll have to get her into the crush to look at her hoof."

Standing in the shelter of a doorway, I watched him slowly approach the animal and slip a halter around her head. She seemed compliant enough as he led her towards the crush, but before they reached the opening she stopped dead in her tracks and refused to take another step.

"Yosh, yosh, yosh!" shouted Dan, flapping his arms at her. "Get in there, you monkey, get *in*!"

Far from helping matters, this only roused the cow, who began shaking her head and skipping sideways. Patiently, Dag tried to coax her into the crush, but she was having none of this, and stood with her head down, looking the picture of stubbornness. Finally, he looped the end of the rope leading from her halter around a bar of the crush, and secured it firmly. All the thrashing around had caused him to sink further into the muck, which was now perilously close to the top of his boots.

"OK, Dan," I heard him say. "We're going to push her in."

Attempting to move anything so big and so unwilling seemed a futile endeavour to me, but the two men were determined. They leaned their backs against the cow's buttocks and heaved, as if she were a car they were trying to push up a hill. Keeping their footholds in the quagmire was almost impossible, and they slithered and slipped about, heaving with all their might. Despite such valiant efforts, however, the cow didn't move an inch.

"Okay, we'll try something else," gasped Dag, when finally they gave up. Mud caked one of his cheeks, from his eye down to his mouth. "You slacken the rope, Dan, and I'll round up a couple of the other cows and send them into the crush first. With a bit of luck she'll follow them."

Wading through the muck and waving his arms, he persuaded two animals into the crush. Hope flickered as the cow took a single step towards them. Then she stopped dead once more.

"I'll fecking shoot you!" Dan yelled at her in fury. "I'll put you in a hole in the ground, you monkey!"

By now I was beginning to rather admire the tenacity of this cow. The farmer and his vet, on the other hand, were utterly exasperated and had resorted to extreme measures. Taking one leg apiece, they strained to lift the back end of the cow a few inches from the ground, pushing forwards at the same time and forcing her to take a few steps on her front hooves. After ten minutes of this desperately hard work, the cow's nose was almost level with the entrance of the crush and the men were exhausted. They stopped for a break, and while they were stretching their backs and gathering strength for the next assault, the cow had a change of heart. Without any encouragement, she trotted casually into the crush.

"She's normally so quiet," said Dan, as Dag began paring down a crack in her hoof. "What in God's name could have made her so contrary today?"

"Women just get that way sometimes, Dan," said Dag, turning to wink at me.

"You're right there, boy. But I'd rather deal with a bold cow than a bold woman. That's the truth, now!"

In St. Finian's Bay, huge foaming waves rolled in from a malevolent grey-green sea, and smashed down onto the yellow strand. Below the exposed cliffside road on the way to Bolus Head, the wind blew clouds of spray off the crests of waves as they reared up, before exploding violently onto jagged black rocks. The farm we were heading for was near the end of the road. Dag's job there was to treat a cow with an injured back.

"How does a cow injure its back?" I asked him.

"Maybe she lifted something awkwardly," he teased me. "Or she got out of bed the wrong way. Or maybe it was a two-thousand-pound bull mounted her a bit too vigorously. What do you reckon?"

We were flagged down by Liam Sullivan.

"It's a fine fresh breeze we have!" he greeted us. A woolly hat was pulled down over his ears and the end of his nose was bright red with cold.

Liam had called Dag out on behalf of his Uncle Peter, who owned the cow with the bad back. We followed him across a field of boggy grass, past a tractor with a wooden pallet attached to its pick-up, to a crowd of men and children gathered around a prone cow. Other cows wandered close by, gazing curiously at the sick animal, and pied wagtails hopped among them. Uncle Peter was a small man with loose false teeth that moved about his mouth as he spoke.

"She was bulling, and one of the big cows kept leaping up on her back," he shouted, above the noise of the wind. "Until yesterday she was walking normal, but then she started to go about like this."

Splaying his legs, he staggered around in imitation of the cow, sending the children into fits of giggles.

"When I came out here this morning, she was down, and now she won't get up."

Dag reached into his pocket for a penknife, opened the blade and pricked various points on the cow's back end to test her sense of feeling. The muscles twitched and her tail flicked until he pricked her haunches, to which she didn't react. Next, he worked his hands carefully along her spine up to the neck. Finally he stood back to survey her from several different angles.

"Her pelvis has dropped three-quarters of an inch," he told Peter. "All I can do is give her painkillers to make her comfortable and anti-inflammatories to bring down the swelling. The rest she'll have to do herself. It's important that you get her inside, somewhere with a floor that she won't slip on when she tries to stand up. You might even want to spread a deep layer of manure around to give her a secure footing. Can you do that?"

"We can, so," said Peter.

Liam reversed the tractor so that the wooden pallet almost touched the side of the cow. As the men rolled her onto it, she lowed pitifully.

"Ah, 'tis terrible to see a creature in such pain," said Peter sadly, while Dag was injecting her. "Some whiskey would do her good."

"I don't carry it as a rule," Dag told him.

"Do you not? Years ago there was another vet in these parts who swore by the whiskey. There was many a time I saw him pour it down the throats of animals. Why did it ever go out of fashion, now?"

With whiskey on our minds, we stopped off at a pub in Portmagee, hoping to get warm and dry. The fire we sat next to was about to splutter out, so we ordered more bricks of turf and a firelighter along with our hot toddies.

"Is it cold you are?" asked the barman. "Ah, 'tis poisonous weather, alright."

"We have a southwest wind, and that's the home of the rain," said a man with a neatly trimmed beard, who was sitting at the bar. "You've come too early for your holidays."

On hearing that we were living here awhile, he joined us at our table. Dermot was a South Kerry man who had moved to London twenty years ago, but came home for a visit every Easter.

"Portmagee's a different place altogether now. The houses weren't painted when I was a young man, everything was grey. There was a bar called Mary Ellen's, it was dark and dirty, and the men who drank there were sad and lonely, with nothing to do in their spare time but complain to each other and weep into their pints. When the tourists would ask me about a nice pub for a drink, I always sent them to Mary Ellen's. I'd laugh to think of them walking into that dirty place with its weeping old men."

He was surprised to hear we'd been in Kerry since February.

"No one in their right mind would choose to be here in the winters," he said, "for they're long and depressing. It's worse if you're on your own, of course. Those old farmers over in the Glen, they have a terrible time of it. There's no pub down there and no bus to town. A few years back, three bachelor farmers hanged themselves, one after the other. It was contagious I suppose. It was the loneliness that got to them, and the isolation. This is a terrible place for a man to live on his own. There's no women for marrying and nothing to do in your spare time but drink. I'm divorced now, and my children are grown, but I'd never come back to live. Never."

He took a long draught on his pint, then stared out of the window at the fishing boats tied up by the pier.

"There's nowhere like South Kerry. I miss it, really I do, and when I'm away I can't wait to come back."

✛

CHAPTER TWENTY

Easter Friday was a busy shopping day in Cahersiveen, with everyone stocking up for the long weekend. The butchers did a brisk trade in legs of lamb, and by noon Johnny Apple had practically sold out of Brussels sprouts. Between three and four o'clock in the afternoon, however, the streets emptied and became eerily quiet. This was the "holy hour," marking the death of Jesus on the cross, when most people attended Mass and the Stations of the Cross in church, or stayed at home and watched them on television.

Things remained quiet in town for the rest of the day and evening. No alcohol was sold on Good Friday; in the supermarket, sheets covered the shelves of wine and spirits, the off-licence stayed closed all day and the pubs never opened their doors. Only the well-prepared could drink on this night—which is why, we later surmised, Dennis McCarthy finally decided to pay us a visit.

I was peeling potatoes at the kitchen sink when a tap at the window made me glance up. An old gnarled face was pressed against the glass, its mouth hanging open, its eyes staring intently at me. I froze, gazing at this spectre in mute terror. Only when the lips began to move did I realize the face belonged to Dennis. He was calling something to me. I didn't hear him at first; blood pounded too loudly in my ears. Looking at me crossly, he shouted, "Are ye *home*?"

I put extra turf on the fire, and brought Dennis an ashtray.

"You scared me witless," I told him. "I think we both need a big drink."

"We do," he vehemently agreed. "Is it a whiskey you're having?"

While I poured out two large measures, he tapped his cigarette against the edge of the ashtray. His arthritic fingers moved slowly, his long, purplish nails had thick dirt caked beneath them.

"I'm sorry I frightened you. I didn't see your man's car. I wasn't sure if it was right to call on you. But I'd walked a step; I didn't want to walk back only to have to turn round again."

Tipping up his glass, he drank half the whiskey in one swallow. He wiped his lips, then continued on in his slow, measured tones.

"There were some tourists here, one midsummer. I came by at dusk to greet them. I had a pitchfork with me; why that was I can't remember. I knocked it against the glass of the window in this room. There was a woman sat where you are now. She looked up, and she let out such a screech that I ran away in fright. She and her husband left the next day, I heard. They went to stay in a bed and breakfast place in the town."

He had refused to take off his coat and was sitting close to the fire, his feet in their big boots planted on the hearth, his face quickly turning a deep shade of red. I had been wondering how old Dennis was, guessing that, like many of the farmers I had met, his lifestyle had aged him beyond his years. But when I asked him, he hedged around the question.

"I have a doctor in town. When you ask him a question, he never gives you a straight answer. I've a lot to learn from him. Isn't that your husband's car I heard coming?"

With another man in the room, Dennis relaxed.

"I've got a colour television, a radio and a telephone," he told us. "There's only one thing I don't have. Know what that is?"

"A fax machine?" I stupidly guessed.

"Conversation?" offered Dag.

"You've got some brains!" cried Dennis, grasping Dag's knee. "And you're a man who has travelled far. It's a long time since I looked at a map. The Great Lakes—they lie between Canada and America, isn't that so? There's a man I met. He told me there are wild horses south of those lakes. Black horses. Have you seen them? And in Canada, do you have Appaloosas? They are a lovely animal. They were first brought to these parts by a circus. A woman came all the way from Dublin to see me about an Appaloosa she had. She was trying to trace its line. Everyone, even people as far away as Tralee, told her to talk to Dennis McCarthy. She asked if she could use a tape-recorder. I told her she could. Then I told the history of that horse, ninety years back."

I asked him about the ponies he kept on the mountain.

"They are a hobby," he said. "Once I had two ponies that pulled the plough for me when I was preparing the ground for seed potatoes. Those ponies knew everything. At twelve o'clock they'd stop, walk over to the stream and take a drink. I'd give them a feed of oats, and then they'd work again. Now I just have the ponies as a hobby. You only have your health if you have a hobby you like."

He refused our offer of dinner, and a ride home, and after quickly downing two more whiskeys eased himself out of the chair.

"Anytime you need help, Dennis, just call me and I'll come over," Dag offered.

"I know that," he said. "But I don't need a vet. I know how to look after my animals properly. There's those that don't, but I do."

Easter Sunday dawned cold and sunny. Dag was on call, but as Mike O'Leary had predicted, things were quiet.

"The farmers will all be at Mass," he had said, "and then in the pub."

In the early morning a few farmers came by with ewes or lambs that needed attention. In between calls, Dag prepared a leg of lamb for our dinner. He wanted to marinate it, but could not find a pot big enough for the job. So he decided to use one of his long surgical gloves. He pushed the leg inside it, poured the marinade on top and knotted the end. It was an ingenious solution, but the sight was disgusting, with the transparent plastic of the glove stretched against the raw meat, and the brown marinade seeping into the fingers and thumb.

Around eleven I cycled into town to pick up the Sunday newspapers. The newsagents thronged with well-dressed people buying last-minute chocolate Easter eggs before hurrying to Mass. Outside the church, two elderly men were selling paper Easter lilies, commemorating the people of Kerry who died in the 1916 Easter Rising. I bought one, and pinned it to my lapel in memory of my father, a staunch Republican all his life.

Crowds streamed by, up the steps and through the high doors of the church. Part of me wanted to follow them, to celebrate Easter with them. When I was a child, my parents used to take me to Vigil Mass on Easter Saturday night. The church would be in darkness; everyone in the congregation held a candle, and we lit them one by one. I remembered excitedly grasping the candle, and my father leaning down to cup his hand around it, ensuring that the wick would catch fire. The magic of the ceremony entranced me: the church aglow with hundreds of flickering flames casting weird shadows across the high, vaulted ceilings when all the candles were lit. Then the tense expectant silence until the priest's voice boomed out,

"CHRIST IS RISEN!" and light suddenly flooded the church, making my scalp prickle.

People stood in the doorways of the church; it was full to capacity. I heard the drone of responses—*Lord have Mercy on us, Christ have mercy on us*. Mass had begun. I hesitated, then pushed my bike to the road. I had been too long a lapsed Catholic—there was no going back.

I got home to find Dora tearing off and swallowing clumps of grass, something she had begun to do only days before. She had also developed a taste for flowers, and I watched in consternation as she bit off the heads of buttercups, daisies and Teesdale violets. There was now no doubt that our lamb was well on her way to becoming a sheep: she had doubled in size, her neck had filled out and her knees no longer knocked together when she walked. As I parked my bike, she wandered over to the shelter of a stone wall and settled down against it, looking very relaxed. Then a spasm passed across her flanks, as if she were hiccuping badly. Her face took on an alarmed expression; her lower jaw began moving from side to side, at first tentatively and then with vigour.

"She's chewing her cud at last," said Dag proudly, when I called him out to see this. "Just watch now, in a minute she'll swallow what's in her mouth, then there'll be another hiccup and she'll start all over again."

In their wild state, he told me, sheep, like other ruminants, are fugitive animals, forever having to flee from predators. Their digestive system is adapted to their snatching a quick meal and later finding a safe place to masticate and digest it.

"She's definitely ready for weaning, Maria."

I knew he was right. But at a quarter to one, when Dora began calling insistently for her feed, I caved in, promising myself I would start the weaning process tomorrow.

Things stayed quiet all afternoon. Dag put the meat in the oven to roast, and I prepared the vegetables. By seven, our dinner was almost ready.

"Don't be too long," Dag said, when I popped out to give Dora her last feed. After she'd drained the bottle, I sat for a while on the wall at the back of our garden. Dora stood quietly beside me. More storms were forecast to blow in the next day, but for now the night was strangely calm, with no wind or scudding clouds, just a half-moon with a lone star twinkling below it, hanging in a navy blue sky. Some small creature, a mink perhaps, rustled about in the grass. A bird fluttered in the branches of a nearby sally tree, and sheep called mournfully from the field behind us. Dora shook her head, and gave a quiet bleat. As I leaned down to scratch her between the ears, I heard the sound of a car approaching. Presently its lights appeared, growing larger and finally sweeping up the track towards our cottage. Before the car stopped moving, the passenger door was thrown open.

"Is the vet home?" a man cried. "We have a ewe here in trouble, she's been gaining for hours."

Dag hurried out, carrying a bucket of water. Soon he had his hand inside the ewe, which lay puffing and groaning on the grass, her two back legs held skywards by one of the farmers. When I went to get more water and some newspapers from the kitchen, Dora followed me. I was happily anticipating this Easter birth, and looked forward to Dora's reaction to a new lamb, coughing and shaking its head on the grass beside her.

But when we went outside again, something was oddly out of place. Instead of cheerful banter, there was an atmosphere of strained silence. Dag's arm was now encased in a surgical glove, which I'd never seen him wear for a lambing, and a cardboard box lay by his feet.

"The injection's working," he told the two men. "She's not feeling much now."

"That's a blessing," said one.

They carried the ewe round to the picnic table. Two little legs protruded from her back end; birth seemed imminent.

"This could be a smelly one," said Dag.

Before I could ask why, he reached for the scalpel he'd left on the table, cut around one small hoof, then sliced through the skin along the length of the leg.

"What are you doing?" I gasped, as a skinned leg came away in his hand.

"Lamb's been dead a while," he said, throwing the severed limb in the box. He started work on the other one. "It's bloated and rotting inside the mother. This isn't my favourite job."

Dora had her head in the box, sniffing at its contents. In the shadows I saw our neighbour's old dog lurking about.

"I'll put Dora away."

Before I could escape, Dag asked me to get a bottle of lubricating gel from the boot of the car.

"Squirt it over my hand, would you," he said, holding out his hand and arm. "She's really dry inside."

Carefully, he manoeuvred his hand back inside her.

"Here we go. I just hope he comes away in one piece."

A dreadful stench arose as he began pulling on the rest of the lamb. The farmer holding the ewe turned his face sideways, his nose wrinkled in disgust. A head appeared, with big horn buds, quickly followed by the rest of the body, a grisly, foul-smelling, mutilated rag doll that he dropped into the box. The farmer let go of the ewe, and turned away to cough and spit into the grass.

"At least the poor mother will feel better now, thank God," he said, when he'd recovered.

But the ewe was exhausted, and terribly enfeebled by her long ordeal. As Dag was preparing to inject her with some antibiotics, her eyes rolled back, her head went limp and she died, quietly and without fuss. We all stood for a few seconds, staring down at her.

"Ah, well," sighed the farmer. "'Twas a wasted journey, I suppose, but at least we gave it a try."

He and his friend hauled the corpse and the cardboard box over to the car, then went inside our house to wash their hands. I walked Dora across to the haggard and she trotted inside it without complaint, only bleating once or twice in protest when I fixed its door shut.

"Good night, little one," I said, rubbing the nose that she stuck through the fox wire.

The aroma of roasting lamb, garlic and rosemary filled the kitchen. The two men sat at the table, drinking whiskey. Dag stood at the sink, furiously scrubbing his hands.

"Even with plastic gloves, the smell of a dead lambing gets into your skin," he complained.

I poured myself a large measure, hoping to build up enough courage to face our dinner.

"I'm sorry about your ewe and lamb," I told the farmer.

He shrugged, and ran a hand over his stubbly chin.

"Ah, that's the way of it," he said with a sigh. "Birth and death—when you're a shepherd you get used to them."

✦

CHAPTER TWENTY-ONE

By six-thirty on the morning of Easter Monday, we were driving towards Cahersiveen and arguing about our lamb. We planned to spend much of the day with Ted Donnelly, going up the mountain with him when he checked his flocks. I had wanted to leave a note on our neighbours' door, asking them to feed Dora in the middle of the day, but Dag insisted that this was a perfect opportunity to start seriously weaning her.

"She'll get hungry!" I wailed.

"Exactly. And when she's hungry enough she'll start to eat more grass."

"How could you be so *cruel*?"

"Have you seen how ewes wean their lambs, Maria? They kick them away from their teats. Dora's a sheep, not a baby."

As we drew up to Ted's small white bungalow, the dark green front door opened and he stepped out. He wore a parka over his tweed jacket. A pair of binoculars hung around his neck and he was holding three walking sticks carved from hazelwood crooks.

"Hello. How are ye? Shall we away up?" He handed us each a stick. "These are for you to keep, now. I make them myself. You shouldn't be out walking on the mountain without a stick. And if you're ever out at night, be sure to take them along and you'll be in no danger from the fairies, for there's great goodness in hazel. Hold on for me, now, while I get Lass."

Muffled barking came from a thatched shed across the yard. Ted pushed open the door, and a sheepdog snaked out. Lass was a small, gentle creature, with one blue eye and the other brown. She followed Ted to his car, jumped into the boot and curled up among a jumble of starter cables, ropes and tools, making no protest when he closed the lid on her.

"We'll go altogether in the one vehicle," Ted suggested. "That way I won't lose you."

Earlier in the morning, Ted had been to check on the sheep in the fields next to his house. These were his "twin lambers," ewes he had kept down from the mountain in late February after an ultrasonic scan had shown them to be expecting twins. The rest of his sheep were on the slopes of Teermoyle, the highest peak on the Iveragh Peninsula, whose name in Irish meant "bare and unprotected mountain."

Ted drove fast along narrow, winding lanes, between stone walls daubed with pale yellow primroses. After several miles we turned onto a track and entered a wide lonely valley, speckled with sheep and patterned by stone walls reaching high up towards the desolate summit of Teermoyle. A series of sheep grids, rounded iron bars set across ditches, slowed our progress.

"This is all my land now," said Ted, as we bumped across the first grid. "And what is it you see here, Dougeen? Rock, isn't that it? Only rock with only a bit of grass between, and we eejits call it fields. There's nothing you can do with this land, it's only good for sheep. Ah, but you're coming into remote country now. We're twelve miles from the nearest village, and it was 1957 before any vehicle came up here. I remember the day a car first drove up; it belonged to a man who lived beyond this land. I was working here for a farmer, helping him shear his sheep. We all stood out to watch that car go by. There wasn't another vehicle seen here for a good while after that."

In a field alongside the track, he spotted a couple of lambs tucked away in the shelter of a clump of reeds.

"The ewe will have put them there for protection from the elements while she went off to graze," he explained. "Sometimes they put them in hollows or among the roots of a tree. You have to know where to look. During that snowball rain we had last week, Carmel found a lamb inside an old washing-up bowl she'd thrown out in the yard. The bowl was lying on its side and wasn't the lamb within it, safe from the wind and the rain while the mother ate the grass nearby."

Farther along the track, he rolled down his window and stared out at a sturdy little lamb with unusual markings. One leg and half of its torso were black, the rest of it was pure white.

"He's a fine young ram," said Ted. "Born twelve days ago."

"You remember him?" I asked.

"Of course, Marie, of course. I remember all my sheep. The shepherd lives with his flock. And the sheep, she'll keep to a certain part of the mountain, and her daughter will keep to that part too. So I can look up at the mountain and always know where the different sheep are."

At the end of the track we came to a dilapidated, two-roomed cottage. Ted had bought this place, and the land that went with it, some fifteen years before, and often camped overnight here during the lambing season. His bed was a narrow rack set under the window, heaped with blankets, a pillow and several copies of the *Irish Sun*. A few cracked and stained mugs, a box of tea bags, a bottle of milk and an electric kettle stood on an old wooden table. The wall above the large, open fireplace was blackened from decades of smoke. Above a heap of fresh turf ash, a pot hung from an old, hinged cooking crane. Ted swept the ash aside, and stacked up a pile of twigs and some bricks of turf. Within minutes, a fire was spluttering into life.

"This will still be glowing when we get back," he said. "We can warm our toes on it then."

From a triangular cupboard in a corner of the room, he produced a bottle of whiskey, already half-drunk, and three glasses, and poured us each a large measure.

"Wash that down now, and then we'll go."

When he opened the boot of the car, Lass jumped out, her tail wagging. Keeping close by his heels, she followed him towards a field behind the cottage. Most of the ewes grazing there had lambs by their sides, but one, standing close to the gate, was heavily pregnant, with red membranes trailing from her back end. Ted leaned on his stick, carefully scrutinizing her.

"She's gaining steadily. There'll be a lamb before the afternoon."

Slowly, he opened the gate, making noises like soft bleats in the back of his throat. The ewe stood very still, watching him cautiously. But when she caught sight of Lass by his heels, she put her head down and charged the dog, chasing it around the field and thrusting at it with her horns until Ted gave a high whistle. Instantly, Lass turned and ran back to him.

"We'll leave her be for now and check her later on," said Ted. "Let's see what we have in the other departments."

We walked at a fast pace, hopping over the streams that separated fields and wading through boggy areas. On the bank of one stream, a ewe with a black star on her forehead stood close to a furze bush, bleating forlornly.

"Look at the poor creature," said Ted. "She lambed two days ago, lying right here by the stream. The lamb dropped in the water and by the time I found him it was too late, and he had drowned. So I put the body under that bush, and the mother has stayed by it day and night ever since."

A little farther along he stopped abruptly, pointing with his stick to a patch of bloody membrane on the grass. "There was a ewe gaining here last night, just after midnight. I haven't seen her yet this morning."

His dark eyes searched the large field.

"There they are." He singled out a ewe and her lamb that to me were indistinguishable from the rest of the flock. "The mother is a small little sheep; I was worried about her. But will you look, she shat out a lamb nearly the size of herself, and they both look healthy enough, thank God."

Whenever he found a telltale patch of membrane, he looked for the newborn lamb, often peering into clumps of reeds and rushes. Once he found it, he checked its rear end for traces of the black feces it passed after sucking the beestings. If the mother wasn't close by, Ted called her back by imitating a lamb's high bleat. Inevitably she came running, stopping in her tracks when she caught sight of Ted and gazing at him with puzzlement before turning her attentions to the baby.

We were on our way to the higher fields when we came across a ewe in labour. Lying in the shelter of a stone wall, she was puffing and groaning in obvious discomfort.

"I'd say she's doing fine on her own, what do you think, Dougeen?" said Ted, after quietly observing her for a while. "We can carry on and leave her to herself."

Dag decided he'd like to stay and take some photographs.

"It's not often I get to see a normal birth," he said, lying down on his stomach on the wet grass, and aiming his camera at the ewe's back end.

Ted turned to me with a bemused expression. "Isn't it a wonder what a man will do in his free time? We'll leave him to his own devices. Are you ready for some mountain climbing, Marie? There's more travelling we have to do yet."

I struggled to keep pace with Ted as he climbed nimbly over walls and up steep slopes. After ten minutes I got a welcome break, when he stopped and sent Lass ahead to round up a group of ewes and lambs, so he could get a closer look at them.

"Get up! Get back!" he yelled to her, whistling and pointing his stick to where he wanted her to go. Sleek and fast, she raced around the small flock, bringing it down the hill and cornering it between us and a wall.

"These sheep, they usually live high on the mountain, between here and the sky," said Ted, as he looked them over. "I brought them down for gaining, and now they're mad to return. Do you see that gate up there? They're always by it, rubbing against it, hoping to go through. Early next month, my son and me and Lass will bring the whole flock to the shed by the house for marking and dosing. Then these mountainy sheep will get their chance to return to where they want to be, close to heaven."

We stood with the mountain rising up at our backs. Tiny flowers—white woodsorrel, blue spring gentians and purple dog violets—bloomed among the dried remains of last year's bracken. Hills stretched away into the distance, their outlines almost transparent. High above us, grey clouds were building up and streaming across the sky, threatening more rain. Ted's face was pinched with cold, and the tips of his fingers were white. Lass lay quietly at his feet, her head resting on her paws.

"It's tranquil up here, Marie," he said quietly. "But it's bad land, only of use to the sheep and those who raise them."

As we headed back down, he talked about the rhythms of his life. Every November, he told me, ewes that were eighteen months and older were brought halfway down the mountain, left out for five weeks with the rams to be impregnated, then sent back up to high slopes. In February, they came down again for scanning, and those carrying twins remained in the fields close to his house. By March, all the pregnant ewes came down to lower ground. Lambing was in April. In May, all the ewes and lambs were treated for ticks and vaccinated for orf, a disease causing blisters around the lips, then sent back up the mountain. In June, the ram lambs returned for castration. In July, all the sheep came down for shearing, which Ted and his son did by hand, without the help of electric shears. At this time he picked out the lambs to be sold. During the month of August, the sheep were left in peace to graze on the mountain. In September, the doomed lambs descended straight into trailers headed for the market, and new rams replaced the ones that, according to Ted, had "run out of steam."

"So all the sheep are up the mountain in October," he concluded. "Except for the rams, which we keep below and feed with oats, ready for their work in November. And then it starts all over again."

"All that running up and down the mountain sounds exhausting."

"We do a fair bit, but the dogs do more."

"Isn't it hard on the sheep, moving them about so much?"

"It's not so much really, Marie. There are only five, maybe six, days a year when the sheep are heading up and down. The rest of the time they're mostly settled."

He had taken a detour to show me a large, sloping boulder. Etched into it were two perfect circles, one within the other, with cup-shaped hollows on either side of them. This was prehistoric art, made by people hammering stone or metal points onto the rock surfaces. Examples of this "rock art" exist all over the Iveragh Peninsula, probably dating from the late neolithic age. Its meaning and purpose remain a mystery.

"It's my opinion that these marks had something to do with the worship of the sun," said Ted. "Though I've heard others say they could be maps of the stars."

He pointed with his stick to a grassy mound higher up the hill. "Over there is another antiquity, an old ring fort built by our distant ancestors. It has places that go underground, but I never went inside it, even when I was a child. It's said that if you go inside such forts you get a bone disease."

By the time we came down the hill, the subject of Dag's photographic study had produced her lamb, which was already suckling. The ewe that chased Lass had also successfully given birth, and her tiny ram was taking his first shaky steps, while his mother licked and nuzzled him.

"There's someone new to this world," said Ted proudly. "Look, she's mad about him. Isn't nature a fabulous thing?"

Back in the cottage, we sat around the turf fire, warming our hands and feet and drinking another round of whiskey.

"When we go home now," Ted cautioned us, "don't be telling herself about the drink."

"Herself" was his wife, Carmel, a strongly built woman with short fine hair permed into curls, green eyes and a direct, generous manner.

"There's no need for that," she chided me, as I started to pull off my boots in the doorway of her kitchen. "We often have dogs and cats and lambs in here."

The room was warmed by an old-fashioned, turf-burning range. A kettle steamed on top of it, and from the oven Carmel took out plates filled with fried bacon, pork sausage, black pudding, liver, egg and tomatoes, and set them on the table before us.

"I've been keeping this warm for you," she said, adding slabs of thickly buttered white bread and mugs of strong tea. "Eat all around you now, I can easily make more of everything."

Ted ate quickly, making no conversation during the meal. Several times he glanced through the window to the sheep and lambs in the field outside.

"He loves his sheep," Carmel told me. "Three hundred ewes we have, and he knows every one of them. I go out to check on the twin lambers and I come back and tell him one of them is gaining, and he asks me 'Which one was it?' I say, 'Are you raving, man? It was a sheep, they all look the same to me.' But he recognizes them; he knows the marks on their faces."

She paused, and smiled fondly at him.

"Ah, but I love the life, too. Of a spring evening I can stand for hours by the wall and watch the lambs play. I'd rather that than see the soap operas on television. It's true, I'd rather do that instead."

Sitting with us in the kitchen was the couple's youngest child, nineteen-year-old Sile. She was slight and pretty, with her father's large dark eyes.

"Bring your pet lamb in, Sile," said Carmel. "Show Marie your lamb."

The lamb, a pretty Scotch Blackface, came careening into the kitchen ahead of Sile and ran excitedly from person to person.

"You *are* a pet," said Carmel, patting it. "You're a spoilt pet, that's what you are. I know what you're after, but I've got nothing for you, you've been fed already, you have."

"This lamb was born eleven days ago, Dougeen," said Ted, setting his knife and fork on his empty plate. "I checked the mother at ten past ten in the morning. The lamb had just come and they were both right as rain. I got into my car and

184

drove into Cahersiveen for a message. By the time I got home again it was no more than five past eleven. And wasn't the ewe lying there stone dead, with the lamb crying beside her. She had been eating the afterbirth, as they always do of course, but she choked on it. Had I only been here to see, I could have saved the poor creature."

"I hear you've a lamb, Marie," said Sile shyly.

I nodded. "Dag reckons I'm treating it more like a baby than a sheep."

"That's not what I said!" he protested.

"Ah, you can't help spoiling them," Carmel reassured me. "You'll miss her when you're gone. I always do. You let the pets away up the mountain and they have their own lamb and then they're sheep and pets no more. But when they come down from the mountain, I know the faces of all my pets. "

"Do they recognize you?" I asked.

Carmel put her head on one side, considering the question.

"Ted tells me to go out and talk to them. And when I do that, I'd say they know me alright."

Sile smiled. "I don't think so, Mam. I'd say you're imagining that."

I turned to Sile. "Would you like to be a sheep farmer?"

She shook her head vigorously. "Ah no. I'd rather the town life."

"She'd be a fine farmer if she wanted," her father interjected. "Tom, our eldest boy, he drives heavy machinery for a living, and he has no interest in the sheep, no interest at all. But Joseph, the younger of the two boys, he's a great shepherd altogether and he loves the work. He's too busy to help out this season, on account of his bartending job, and the boiler he has for himself now."

I look blankly at Ted. "A boiler?"

Sile giggled and blushed. "Ah, dad, that's not nice."

"A kettle," explained Ted. "A kettle on the boil."

Registering my incomprehension, he said, "A young *woman*, Marie!"

Carmel cleared away our plates, and set a fresh pot of tea and a sponge cake on the table.

"Maybe Joseph or Sile will take over from me one day," said Ted pensively. "It's up to them, of course, and whoever they marry. But you have to love the life, because if you don't, it's too hard to face into day after day. That's why I'd never push my children into following on from me. What would be the use of that, Marie, to make them do something they hadn't the heart for? 'Twould be no use at all."

✦

CHAPTER TWENTY-TWO

The late April morning was humid, with a low, dense covering of cloud and barely any wind. Groups of ewes and their lambs lay along the track leading from our cottage, preferring its hard-packed earth to the dew-damp grasses in the surrounding fields. When it was time for Dag to leave for work, I ran down the track with Dora at my heels, scattering the sheep to make way for his car and opening the gate so that he could drive through without stopping.

As we walked back up the track, Dora kept pausing to nip off the new, curled-up green heads of ferns. Worriedly, I shooed her away from these, remembering Dag's warning about bracken being poisonous for sheep. But there was little else to disturb my peace of mind on this calm morning. A pair of stonechats perched either side of the track on furze bushes, warning me away from their nest with piping cries—"*wheet-tsack-tsack-tsack!*" From somewhere up the mountain came the lovely, deep-throated *"pruk-pruk"* of a raven, and over on the other side of the valley, one of Peggy's cows began lowing plaintively. Sheep called to their lambs, who replied with childish bleats. Underlying all this was the rhythmic beat of the sea, as it lapped the harbour and broke against the exposed headlands and cliffs beyond.

Dora spent all morning grazing and chewing her cud. I had successfully weaned her off her one o'clock feed and she made no fuss when I left to cycle into town. In the fields along the lane, Kevin O'Shea's mountain lambs had turned into teenagers and were running about in gangs, scrambling up boulders and playfully pushing each other off the tops. Like Dora, they were growing fast and becoming more independent by the day. Though it was a joy to see them so strong and healthy, it reminded me that our time in Kerry would soon be drawing to a close. The grass was growing well, the animals were thriving. Lambing was almost over, the rate of calvings was slowing down and soon the O'Learys would have no need for an extra vet. Signs of the approaching summer were upon us: fresh green shoots grew among last year's high, desiccated reeds, and the carmine buds of fuchsia were unfurling into delicate pendants of purple, pink and red petals. Cow parsley bloomed in the hedgerows, and the clumps of montrebretia leaves were more dense and green by the day. As I cycled along the high road, I breathed in the sweet heady scent of hawthorn blossoms and tried to forget that by the time summer arrived, we would be gone.

In Cahersiveen I stopped at the crossroad by the library, where I dismounted to pull a couple of well-sealed plastic rubbish bags from my bike panniers. The council rubbish trucks didn't come down our valley, so we were responsible for the disposal of our household refuse. Dag took any veterinary waste away to the surgery, while I burned all our paper in the fire, put our fruit and vegetable peelings on a neighbour's compost heap and tried to avoid buying anything in a tin. This left us with a couple of small bags of rubbish a week. When I'd asked our landlords what to do with these, they had advised me to dump them in the town litter bins. These bins, of which there were a number along Main Street, were made of sturdy concrete, with a removable wire basket inside. I'd never been very comfortable leaving our rubbish in them, but the only other alternative was to take it to the council tip, which was a long way out of Cahersiveen, and always closed whenever Dag was not using the car for work.

As this was a fair day, the bin opposite the library was already half-full. I shoved my bags on top, pushing them down as far as they would go. I looked up from the bin to see three men sitting on the bench outside the library, looking solemnly at me. I recognized a couple of them and waved in greeting; they raised their hands and smiled in return. More familiar faces stood around Johnny Apple's fruit and vegetable stand, examining the seedling cabbage plants he had for sale. As I wheeled my bike past the market stalls, several people called out to me, and even the Coffey man who sold boots and shoes offered me a gruff hello.

I was carefully leaning my bike against the window of Curran's butcher shop when a Jack Russell terrier ran out and lifted its leg against one of the wheels. Behind the counter, James Curran hacked through a side of lamb, turning it into chops. He was a big man, with a fleshy red nose. His manner was kindly and shy, and he found it hard to meet my gaze when we talked.

"How are you?" he inquired, staring down at the dead lamb. "And how's himself?"

Much more outgoing than James was his elderly mother, the undisputed boss of this shop. Dressed in her uniform of a full pinafore over a thick tweed skirt and hand-knitted sweater, she hurried about purposefully, keeping an eye on everything through thick spectacles. Rumour had it that while his mother was at Mass, James would often attempt some slight changes to improve the display of merchandise in the shop, rearranging the meat in the refrigerated display case, or moving a sack of potatoes from one wall to another. But he was never able to test such innovations, because as soon as his mother returned, she checked the premises and quickly changed everything back to how it had been before she'd left.

"Now let me talk to you," she said, holding my hand. Her hair was held in place by a net and grips, and a web of fine veins showed through the delicate skin of her cheeks. "I've been meaning to ask you this. Do you have any Irish relatives?"

She was delighted to hear that my father was from Cashel, in County Tipperary.

"I'm from Michelstown myself. That's on the border with Cork, but when I was a girl I used to often go to dances in Cashel. Where are you living? Over the Water, is it? Which side of that valley is your house? How close to the harbour? Is it above or below the holy well? You must have a little car to get there. No? By bike you go? Well, isn't that marvellous, you don't mind the hill? Ah, but you're so nice and slim. Do you own the house Over the Water? No? Ah well, maybe you'll buy a place here in time."

"This girl has a Suffolk lamb," James told her, carrying some chops over to the display case. "John Joe O'Sullivan made her a present of it. It's a pet."

"A pet lamb!" she cried. "Well now, James, do you have any advice to give her?"

He smiled at me. "I wouldn't dream of giving advice about a pet lamb to the wife of a vet."

No one in the East End Bar, where I stopped for lunch, was in the least bit reticent about giving me advice on my pet lamb. The usual crew was there, and while I waited for my glass of stout and plate of cheese sandwiches, they all had a comment to make.

"Have you that lamb weaned yet?" asked Ted Donnelly.

"Sheep nuts is what you need," said Francis, a freckled-faced building contractor.

"Ah, nonsense," Mike Falvey contradicted him. "Just let the creature out in the field to watch what the other sheep do, and she'll be doing the same before long."

"Won't you have ham in your sandwiches as well, Marie?" asked Noreen, putting her head around the door to the kitchen. "Ah, do. Cheese won't get you far on that bike."

"I hear you will be leaving us," said Florence O'Sullivan. "What will you do then with your lamb?"

"Peggy O'Sullivan is going to take her," I told him. "She hopes to breed her."

He nodded approvingly. "She's going to a good home. Peggy knows how to care for her sheep. She does things in the traditional way."

These days, the East End regulars were far more at ease in my presence. Francis insisted on buying me another drink, and regaled me with stories about the fair days he remembered from his childhood. Farmers would walk their cattle ten miles into the town, he said, and sell the animals on the piece of ground called Fairfield, opposite the vet's surgery.

"They brought them a longer step than ten miles," Florence butted in. "Some walked them from as far as Caherdaniel and Glenbeigh. They'd leave by night, with a boiled potato in their pocket, or some pudding to keep themselves going. At the Carhan Bridge on the east end of town and the Oghermong Bridge on the west, there'd be a jam of animals at dawn, with people bidding on them, hoping to get a better price than in the mart."

"On fair days you met *everyone* you knew," Ted Donnelly added. "You could buy a drink in the town at six o'clock in the morning. Ah, 'tis all very different now."

Noreen placed another round of sandwiches and a glass of stout on the counter in front of me.

"These are on the house," she said.

"This pub was a very different place, too, before Noreen got here and changed it all," Francis said mischievously.

Noreen smiled. "Get away with you, Francis."

"The bar was over on the far wall where the fireplace is now," he continued. "I remember sitting there with a pint of stout on a fair day in 1957, watching twenty-one head of cattle being driven though this room and into the backyard."

"Oh come on, now," I said. "Cattle in the bar?"

"It was a regular sight. Ask John here. The fair started early in the morning, so that the people who arrived the night before needed a place to keep their animals. John's father would let a herd stay in the back garden; I suppose he collected a few pounds for his trouble. The bar was the only way through for the animals, so in they came."

John Curran was leaning against the counter.

"Francis is right," he said. "And it wasn't only my father who did it. There was a woman who lived next door to here, she used to let animals through as well. I remember one time she left her washing on the line, and didn't the cattle get in among it, trampling the poor woman's sheets into the ground."

"One time I saw a horse and car pulling up outside a house," Ted chipped in. "It was at the west end of town. I looked away for a second when the man was taking the car off the horse. When I looked back wasn't the car standing there alone and the horse gone. The man had led it into the house, through the kitchen and into the garden. There's not many women these days who'd tolerate horseshit in their kitchen, isn't that right, Noreen?"

"The cattle were long gone from here before Noreen arrived," John told him. "The last time I saw any was 1968. Five bulls came through then. I was only a little lad. They were sculling them out in the backyard; six men would hold down one bull, while another took off his balls. Christ, it was like a rodeo out there."

Two hours later, I emerged from the East End Bar and cycled home, filled with several pints of Murphy's stout and an enormous sense of well-being. The sun broke through the clouds, and a gentle breeze raked the blue waters of Dingle Bay. Halfway down the lane I met Chloe, chomping on the new growth along the hedgerow.

"She's enjoying the long acre!" called Peggy merrily. She was standing in one of her fields, close to the stream, holding a lamb while its mother fretted close by. "How's Dora? Is she weaned yet? This lamb here has a bad scour. Would you ask your man to call in later to see her? And come by with him for a drop of sherry."

When I pushed open the gate at the bottom of our track, Neddy the donkey ambled over towards me. I fished around in my panniers for one of the carrots I'd bought from Johnny Apple and offered it to him on the palm of my hand. He gathered it up in his soft lips and began ponderously chewing on it.

Feeling at peace with the world, I carried the bags of groceries into the kitchen. I was unpacking them, happily humming to myself, when the phone rang.

"Is that Maria Coffey?" asked a soft, unfamiliar voice. "This is Cahill McCarthy from the council office."

A long pause followed.

"Yes?" I cheerily prompted him.

"Well now, Maria. I'm sorry to bother you. But I wonder if you've heard about the campaign that's on in Kerry, to stop people from the country areas dumping their rubbish in unsuitable places."

I was too buoyed by alcohol to consider why he was asking me this. I told him I had indeed heard about the campaign, that I thought it was a very good thing. I said I'd lost count of the times I'd peered over a cliff to see the slope below littered with rubbish, or come across the hulks of cars, old mattresses and rusting farm equipment lying in fields among beautiful scenery. I wanted to add that only recently I'd read in *The Kerryman* about a man who had been fined for throwing bags of rubbish into a stream, but I didn't get a chance, because Cahill interrupted me by loudly clearing his throat.

"Well now, Maria. We had the inspector from Tralee here with us in the office today. He was sitting with me when someone came in with two bags of household rubbish—"

The phone was on the living room windowsill. Dora emerged from her haggard, caught sight of me through the glass and ran over to the cottage, bleating insistently.

"I'm sorry, I can't hear you," I told Cahill. "Please speak up."

"The two bags of rubbish were found—"

"It's my lamb." I carried the phone to a chair by the fireplace, out of Dora's sight. "She's after her five o'clock feed already. I'm trying to wean her, but you know what it's like. Sorry, what were you saying?"

Cahill cleared his throat again. "The inspector wanted to write a letter to you. You could be charged for this, of course, but I suggested that maybe I could talk to you in person, to avoid anything unpleasant."

It was my turn to be silent.

"Charged?" I said at last. "For what?"

"For dumping the two bags of household rubbish that we found today."

"I didn't dump them," I protested. "I put them in a bin in town."

"Those bins are for litter," said Cahill. "There's a tip a few miles outside the town for household rubbish. It only costs a few pounds to dump a whole trailerful of it."

"Whenever the tip is open, my husband is using our car," I told him. "And we don't have any place where we can store our rubbish. We haven't even got a dustbin outside. And even if we did, there are mink and foxes and dogs around here, and they'd get into everything."

"The council can provide you with a suitable bin," Cahill offered. "You've probably seen them around the town on a Monday morning, when the rubbish lorries go around. They're big and strong, with well-fitting lids. And they have wheels you can pull them along on."

"One of those would come in very handy," I said gratefully. "Do they cost much?"

"They're provided free of charge. But you'd have to buy a sticker with it, and they cost sixty-two pounds for six months."

"What's the sticker for?"

"The bins are emptied once a week by the rubbish collectors, and the sticker shows that you've paid for the service."

"The rubbish lorry doesn't come down this valley," I reminded him.

"I know that. We can still provide you with a bin, but you have to buy the sticker."

"Why?"

"Because otherwise we'd just be giving it away, and then every farmer in the country areas would want one, and he'd be storing his turf in it and still throwing his rubbish in the field."

"I won't be here for six months," I said. "Can I just buy one of these bins?"

"You can't have it without the sticker."

I had passed through the euphoric phase of my drunkenness, and was entering the aggressive stage.

"What you're telling me, Cahill," I said testily, "is that I can have a bin as long I buy a sticker for a service that I can't get."

"You could if you took your bin to the top of the lane by the high road every Monday morning. The rubbish lorry stops there then and it would empty it. As long as it had the sticker on it, of course."

"And how exactly do I get the bin up the lane?"

"You could push it."

"Cahill," I hissed. "It's a *mile* from here to the top of that hill. Why can't the lorry come down to the harbour?"

"It's too narrow a lane. There's nowhere for it to turn around."

"The school bus manages it, twice a day."

"Ah no, it would be too much of a risk."

I moved the phone from one ear to the other, trying hard to keep my temper in check.

"Lots of people must have the same problem as me. Why doesn't the council put a big skip in town that can be used for free?"

"Because it would fill up in no time," he said.

"*Isn't that what rubbish skips are for?*" I cried in exasperation.

"Yes, but the thing would be overflowing from day one. There'd be old mattresses and dead dogs and God knows what else lying all around it. We learned from experience that the more we provide for people in town, the worse it gets. Next week we're starting to take away some of the litter bins."

"You must be joking," I said, in disbelief. "That makes no sense."

I could tell from his tone that Cahill's patience had begun to wear thin.

"I'd be grateful, Maria," he said, carefully pronouncing each word, "if in future you could dispose of your rubbish in the proper way, by taking it to the council tip."

"The more litter bins you remove," I persisted, "the more rubbish you'll have on the street."

"I've no doubt Canada is far more advanced in this matter than Ireland," he said, his voice heavy with sarcasm. "But as you're here on your holidays for a relatively short period of time, I'd be glad if—"

"Just a minute," I interrupted him, as the alcohol haze in my brain suddenly cleared. "How did you know I'm from Canada?"

He paused.

"You have a bit of a twang there, Maria."

"I have an *English* accent, Cahill," I said. "And how did you know it was me who put the two bags of rubbish into that bin?"

He answered too quickly. "We looked through them and found a letter sent from Canada with your name and address on it."

I was suddenly very sober. A cold, hard realization was creeping up my back.

"That's not possible. I hardly ever throw letters away. And when I do, I burn them."

"Ah well. You must have let this one slip, I suppose." Cahill's voice had turned brisk and decisive. "I have someone waiting here to see me, Maria, so I must go. Maybe we'll have another chance to talk about this soon. Goodbye now."

By the time Dag came home, I had constructed a conspiracy theory around the discovery of my rubbish bags. The farmers outside the library had seen me dispose of them. Hearing my accent, and feeling ill-disposed towards the English, they turned them in to the council, mentioning that I was the wife of the new vet. The council needed a scapegoat for their new campaign, and I was to be it. This was only the beginning: a nasty letter would soon arrive, a court case would ensue and a headline in *The Kerryman* would blare, "Englishwoman Fined For Dumping Rubbish In Town."

Dag found the whole thing hilarious.

"It wasn't those old guys who shopped you," he said. "Why would they? The Irish are always on the side of an outlaw. I'm sure it was Cahill whatshisname who found the bags. He was probably on his way back to work from the pub, saw you dump them and figured that this was a way to score some brownie points with his inspector."

"But how did he know who I was?"

"Maria, how many Canadian vets' wives are there in Cahersiveen? Everyone knows you and your old bike. You stick out a mile."

"I was really starting to feel comfortable here," I said unhappily. "I thought that, what with the lamb and everything, people were beginning to accept me. Now I feel like an unwelcome foreigner all over again."

"Of course, people are accepting you," said Dag. "They're accepting both of us."

He stopped, and reflected for a moment.

"We'll always be strangers here, Maria. No matter how long we stayed, even if we lived here full-time, we'd be seen as different. We *are* different. Even you, with your Irish background, you come from another world. That's just how it is."

I sank into a bruised silence. Dag was looking through the fridge for something to cook for dinner when we heard a knock at the door. Jer O'Donaghue stood on the step. He was wearing yellow oilskins and held a plastic bowl containing six or more huge crab claws.

"There's nothing I can do for those crabs, I'm afraid," joked Dag. "They're beyond help."

Jer laughed. "The rest of the crabs aren't worth eating. We throw them back in and leave them to grow new claws. I'm just up from the harbour with these. I promised your wife some crab and here it is, the first of the season."

He wouldn't accept payment and refused to come in for a drink.

"If you'd like to go fishing one evening before you leave," he told Dag, "we'd be happy to take you. Goodbye now and God bless."

Dag steamed the claws. He served them with a loaf of freshly baked soda bread that a farmer's wife had given him earlier in the day, and a delicious butter and garlic sauce. We ate by the fire, laying the claws on the hearth and cracking open the sturdy shells with a poker. Using a fork, I pulled out nuggets of sweet, tender meat. It was food for the spirit, straight from the sea, and with each mouthful I began to feel much better.

✛

CHAPTER TWENTY-THREE

For the past two and a half months, both indoors and out I'd worn sweaters, jeans and woolly socks. But on the first day of May, traditionally the start of summer in Ireland, the temperature suddenly soared to twenty degrees Celsius. Kerry Radio excitedly proclaimed this a heat wave and forecast it to last until the end of the week. Around mid-morning I donned the shorts and t-shirt that, in faint hope of ever wearing them, I had brought with me from Canada. In the most protected part of the garden, I stretched out on a blanket, reading a book and revelling in the unfamiliar feeling of warm sun on my bare skin.

Dora grazed close by, grabbing mouthfuls of grass and jerking her head to tear them off. After a time she settled down next to me, dropping first onto her front knees before folding all four legs beneath her. Then she started chewing her cud. I laid my head on my arms, listening contentedly to this process: the soft burp when a ball of grass came up into her mouth, the clicking of her teeth as she pulverized it, a gulp as she swallowed then, after a brief pause, another burp.

I snoozed for a while, then woke with a start, aware of heavy panting close by. Dora was sprawled on her side, ribs heaving and ears and lips twitching. Scrambling to my feet, I ran inside the cottage, grabbed one of Dag's veterinary tomes and searched for a reference to Bracken Fern Poisoning. With great relief, I read that its symptoms took at least a month to develop. Then I remembered the tick I'd recently found on Dora's neck. A picture of the sheep on Paddy Loftus's farm flashed before me: pathetic brain-damaged creatures, curled up on the ground or convulsing and staggering around in circles. Louping ill! Quickly, I looked it up. A tick-borne virus, its incubation period could be as little as six days. The first symptoms were a fever, incoordination of the limbs and tremors in the lips and ears. Young lambs, the book went on to inform me, usually died from louping ill very quickly. Most were found dead within twenty-four hours.

My hands were shaking as I dialled the surgery number. When Ann answered, I gabbled at her about our pet lamb being sick.

"What's happened to her?" she asked.

"I don't know, but she's panting and twitching."

"Can you bring her in?"

"I've only got my bike, Ann."

"Ah, I wasn't thinking of that. Dag's treating a dog in the back right now. The minute he's finished I'll send him over."

I was waiting for Dag when he drove up to the gate at the bottom of the track. "Dora's panting and trembling," I told him, jumping into the car. "I looked it up in one of your books. I think she's got louping ill."

"I doubt that. There have been no cases of louping ill in this valley for several years."

As soon as we reached the cottage, he hurried towards Dora with a stethoscope and a thermometer. He bent over her for a few seconds, then looked up, smiling. "She'll live, Maria."

"What's wrong with her?"

"She's panting because she's lying in the sun. The twitching is probably because she's dreaming about her next feed."

Dag's successful diagnosis of Dora was the high point of his day, which, as he recounted over lunch, had so far been disastrous. It had begun with a cow who objected to him testing her for tuberculosis and kicked him hard in the shin, leaving him with a huge purple bruise above the knee and a pronounced limp. Then he raced across the peninsula for an urgent calving on a small heifer, only to discover that the calf was dead and had to be cut up inside the mother before it could be removed. When he'd finished this grisly task, the farmer asked him to look at a lamb with a bad cough. He treated it with a drug that was commonly used on sheep, but the animal had a rare allergic reaction to it, and died before Dag had even walked out of the shed.

"It wasn't just any old lamb, either," he glumly recounted. "It was the pet of the farmer's youngest daughter. She was there at the time, and burst into tears."

"Well, I can understand that," I said, rather unhelpfully.

The dog he'd been treating when I called the surgery had strychnine poisoning and was suffering horribly, beset by violent spasms that arched its back into a sawhorse position and made its limbs rigid.

"The farmer reckons it was poisoned by his neighbour," said Dag. "They've been feuding for years about a right-of-way. He says that malicious poisoning of animals is pretty common around here."

I shuddered. "It's barbaric. Will the dog be alright?"

By now Dag looked very unhappy.

"I don't know. He was pretty far gone. It will be touch and go if he survives."

That afternoon I accompanied Dag on his calls, hoping to break his run of bad luck and improve his mood.

"I don't like Ireland when it's so sunny," he grumbled, as we drove towards Cahersiveen. "It bleaches out the colours from the landscape. Clouds and rain suit this place much more."

We stopped briefly at the surgery to find out what was lined up for him. Frank O'Leary was at the counter, relieving Ann for her lunch hour.

"Isn't it a fine day? Have you been swimming in the harbour yet, Marie?"

"Very funny," I said. "The water's freezing."

"Ah, it's not so bad, about nine or ten degrees, I'd say. I was in there myself at seven this morning and it was grand."

As I gaped at him incredulously, he turned to Dag.

"I've got something interesting for you here. Have you ever been out to Mrs. Murt at Shanavagh? She has a billy goat with a teat that's full of milk, and she says it's getting in the way of his real business."

It was Dag's turn to gape.

"A billy goat with a teat? I've never heard of a case like that. If he's a breeding goat I'd be wary about giving him hormones. What else could we do?"

"The fact of it is, Dag," said Frank, his eyes twinkling mischievously, "I don't have a clue any more than you. But seeing as you're a good bit younger than me and mad for experience into the bargain, I thought I'd send you along. Do what you can. It will be a good story for when you get back home, if nothing else."

As we were leaving the surgery, Frank called me back.

"Mrs. Murt has an ogham stone on her land, Marie. She might show it to you if she's in the mood. Do you know about ogham? It was the first written form of the Irish language. The Celts carved it onto standing stones."

All the way to Caherdaniel, Dag worried aloud about the goat.

"A billy goat with a teat? What am I supposed to do with that? Is this Frank's idea of a joke?"

I was only half-listening to him.

"I'd love to see that stone. Maybe we could ask Mrs. Murt when you're finished with the goat."

"Let's find her place first. Do you know where we are?"

Frank had mentioned that Mrs. Murt had white gateposts with plaster dogs on top of them. Soon we spotted two large red Alsatians flanking the entrance to a driveway that led to a bright yellow bungalow. A stocky woman in a purple sweat suit was sweeping the crazy paving outside it. She leaned on her broom to watch us approach, coldly eyeing the number plates on our car.

"Is this the Murt's place?" asked Dag through his window.

"It is. And who wants to know?"

"I'm the new vet. I've come about the billy goat."

Upon hearing the word "vet," Mrs. Murt's demeanour then changed dramatically.

"The *vet*! Jesus, why didn't you say so in the first place? Aren't those English registration plates you have on your car? I was thinking you were more tourists come looking for the old stone. And I was thinking, 'tis bad enough the way they come around in the summer, without them turning up in the spring as well. Me and Mr. Murt have had our fill of people ripping open our gates and forgetting to shut them, and tramping over the fields. My neighbour set his dogs on some tourists last year. He got into mighty trouble with the council for it, but you can't blame him now, can you?"

"Mrs. Murt," said Dag hesitantly. "About the goat—?"

"Ah, poor Old Billy. He's in a shed round the back. Come after me now and I'll show him to you."

Old Billy was a big, muscular, white-haired goat, with a long beard, impressive horns and a ripe smell. He would have been quintessentially male, had it not been for the teat-like sack hanging between his back legs. Dag briefly examined the sack, then stood up, scratching at his head in obvious puzzlement.

"Well now, Mrs. Murt—"

"It's a queer thing," she interrupted him. "It's happened from time to time, but never as bad as this. He's a pure Saanen. They're a milk breed, of course, and I've heard it said the males have mammaries of a kind that can produce something like milk now and again; nothing that's of any use, of course, but there's a scarcity value in it, I suppose. When it's happened before I've managed to squeeze the stuff out and then the teat has disappeared of its own accord. But this one has got bigger and bigger and he can't mount the females on account of it. I thought of trying to open it myself, but I wouldn't want to be interfering with the poor creature, and isn't it a better thing for his dignity if a man does the job?"

Dag's face had relaxed.

"Of course, Mrs. Murt, I can take care of that quite quickly. I'll just go back to the car and get a few things."

While he was gone, Mrs. Murt patted the good-natured goat between his horns.

"I don't mean to be telling a priest his prayers, now," she said. "If Mr. Murt was here he'd be scolding me. He says I have a terrible habit of pushing my own opinions on people."

"Dag won't mind in the least," I reassured her.

I looked through the shed door and over the fields.

"This old stone the tourists come to see," I casually asked her. "Where exactly is it?"

A glimmer of suspicion appeared in her eye.

"In the field," she said, "where Mr. Murt intends to keep the bull this year."

Dag returned with a large-gauge needle, which he stabbed into the sack. A slightly viscous, milk-like fluid spurted out.

"There we go," he said, as he inserted a small yellow cannula. "This will allow the fluid to drain freely."

"You're a great man, you are," Mrs. Murt told him. Glancing at me, she continued, "And won't Mr. Murt laugh to hear that I took you for a pair of eejits come to look at the old stone in our field."

On the way back towards Cahersiveen, Dag stopped at a phone booth to call into the surgery. He returned to the car looking tense.

"Tommy Heggarty at Briska has a heifer that's calving. She's not even a year and a half old, so it might be a Caesarean. Ann says the place is really primitive, and that Tommy might be having one of his turns, whatever that means."

Ann's directions took us off the main road and down to a stretch of rocky coastline with tiny coves and small, intertidal islets. After half a mile or so, we drove by a tumbledown house with slates missing from its roof, dirty curtains flapping through broken windows and a door tacked together from scrap wood. Dag braked abruptly.

"I think this is the place."

"It can't be!"

"It's got a telephone line running to it. And look, there's a TV aerial."

He beeped the horn. From inside the house, a dog started barking furiously. The door was yanked open and a man ran out, clutching at the waist of his oversized trousers with one hand.

"Down there away, down there away, sick with calf!" he shouted, pointing to the fields running towards the sea.

Tommy Heggarty was a big, powerfully built man. It was hard to estimate his age—he could have been anywhere from thirty-five to fifty. He had a pronounced underbite, and several of his front teeth were broken or missing. His hair was rumpled, his eyes were wild and his breathing heavy, as if he were in a terrible panic.

"Down there away!" he hollered, as Dag got out of the car.

"Is she loose, Tommy?"

"She is, of course!"

"Well, we'll have to catch her then. Do you have a place where we can put her to calf?"

"I do."

Tommy hurried across a yard littered with discarded bottles and ripped silage bags, to a stone shed. The latch on its wooden door was so badly rusted that only a thick growth of brambles kept it in place. With his free hand, Tommy yanked back the prickly plants and pulled open the door. Beads of blood oozed from the scratches on his fingers. Dag and I poked our heads through the doorway. The muddy floor was covered with rubbish, and the only sources of light were a tiny window and some holes in the roof.

"Let's round up the cow," suggested Dag. "And Tommy— why don't you get some baling twine for your trousers?"

Ignoring this, Tommy cried, "Over here!" and headed off at speed into the fields.

When the heifer saw a wild man bearing down on her, hollering and flapping one arm, she understandably turned and fled.

"Get by that gap in the hedge," panted Dag, as we ran to catch up with Tommy. "Fend her off if she tries to get through it."

I stood in front of the gap with my arms outspread, watching Tommy dashing about and Dag limping along in his wake, simultaneously trying to calm him and reassure the frightened animal. For ten minutes, the two men executed a bizarre dance with the heifer, until she outmanoeuvred them, running back towards the house and into a field behind it. Still clutching his trousers, Tommy followed at a gallop, with Dag huffing along behind him. They cornered the cow by the shed, but before Dag could get a rope on her she escaped, down into the fields towards the beach.

"I give up," sighed Dag, as Tommy set off in pursuit. "Let him catch her himself."

A horizontal band of cloud stretched above the horizon; we stood watching as the shimmering globe of the sun slid behind it.

"Please God, don't let this be a Caesarean," said Dag quietly. "It will be dark soon, there's no electricity in the shed, there's no hot water . . . and there's Tommy."

It was twenty minutes before Tommy returned, herding the heifer into the field next to the house.

"Now's our chance, Maria," said Dag. "I'm going to try and help Tommy get her through the gate. I want you to stand on the track, above the shed. Whatever you do, don't let her get past."

He took off, and that was the last I saw of either of them for over half an hour. As the sun slipped away, the cloud bank turned a hazy pink, the sea took on soft shades of violet, and the surrounding fields faded from the bright colours of the day to gentle pastels. A rooster with a crooked comb strutted around the yard, crowing feistily; thrushes chirped in the trees along the track; in the distance I could hear the soft murmuring of waves breaking on the shore, and Tommy's occasional shouts of "Yup yup yup! Hoa hoa hoo-ah HOOO!"

When the two men appeared with the heifer, I spread my legs wide apart and waved my arms in readiness. Before she got anywhere near me, however, she turned and ran down the track, through an open gate on its far side and into a field above us.

"I don't believe this!" cried Dag in exasperation. "I'm dreaming, or maybe we're in a movie, but this is *not really happening*."

After a few more desperate manoeuvres, Tommy finally got the heifer into the yard. With Dag's help, she was persuaded into the gloomy shed, and the two men followed her, wrestling the door shut behind them. I heard muffled thumps, scuffling, cries of pain, cursing and Dag's voice repeating, "Steady girl, relax, let's take it easy. Slow down Tommy, hold her Tommy, steady now. Hold her, relax . . ."

When finally they came out of the shed, blood was oozing from a gash on Tommy's forehead, and running down his face to his chin.

"That looks bad," Dag told him. "It might need stitches."

But Tommy didn't care about his forehead. "The calf?" he asked urgently. "What about the calf?"

Dag shook his head. "She's not calving down yet."

For a moment Tommy was silent, taking in this news. Then he flew into a rage, spitting blood and foam as he screamed, "She *is*, she's sick with calf, she's *sick*!"

"Tommy, listen to me," Dag insisted. "The heifer started pressing because a hoof is sticking up into her pelvic canal, but she isn't ready to calf yet. She won't be ready for two or three weeks."

"No. *No!*" Tommy's voice had gone up several pitches and he looked close to tears. "She's sick with *calf*."

Dag laid his hands on Tommy's shoulders and looked him straight in the eye.

"You know what, Tommy? She's just thinks she's sick with calf. She just *imagines* it."

In silence, Tommy returned Dag's gaze. He nodded slowly and his body relaxed. "She *thinks* she's sick," he repeated. "Alright, alright."

"She might even calf on her own."

"Yes," agreed Tommy

"Let's hope so," added Dag fervently. "Let's pray for that."

I was light-headed with relief that Dag didn't have to perform a Caesarean in this bizarre place. All he had to look after now was the gash on Tommy's forehead.

"That cut—" he began, but Tommy backed away from him.

"No! I'm strong."

"You certainly are," I told him truthfully. "You've just run the equivalent of a marathon."

"Whiskey," he gasped, turning towards the house. "You'll have a whiskey before you go."

We stood in the yard for what seemed like an age, while Tommy crashed about inside, constantly yelling at the barking dog.

"I've managed to get a few more kicks," Dag told me, rubbing his shin. "You wouldn't believe what it was like in that little shed. Tommy was trying to catch the heifer with a rope, but he kept tripping over because he'd let go of his pants and they were down around his ankles. So there was this heifer going crazy, and Tommy falling about with his big bare ass shining through the dark."

When Tommy came out, the transformation was remarkable. He'd wiped most of the blood from his face, stuck toilet paper on the cut and hitched up his trousers with a belt. In one hand he was holding a new bottle of Jameson's Whiskey, and in the other a whiskey tumbler, made of expensive cut glass and wiped to a gleaming shine.

"Only one good glass left," he mumbled apologetically. "You can share."

A lump formed in my throat as he handed the glass to Dag and filled it with whiskey.

"We should have a toast," said Dag.

"A toast!" repeated Tommy happily.

"Let's toast the heifer." Dag clinked the glass against the bottle in Tommy's hand. "To its health!"

"You're in one piece, thank God," said Ann, who had been anxiously hanging on for us in the surgery. "Was Tommy having one of his turns?"

"I hope so," said Dag. "I'd hate to think that was him behaving normally."

She listened carefully to his account of the visit.

"Ah, that wasn't so bad," she commented, when he'd finished. "He can be far more difficult than that. One time he left a dead cow lying on the beach, and when it started to smell people complained to the *gardaí*. They went up to the house and he took a swing at them, so they put him in handcuffs but he broke out of those soon enough. He was on such a rampage they just drove away and let him be."

"I'm glad you didn't tell me that before we went there," said Dag.

"The poor soul is harmless enough most the time. His parents passed away when he was a young man, and left him that farm. His fields go right to the beach, and the estate agents are always at him to sell, but he won't part with a square inch. For years he's been getting EU subsidies and grants, so he must be made of money. He could be living in every comfort, but he chooses to stay in that wreck of a house, with the rain pouring in on top of him."

"Can't anyone do anything to help him?" I asked her.

"He won't take his medicines and no one can force him. But there's many a one around here keeps an eye out for him, and makes sure he has enough turf in and a hot meal to keep him going."

As she slipped on her coat, she added, "And a prayer is said often enough for Tommy Heggarty at Mass, without ever him knowing it."

✦

CHAPTER TWENTY-FOUR

In Ireland, May is the month of the Virgin Mary. Peggy O'Sullivan had told me that when she was a child, altars were set up in honour of Mary out in the fields or between the low boughs of trees. It was always the children who'd made these altars, she said. Nowadays they had no interest in such things, they were mad for the television instead and the custom was dying out.

A vase of bluebells, red and purple fuchsia and yellow cowslip appeared in front of the statue of the Virgin Mary, in the shrine along the lane.

"Was it you who left the flowers there?" I asked Peggy, when she telephoned me early on the first Saturday in May.

"It wasn't. I'd say it could have been the work of old Mrs. O'Donaghue. She's the wife of the man who gave you the crabs last week. We saw him on his way up to you from the harbour. How did you enjoy them?"

She had phoned to ask if Dag and I could stop at her farm on our way out to the day's calls. Chloe had developed a limp; she thought it might be foot rot. We found Peggy in the flower bed outside her house, weeding among hydrangeas, pansies and a stand of *Zantedeschia*, known in these parts as Easter lilies. The tall, impressive lilies had glossy, dark green leaves, large white funnel-shaped flowers and bright yellow stamens. In 1916 they had been adopted as a Republican emblem, and it was one of their paper facsimiles that I had bought outside the church on Easter Sunday—even though, as Peggy now told me, they rarely bloom as early as Easter.

A fence of fox wire and netting surrounded the flower bed to preserve it from the ravages of the sheep that often wandered through the yard. Peggy climbed over the fence, and went to catch Chloe, who was grazing in an adjoining field. After luring her with a digestive biscuit, she grabbed her by the horns and held her while Dag examined the hoof.

"It's foot rot, alright," he said.

He was paring at the hoof, when Michael came out of the house and walked slowly towards us, leaning on his stick.

"What do you think about this weather, Michael?" Dag asked him. "Will it last?"

Before his stroke, Michael had done a lot of fishing. He looked out to Dingle Bay, as if searching there for an answer to Dag's question.

"There's no swell on the sea, and that's a good sign. I'd say we're in for a fine spell."

"I'd say you're wrong," said Peggy. "The swifts are back, but they're flying low over the fields. That means it will rain. I haven't heard the cuckoo yet this year either, and that's a bad sign too."

When Dag had finished with Chloe, they asked us in for tea. But Dag was already late for his visit to Tappy Murphy's farm, where there was a bullock waiting to be dehorned.

"It's not my favourite job," he admitted.

"Dehorning was easier in the old days," said Peggy. "The farmers handled the cows more then, so they were quieter and they didn't make the fuss they do now. A few men wrestled a cow to the ground, three more sat on her back to hold her down and another cut off her horns with a saw. It was no bother."

"That sounds like a lot of bother to me."

"Ah no, it wasn't," she assured him. "It was no bother at all."

Tappy Murphy was waiting at the farm gate, a pair of enormous forearms crossed over his chest. I'd met him once before in the East End Bar, where he told me his real name was Patrick. As a small child he had always been called Pat, which he had taken to saying backwards, until the nickname had stuck.

"I feel badly about the bullock," he told Dag. "He's lost his balls already and now we're robbing him of the rest of his equipment, the poor bastard. But he's like a Spanish fighter. I can't sell him in the market the way he is."

The animal in question was as muscular as his owner, and had a set of impressive horns that he didn't seem happy about losing. While Tappy struggled to restrain him with a rope halter, Dag injected anaesthetic under a bony ridge that ran from the bullock's eyes to the base of the horns.

"When the horns are this big, it's hard to block the pain," said Dag. "There's a nerve that goes around the back of the horn that we can't reach."

I was standing by with the dehorning tool, an alarming contraption that was a cross between a pair of shears and a miniature guillotine. Dag slipped it over the first horn, and brought down the sharp blade by squeezing hard on the handles. There was a sickening crunch, and the horn tumbled to the ground. The bullock bellowed in fury, and struggled to free his head from Tappy's grasp.

"Ah, you poor man!" cried Tappy.

Quickly, Dag chopped off the other horn. The hollow stumps were so raw and exposed they looked obscene. Blood spurted out from them in narrow streams, like leaks from a pipe. Dag twisted off the blood vessels, and stretched a band cut from the inner tube of a tire across the stumps. Finally, he sprayed them with disinfectant. Released from the crush, the bullock stood in the farmyard, forlornly shaking his head.

"I hate doing that," said Dag, as we drove away. "When I remove big horns that size I feel as if I'm robbing the animal of something."

"Strength?" I offered. "Dignity?"

"I don't know. There used to be an old belief that horns were the receptors of cosmic energy. That's a bit far out for me, but there's certainly something special about a cow with a big set of horns. The problem is, they know how to use them; lots of cows wouldn't think twice about damaging a vet with their horns."

"At least you didn't have to castrate him as well," I commiserated. "That's one job I'm not keen on seeing."

In dazzling sunshine, we were driving up to the mountain pass above Portmagee.

"Didn't I tell you?" asked Dag, as we reached the top. "Our next call is to Pat Falvey. He's got three bullocks that need emasculating."

Below us, the open ocean was flat and shimmering like silk, with the Skellig Rocks almost obscured by haze. The fields of the Glen appeared to be dusted with snow, an illusion created by carpets of newly bloomed daisies. Trees were tipped with fresh leaves, illuminated by the sun to an electric green. As we zigzagged down the narrow lanes, the hedgerows were a blur of colour. Bluebells, whitebells, primroses, yarrow, London Pride and forget-me-nots grew in profusion along them. In the pastures, sheep and cows grazed with their lambs and calves among the yellow, flag-like petals of newly bloomed irises.

Pat Falvey taught at the local school and also ran a small farm. Like most part-time farmers, when he needed routine work done on his animals, he called out the vet on Saturday mornings, before the more expensive weekend emergency rates took effect at noon. He had carrot-red hair, and freckles covering every bit of exposed skin. Waiting with him were his two sons, six-year-old Dermot and five-year-old Colm, who were exact replicas of their father.

Immediately, Pat began apologizing for the three bullocks that needed castration. With his sons in tow, he led us across the yard to the crush, explaining that these bullocks had been bought into the farm the previous November, that he had kept putting this job off, and that now the animals had grown past the usual age for sculling.

Dag listened to him in silence until we reached the crush; then he let out a long, resigned sigh. The wall it was built along had bits of iron bars protruding from between the stones, approximately at Dag's head level. Baling twine tied into a mess of knots held shut the gate at one end of the crush. The bullocks inside it were big, unruly, and already struggling bad-temperedly within its confines.

The two boys watched in fascination as Dag climbed into the end of the crush behind the last bullock, holding a syringe between his teeth.

"Did your man get a wallop?" Colm asked me, observing his stiff gait.

"A cow kicked him yesterday," I said.

Dermot piped up, "Just before you came my daddy told us he hoped the vet wouldn't get a kick today. And here he is with a kick already."

"Whisht, Dermot," snapped Pat, flushing beneath his freckles.

Standing safely outside the crush, he held the bullock's tail in an effort to restrain him. Dag wrestled with the animal's back end, trying to administer a shot of anaesthetic into the base of the scrotum.

"Owie!" cried Colm, as the needle hit home.

I passed Dag a heavy tool called a Burdizzo Bloodless Emasculator. It resembled a pair of giant, blunt nail clippers.

"I could do with something a bit bigger for balls this size," muttered Dag. Reaching between the animal's back legs, he struggled to slide the open jaws of the emasculator over the first testicle, then squeeze them shut. I held my breath, expecting the animal to flail out, but mercifully, he seemed free of pain, and unconcerned about his impending loss of manhood. For a minute or two, Dag left the emasculator dangling from the testicle, to make sure it severed the spermatic cord. The two little boys giggled uncontrollably at this, pressing their hands against their mouths in vain attempts to control their mirth.

Dag repeated the whole procedure with the other testicle. Before long the operation was over and the bullock was through the gate and eating fresh grass.

Things didn't go quite so smoothly with the second bullock. Despite the anaesthetic, it bellowed in outrage when Dag tried to fix the clamp. Kicking back hard, it caught him in the knee, then broke free of its halter and started bucking wildly.

"You got a kick, you got a kick, Daddy said you'd get a kick!" sang out Dermot, watching Dag rubbing his leg. "Does it hurt?"

"Not too much," Dag told the boy. "I saw it coming and I went into it. If you do that you avoid the main force of the kick. Try and remember when *you* start castrating bullocks."

"Did you hear that, Daddy?" said Dermot admiringly.

Pat ignored him.

"I don't know what possessed me to let these lads go so long. And this one here is very bold to begin with."

"We'll do him last, then," said Dag, moving around to the back of the third bullock.

This time, I couldn't bear to watch. Shading my eyes against the bright sun, I stared out to sea, at a peaceful scene of birds skimming the calm water, a fishing boat passing by and distant headlands, blue and translucent. But I couldn't screen out the distressing sounds of struggling animals, stamping hooves and furious swearing.

"Okay boy, that's it, we'll have to sedate you," I heard Dag say, before he crossed my field of vision on his way up to the car.

A dose of sedative injected into the base of his tail calmed the bullock. When the clamp was applied, however, he still attempted a few perfunctory kicks.

"After all those drugs, surely he doesn't feel anything?" I asked.

"No, but he remembers what I'm trying to do to him," said Dag.

Once out of the crush, the bullock meandered a little way up the field, then sank heavily to the ground and lay on his side.

"Is he dead?" asked Dermot in dismay.

"No, he's just having a long sleep," Dag reassured him.

Finally it was the turn of the third and angriest bullock, who by now had worked himself up into a fit. Even after sedation he was still thrashing about inside the crush. I pleaded with Dag to stop.

"He'll *destroy* you," Pat chimed in. "It's never worth it. Let him be, and I'll sell the bastard as he is."

But Dag had become as stubborn as the bullock; he simply wouldn't give up. While he administered a second dose of sedative, he sent me to the car for a better rope to restrain the animal. He had tied this into a halter and was about to slip it over the bullock's head, when he noticed the animal's eyes glazing over. Grabbing the emasculator, he jumped back into the crush. But the bullock's front knees were already buckling; before Dag could attached the clamp, his back legs also gave way, and he sank to the ground. We all gazed in dismay at the recumbent animal.

"Well, now," muttered Pat.

"He's sleeping, too," commented Dermot.

"This poses an interesting problem," said Dag. "Can someone tell me how I castrate a bullock when it's lying on top of its balls?"

Reaching through the bars, Pat and I tried to heave on the bullock's side, but he was firmly jammed between the posts. Dag got out of the crush to help us, and after much pushing and swearing the testicles were exposed just enough for the job to be done. The bullock's eyes were closed and his breathing had become deep and rhythmical.

"At least he won't react now," I said.

"Don't be so sure," said Dag. "When a bullock's escaped you once, no matter how much you sedate him he'll still try to kick you."

Which he did, from his prostrate position, flailing back in dazed fury as the clamp closed shut.

"Thank Christ you're in one piece," said Pat, when it was all over.

He turned to his sons, who were gazing in adoration at Dag.

"On Monday morning lads, when the teacher asks everyone what they did over the weekend, won't you have the best story of all?"

The road from Portmagee back to the main N70 led us through an expanse of peat bog, stretching from the shores of the Valentia

Channel to the lower slopes of Knocknaskereighta Mountain. Heather, black bog rush, purple moor grass and marsh Andromeda grew over its reaches, as well as blankets of bog cotton, their white, wispy seed heads nodding in the breeze. Long brown scars ran across parts of the bog, where mechanized peat cutters had been at work. By the sides of the road, bricks of turf were expertly piled up into ricks shaped like early Christian oratories, waiting to be collected and taken off to the turf-burning power plant.

As we drove through this landscape, I tried to imagine it covered with trees. In ancient times, birch, pine, hazel and oak trees grew here in profusion, until neolithic farmers began clearing them to plant their crops. This was a period of heavy rainfall, and water percolated easily and quickly through the newly exposed soil, washing away its plant nutrients and clay particles and making it more acidic. Before long, acid-loving heathers, sedges, rushes and bog mosses colonized the cleared areas. The soil became waterlogged, and in these anaerobic, acidic conditions, the remains of dead plants were slow to break down. Slowly and steadily, peat accumulated. In places it grew to depths of up to nine feet, covering ancient stone walls and cooking pits, and the stumps of trees that had fallen naturally or been cut down.

Dag kept slowing the car to look out at the piles of gnarled branches and roots, which had been unearthed by turf cutters. A friend of ours in Canada was a wood-turner, and Dag had promised him a piece of bog oak, prized for its hardness and scarcity. He parked at the side of the road and hopped over a ditch to get a closer look at the piles of wood. A tour bus roared by and stopped ahead of our car, just beyond the nearest turf rick. About twenty tourists got out. They wandered around the rick, videoing it and posing for photographs next to it. Behind them, I could see a man approaching on foot, walking briskly and swinging a stick. Even from a distance I recognized him as Patrick O'Sullivan, a retired carpenter. We often saw him on this stretch of road; every day, whatever the weather, he walked six miles along it, from his cottage to the nearest shop and back. He stopped to talk to the tourists, and had his photograph taken with a few of them. By the time he reached us, Dag had returned from the bog, empty handed.

"Here is the new Canadian vet," Patrick greeted us, as if he were making introductions to some invisible companion. "And this is his travelling nurse."

As always, he was dressed in a baggy overcoat, woollen trousers and oversized plastic running shoes. Sprouting from one of his bushy grey eyebrows was an extremely long, thick hair, that hung down almost to his cheek.

"Those people are from America," he informed us, looking back at the tourists. They were climbing aboard the bus. Some of them clutched bricks of turf as souvenirs. Patrick leaned on his stick.

"I meet many a Yank in the summer months. I was on the bog road one day, taking a ramble, and I had just come alongside a turf cutter when these Yanks pulled up in their car. Now, I like to tell the Yanks a yarn. The fact is, I walk along making up yarns for them. So this Yank asks me if I own the turf cutter. I do indeed, sir, I say. Then he asks how much a machine like this might cost. Five thousand pounds, sir, I say. And I ask him, would you be interested in buying it off of me now?"

He broke into cackling laughter, which turned into a fit of coughing.

"And then," he gasped, "this Yank I'm telling you about, he looks over to Valentia Island and he asks who owns that land. I do, sir, I tell him. And he looks at the fields and the stone walls and he asks who runs the farms he sees over there."

Another bout of laughter and coughing ensued before Patrick could deliver his punch line.

"My TENANTS, sir, says I! And he believed that Patrick O'Sullivan was the landlord of that place, like the old Knight of Kerry!"

Using his sleeve, he wiped tears from his eyes. "Ah yes, I have great merriment with the Yanks."

Dag told him he was looking for bog oak, and asked if there was much of it around.

"You find it often enough," he said. "I drag it to my house and burn it. It makes a fierce heat, but you have to dry it a few years first."

"Burn it?" spluttered Dag. "You could sell that stuff for a fortune in North America."

"Is that so? Those Yanks, they'd buy anything. Down at Portmagee Community Centre they're giving lessons on how to make it into tables and what have you. Mostly it gets thrown away, no one sees value in it. When we were cutting turf by hand we'd find it all the time. We found old butter boxes too, that we called ferkins. Some were a hundred years old, with the butter inside them. The butter would melt still, but it was no good for eating."

Kerry used to be famous for its salted butter, which was made from the rich, fatty milk of the Kerry cow, an indigenous breed in these parts.

"There were no creameries until fifty or sixty years ago," said Patrick. "Before then the women made the butter at home. They wrapped it in cabbage leaves and packed it into ferkins. The butter they wanted for themselves they'd bury in the bog to keep it fresh. The rest they sent off with "car men," along the Butter Road to Cork. And from there it went all over the world, to North America and Australia, even to Jamaica."

I told him that as a child I'd watched my Aunt Theresa churning butter in the scullery of her County Longford farm. I didn't like its taste, which was strong and salty.

"Ah, you weren't used to it, I suppose," said Patrick. "The country butter was lovely. You can get nothing like it nowadays."

"I used to go with my uncle to the creamery," I reminisced. "I sat next to him on the horse-drawn cart, and I jumped down to open and close the gates along the lane."

"You don't see many on horses and carts nowadays," said Patrick. "Life has changed, and mostly for the better, I'd say. But the tourists that come here don't see it that way. There was a German man who came by last year, offering me money for my old stone shed. He wanted to live there and put a thatch roof on it. He said the thatch was romantic. *Romantic*, says I! I told him in my youth thatch was a sign of poverty. There was rats and mice living above in it and smoke from the fire blackening the reeds. The rain would be dripping through all sooty and there'd be hens scratching about up there, laying their eggs and dropping their shite on our heads. What in God's name was romantic about that? When the tin roofs came they were a blessing, indeed they were."

While we were talking to Patrick, a tractor had turned out of a gate and was chugging towards us.

"I think that's Mike O'Connell," said Dag excitedly, squinting to see more clearly. "He's the guy whose dog was strychnine poisoned last week. Hey look, isn't that it sitting beside him?"

"Poisoned?" Patrick repeated. "That's a terrible thing. When my poor wife was alive, God bless her soul, she'd be raging at people who did that."

Standing in the middle of the lane, Dag waved down the tractor. On the seat next to Michael, a black and white sheepdog wagged its tail.

"The dog's okay now?" asked Dag eagerly. "That's great!" Mike glanced at the animal.

"He is, I suppose," he said nonchalantly.

"The drugs worked!"

"They did. Isn't that what they were supposed to do?"

"Look at that, he's as right as ninepence," said Patrick, standing on tiptoes to observe the dog. "My wife would be thrilled, if she could see him."

The sheepdog jumped on his master's lap, wagging his tail and enjoying the sudden attention.

"Well, I'm delighted," said Dag. "I didn't think he had a chance. He looked really far gone when you brought him in. This has made my day. No, it's made my week."

Mike seemed puzzled by all the fuss over his dog.

"I'm glad to have met you. You've saved me a phone call to the vet's office. I have a lamb with watery mouth in a shed close by. Can you come by now to see him?"

CHAPTER TWENTY-FIVE

During the second week of May, a sponsored walk was planned in Cahersiveen, to commemorate The Great Famine. Its route was to follow the old "pauper's road," to the ruins of the workhouse in Bahaghs, then on to the Srugreana graveyard, where many famine victims were buried. There would be speeches, prayers, music and refreshments. Several farmers' wives had asked if they'd see me on the walk; I'd been inordinately pleased by this and assured them I'd be there. In one of the crazy weather switches that by now I'd grown accustomed to, the sunshine we'd been enjoying abruptly gave way to gales and snowball rain. On the day of the walk, one squall after another moved across the slopes of Knocknadobar, leaving a dusting of snow on its summit. Wind howled down our chimney all morning and big hailstones rattled against our windows. Sheep huddled for shelter against the stone walls around our garden, and Dora stayed curled up in the far corner of her haggard.

At noon, the storm appeared to be worsening, so I phoned the organizer of the walk and asked if it was still on.

"It is, indeed, in a manner of speaking at least," he said. "It would be grand if you could come. Shall we see you at two o'clock?"

At one o'clock I put on waterproof gear and set off on my bike. A strong wind was funnelling down the valley, and I laboured hard against it, sweating beneath layers of clothes.

As I passed Peggy and Michael's house, I could sense them watching me.

"Will you look at her, out in this poisonous weather on an old bike," I imagined them saying to each other. "Is it mad she is?"

The starting point of the walk was a Craft Centre on the main Ring of Kerry road, a few miles out of Cahersiveen. It was a new stone building, with a roof thatched in the Dutch style. Outside it were picnic tables and a commodious car park suitable for the large tourist buses that regularly stopped during the summer months. A dozen or so cars were there already, and more pulled up as I leaned my bicycle against a side wall. I stepped through a porch, past a small souvenir shop and into a spacious room. At the far end, schoolgirls were serving tea, sandwiches and cakes from a glass-fronted counter. Groups of people sat around tables, talking and laughing. As I scanned the room for a familiar face, a young man jumped up from his seat and shook my wet hand.

"You're very welcome!" he proclaimed.

James, the organizer of the event, had curling, prematurely grey hair, handsome features and an American note to his Irish accent.

"It's a great pity about the weather, but we're masters of improvisation," he said. "Make yourself at home, it won't be too long now before we get started."

I bought a cup of tea and sat at a table with three women I'd met on various farms in the area. In their home environment they'd been friendly and forthcoming, but now, in public, they were shy, and apart from a few platitudes, seemed unwilling to enter into conversation with me. One of them leaned over, and offered me a pamphlet about the walk.

"Did you see this?" she asked.

"'The Great Irish Famine was without a doubt the greatest human catastrophe of nineteenth century Europe'," I read. "'More than two million people (over one-quarter of our population) died or emigrated during the period of 1845 to 1850'."

It was a brief summation of a terrible, long and drawn-out nightmare. By 1845, Ireland was already in a desperate state. During the previous eighty years, the population had exploded to eight million. The country had no industry and no well-developed fisheries, and its farms were too small to require much in the way of hired labour, so chronic unemployment and dire poverty were rife. A census taken in 1841 found that two-thirds of the families in Kerry inhabited one-room, windowless mud cabins, and owned little more than a few pigs and a manure heap. The diet of most people consisted almost entirely of potatoes, supplemented whenever possible with a little buttermilk. Finding a scrap of land on which to grow these potatoes was therefore crucial for survival; as families expanded they divided up their rented small-holdings into ever smaller parcels.

Earlier in the century there had been foretastes of The Great Famine, in the form of crop failures and outbreaks of cholera and typhus. But no one was prepared for September 1845, when people across the country began digging up what appeared to be a splendid new crop of potatoes. They stored the tubers in well-drained pits and covered them with furze and brambles, hoping they would last throughout the winter months. Within days, however, much of this harvest had rotted from the inside out, and turned into a slimy, putrid, inedible mess. A fungus, *phytophthora infestans*, was the cause of this disaster. After spreading from America to England, it had arrived in Ireland, and destroyed forty percent of its precious potato crop.

The following spring, the blight struck again; this time it completely devastated the crop. Across the country, people were starving, yet the English continued to import oats, wheat, barley and livestock from Ireland. In Parliament, the Duke of Cambridge claimed that Irishmen could live on anything, and that there was plenty of grass in the fields for them to eat. The horror continued: in the year that came to be known as Black '47, an epidemic of typhus swept across Ireland, killing tens of thousands. The English passed the Gregory Clause, barring from government relief anyone with a small-holding of under a quarter acre, thus opening the doors to mass evictions. Landlords threw families off their tiny pieces of land and burned down their cabins.

In 1848, when it seemed things could get no worse, the potato crop once again failed totally.

During what became known as The Great Hunger, forty-one percent of Kerry's population abandoned its mountains and valleys. Many of these people walked to Tralee or Cobh, and boarded the infamous "coffin ships." These vessels, which had brought wood from North America, returned to the New World with Irish emigrants as human ballast. Conditions aboard the ships were appalling. Many of the emigrants perished before they reached their destinations, while thousands more died on arrival and were buried in mass graves.

There was a stir in the room; I looked up. A man carrying a large harp was weaving between the tables, greeting people on his way. He was followed by a girl with a fiddle, then two more girls with oboes. They sat by the refreshments counter, tuned their instruments and began playing plaintive Irish airs. The harpist was small and stocky. His grey hair was cut very short and he wore fashionably tiny glasses.

"That man is very talented, he makes the harps himself," a woman at my table whispered to me, leaning over and holding her hand against one side of her mouth. "His name is Adolf. He's a *German*."

The room was filling up. Soon, the noisy chatter and the clinking of cups and saucers almost drowned out the gentle music. James Casey flitted about, chatting to people and glancing worriedly through the rain-streaked windows at trees thrashing about in the wind. An hour passed. Adolf and his girls worked through their repertoire and started at the beginning again. By now I was becoming very bored, but no one else in the room seemed bothered by the long delay.

The parish priest arrived, along with a three-man film crew. In a flurry of activity, the crew set up their camera and lights and did a sound check. James stepped onto the podium, blinking against the glare. After welcoming us, he explained that because of the inclement weather, our itinerary had been changed. The speeches, prayers and music would happen indoors. The walk was cancelled, although it was hoped that sponsors would be understanding enough to cough up the money they had promised to each individual. Later in the afternoon, the Cahersiveen Sunday hiking club would walk up to the workhouse to lay the wreath, and anyone suitably dressed was welcome to join them.

James began the new itinerary by quoting a passage from the work of W.S. Trench, who in 1861 published eyewitness accounts from the famine times.

"'They died on the road and they died in the fields'," he read. "'They died on the mountains and they died in the glens; they died at the relief works and they died in their houses, so that the little streets or villages were left almost without an inhabitant, and at least some few, despairing of help in the country, crawled into the town and died at the doors of the residents and outside the Union walls. Some were buried underground and some were left unburied in the mountains, there being no one able to bury them'."

A hush had fallen across the room. No one stirred as James told a story he said had been passed down from Famine days. While people in the Cahersiveen area were dying in droves, a landlord stored up grain in a warehouse in the town, preparing to ship it to England. One night, an angry mob attacked the warehouse. The *gardaí* were helpless against such numbers; rioting spread until a local doctor took charge, bringing in several tons of Indian cornmeal to the town and distributing it among the starving.

People coughed and cleared their throats while James made his closing remarks. Then the priest took the podium. From his trouser pocket he pulled out a key ring with some beads threaded onto it.

"We'll say a decade of the rosary," he announced.

All around me, people lowered their heads and clasped their hands. As the priest galloped through the Hail Marys, they murmured along with him, dropping the ends of the words and running them into each other. Had the prayers not been so familiar to me, I could have taken them for an exotic incantation:

"Hail mary fulla grace, the loris withee, bless arhou among women, and blessis the fruof thywomb—" Heads nodded as the crucial word was hissed out—"*JESUS* . . ."

Another musical interlude from Adolf's group followed the prayers, then James officially closed the ceremony. I decided to join the group that was walking up to the workhouse. We were led by the hikers, James and a young boy holding a wreath of yellow flowers. As we trudged along, bending our heads into the driving rain, the wind tore a few blooms off the wreath, and one became entangled in a fuchsia bush. I rescued it, and slipped it into my pocket. The film crew had come with us, and the cameraman was running along backwards ahead of the group, his machine shrouded in transparent plastic and balanced precariously on his shoulder.

"Smile!" he kept exhorting us. "You're in the movies!"

"Whatever has possessed that fellow, to want to walk backwards all the way to Srugreana?" said the woman next to me.

Her name was Catherine. I had once visited her farm with Dag, just after we'd arrived in Cahersiveen. Though I hadn't seen her since, she knew a lot about me.

"I hear you've a pet lamb. Last week I was thinking of calling you to see if you'd take two more. One of my ewes died after having couplets and I was bottle-feeding them both. Then another ewe lost her lamb, so I skinned it and sewed the fleece around both the orphans, hoping the ewe might adopt them. I kept all three in a pen, but the ewe would have nothing to do with them. She pucked at them all the time and wouldn't let them near her teats. I told my husband I'd be ringing the vet's wife and asking if she wanted more pets. Then she let them suck, and now she's mad about them."

We had turned onto the narrow lane known as Pauper's Road. It was along here that the evicted, the destitute and the starving had made their way towards their last resort: Bahaghs Workhouse, built by the British in 1846, under the Act for the Relief of the Destitute Poor in Ireland. Like all the workhouses across Ireland, it was a dreaded place. As soon as families entered its gates, they were ripped apart. Men and women were strictly segregated, and children over two years of age were taken away from their mothers. More often than not, they never saw each other again. Most people arrived at the workhouse in a desperate state of health, and, faced with a punishing work regime and only a survival diet, they often died soon afterwards.

All that was left of the workhouse were some high, red-brick walls and a turret and a chimney stack standing bleakly against the grey sky. A cross nailed together from scraps of wood was propped up by its main doorway. The boy laid the wreath against it, and I added the yellow bloom and some flowers I had picked from the hedgerows along Pauper's Road. We stood in silence for a minute, remembering the people who had suffered here. I stared through the doorway of the workhouse, at the remains of narrow, gloomy rooms. A sense of unhappiness clung to this place, as strongly as the ivy that wound around its bricks.

"Did you ever hear of the Bahaghs Martyrs?" Catherine quietly asked me, after the minute was up.

I nodded, surprised that she'd even mention it.

"This place was a prison during the Civil War," she said. "It was from here they took the five men. They blew them up along the lane. There was an uncle of mine locked up here at the time. Word came to him that one of the dead men was a relative of his. It turned out not to be true, but he sat in here grieving for a while anyway."

There was a break in the rain, so our group decided to carry on to Srugreana Cemetery. It was much farther than I'd expected; my feet hurt as I clumped along the hard road in my Wellingtons. But there was much to distract me along the way: Saint Joseph's lilies flowering along the sides of the lane, fields of buttercups and a piebald horse prancing in an orchard of gnarled apple trees.

The cemetery was on a slope, with a gentle view across the green fields of the Carhan River valley. Long grass and weeds grew between the tombs. Some of the headstones were fairly recent, but most were old, their inscriptions weathered away and barely decipherable. One area was covered with scores of stubby, unmarked stones, many of them just rocks stuck into the ground.

"These are from the Famine times, I'd say," Catherine observed. "There's a mass grave around here somewhere. Those in the workhouse who had any bit of strength left were made to bring the dead up here and bury them. I've heard it said that the cloths the bodies were wrapped in had to be taken off and brought back to the workhouse to be used again."

The ruins of a small church, medieval in design, stood in the middle of the cemetery. Its roof had collapsed, but the walls were intact. Just inside the doorway was a ballaun, one of the hollowed-out stones originally used for grinding corn and often incorporated into early churches as baptismal fonts. It held a puddle of grimy water. Catherine and others in the group busily dipped the fingers of their right hand into this, then made the Sign of the Cross. There were more gravestones within the church, and for a while the Famine was forgotten as the newer inscriptions were discussed.

"Keating—Mary Keating—she was my father's second cousin by marriage."

"O'Sullivan—the father, the sons, the daughter—what about poor old Maisie—how is it she's not buried with them?"

"Pat Golden from Kells. What's he doing here?"

"Didn't he live along Old Street?"

Just before we left the cemetery, a man called me over to see some large family tombs built of unmortared stones. The slabs across their doorways had fallen down, and I could peer inside at about fourteen skulls and a collection of assorted bones.

"Doesn't it make you think," the man asked me, "that there's something to be said for cremation after all?"

As we headed back towards the Craft Centre, another woman fell in with Catherine and me. Annette was the wife of a local undertaker in town. When I asked her what it was like being married to a man with such a profession, she laughed merrily.

"He never brings his work home, thank God."

She and Catherine were keen to discuss the horrors of menopause, which they were both presently experiencing.

"I'm burning up with the hot flushes," said Catherine.

"I can't remember things from one minute to the next," said Annette. "And I'm having to pee the whole time."

To prove her point, she hopped over a stone wall into a field and squatted down.

"Ah, thank God for that," she sighed.

"Annette, there's a fellow way up with his binoculars trained on you," Catherine teased her.

"He can look all he likes, Catherine. It won't be doing him a bit of good!"

By the time we got back to the Craft Centre, the rain had set in again. I looked forward to being pushed home by the wind, but by the time I reached the top of our valley it had shifted and was funnelling up against me. I had to pedal furiously to make any progress downhill. As I laboured past the track leading to Peggy and Michael's house, I couldn't help but laugh, wondering what they might be saying about me now.

CHAPTER TWENTY-SIX

The ringing went on and on, reaching into my dreams and pulling me from sleep. Dag was curled around me, his breathing deep and steady. Without opening my eyes, I took hold of his hand and shook it gently.

"The phone," I muttered.

It continued to ring; Dag grunted in his sleep. Turning in his arms, I located one of his ears.

"Phone!"

He woke instantly, lurching up like a behemoth, and as he fumbled blindly for the switch on the reading lamp he knocked the phone off the table. It hit the floor with a bang, the ringing stopped and was replaced by a tinny "Hello? Hello?"

Dag clicked on the lamp and slid out of bed.

"What? Where?" I heard him say. "Can you speak more slowly?"

Farmers were often so panic-stricken when they rang in the middle of the night that they blurted out the details of the emergency at great speed, their Kerry accents thicker than ever with the anxiety.

"Don't hang up!" Dag cried. "Just say it again. What's the problem?"

Stark naked, he was crouched on the floor in a pool of yellow light, poring over an *Ordnance Survey* map, with the phone receiver pressed to his ear. I glanced at my watch. It was five minutes past two.

"How long has she been calving? OK, I'll come right away. Can you get some help? What? Well, get whoever you can. And have lots of hot water ready."

He rang off and began to dress. I stretched and yawned, then burrowed luxuriously beneath our duvet, feeling sorry for him having to go out into the cold.

"It's a cow down by Caherdaniel," he said, his voice muffled through the covers. "She's been calving a long time. This could be a Caesarean."

I'd yet to witness a Caesarean on a cow. Dag had told me that big burly farmers sometimes went into dead faints during these long operations, and despite all the blood and gore I'd seen over the past three months, he was worried that I might find it too grisly a spectacle. I hadn't argued; most cows seemed to prefer the depths of night for giving birth, and I was always happy to stay in the warmth of our bed when he was called out at some unearthly hour like this.

"Would you mind coming along, Maria? Eileen McCarthy's a widow and it sounds like she might not be able to get much help. I could really use an extra pair of hands."

I slid my head out just far enough to squint at him.

"You're not serious, are you?"

He was. Summoning up all my willpower, I swung my feet onto the cold floor.

"Do we have time for a cup of tea before we leave?"

"Tea? Are you kidding? This is an emergency. Put your clothes on, let's go!"

Outside, the air felt fresh and clean against my face. A strong wind had chased away the clouds, and stars glittered brightly against a dense, velvety black sky. As we drove away from the cottage, our headlights picked out the eyes of sheep lying on the track. I got out twice to shoo them out of our way, and once more to open and shut the gate onto the lane.

Dag drove fast along the deserted roads, through Cahersiveen, to Waterville and beyond, along high, coastal cliffs. A yellow quarter moon cast a shimmering path across the long rows of swells moving in from the Atlantic, but the Skellig Rocks, eight miles out at sea, were lost in darkness.

Just before Caherdaniel we left the main road and turned up into a valley. Soon we were following a track that suddenly branched off into three different directions. Dag gambled on the middle branch. Frank O'Leary's adage was proved right yet again: just as we were convinced we were lost, the track took a sharp bend, then a light appeared and we drove into the yard of a two-storied farmhouse. A small woman appeared, shading her eyes against the glare of the car's headlamps.

"Are you the vet?" cried Eileen O'Sullivan anxiously. "How quick you came!"

She was an edgy, nervous woman in her late sixties. She spoke rapidly, emphasizing her words with hands that flitted through the air like birds. She wore thin nylon stockings under her rubber boots and a heavy outdoor coat over a tweed skirt and a twin set. Her "help" consisted of Michael and Albert, two old men dressed in dark suits and flat caps. We knew Michael from Mary O'Donaghue's pub, where he was a regular. I thought back to the time he was so drunk he couldn't walk up the road to the church, and Mary drove him there instead.

"We've met before," I told him.

"We have not," he retorted, sucking in his cheeks. "I have never in my life set eyes on either of you."

"Where's the cow, Eileen?" asked Dag.

"She's in the shed. There's no electricity in there, but we have a torch. Mind yourself now, for she's a bold cow."

We all trooped inside the low, dark, stuffy shed. Albert brandished the torch, shining it onto a big rusty-coloured cow. She was lying among piles of dung and dirty straw and was tethered tightly to a metal ring on the wall.

"She would have to be a Limousin," said Dag ruefully, referring to a breed with the reputation of being wild and unmanageable. "Can someone loosen the rope so that she can get up?"

While Michael fumbled with the knot, Dag slapped the cow on the back, encouraging her to stand up. On struggling to her feet, she discovered that Michael hadn't just loosened her rope but untied it completely, and she made a dash for the door. Eileen fled through it ahead of her, leaving it wide open. Dag leapt in front of the doorway just in time to block her escape. Veering away from him, she began charging wildly around the confined space. The torch beam strafed the walls of the shed as Albert flapped his arms at the cow, and Michael scuttled behind him, yelling "Whisht! Whisht! Whisht!" I backed myself into a dark corner, fervently hoping I'd be safe there from this wild-eyed, unrestrained animal.

"LET'S ALL CALM DOWN," Dag called over the confusion.

By holding out his arms in front of the cow and talking quietly to her, he slowly manoeuvred her into a corner.

"Anyone have a rope? Let's get a halter on her."

A rope was produced and the cow safely tethered to the wall. By now she was far from happy and tried to kick Dag while he examined her.

"She's got a bad torsion, a twist in the womb," he said. "We'll have to do a Caesarean section on her, but the calf might be dead."

"Oh my God!" wailed Eileen, who had crept back into the shed.

"Eileen, I'll need more light, more rope and lots of hot water. Is there any chance of getting some extra help?"

"I'll wake my neighbour's son, Brendan Joe. Come with me now, Albert and Michael, I need the both of you."

Dag stripped off from the waist up and pulled on his calving gown. While I held the torch, he carefully laid out his surgical instruments and suture material on a bale of hay, which was the best thing he could find to use as a worktable. The cow had settled and was standing calmly against the wall. It was peaceful and quiet in the shed: the cow's laboured breathing, the swishing of Dag's rubber gown and over-trousers as he moved about, and the rustle and squeak of mice in the cobwebby rafters above. Then footsteps and querulous voices came from outside and the two old men were back. Michael carried a bucket of steaming water in each hand, and Albert held a bedside lamp. It resembled a brass candlestick holder, and had a bare sixty-watt bulb powered by two long extension leads trailing through the door and across the yard to the farmhouse.

"Is that it for light?" asked Dag in dismay.

"It is," confirmed Albert.

While Dag was scrubbing his hands and arms, a car pulled up in the yard.

"Here's Brendan Joe," announced Michael.

Dag glanced up nervously from the bucket; when a young, strong man strode purposefully through the doorway, his face relaxed.

Soon, we were all positioned and ready for the start of the operation. I held the bedside lamp aloft, Brendan Joe steadied the cow's head and Michael and Albert leaned against one side of her rump to keep her against the wall. Dag had attached a long rope to her back inside ankle and left it trailing across the ground. If the cow started to go down, he told the men, someone must grab the rope and pull it as hard as they could, to ensure she fell inwards to the wall rather than keeling over towards us.

"Otherwise," he warned them, "her guts will come spilling out all over the floor."

I passed him syringes filled with local anaesthetic, which he administered into the base of the cow's tail and deeply into the muscle along her spine. Like most of the cows I'd met in Kerry, she wasn't partial to needles, and when she felt them prick her she snorted, struggled with Brendan Joe and tried to kick out at the old men.

"You whoore," they muttered darkly. "You wilful blaggard!"

Once she was calmer, Dag rubbed a soapy iodine solution into the hair on her flank, then shaved it until there was a rectangle of bare skin the size of a coffee-table top. Eileen, who had been hovering in the doorway, suddenly emerged into the small circle of light. She was holding a bottle filled with a clear liquid, which she began sprinkling over the cow, the vet, his surgical tools and his helpers, murmuring all the while under her breath. Dag paused from his work to stare at her, looking utterly perplexed.

"It must be holy water," I whispered to him.

Overhearing me, Eileen launched into an explanation.

"It is indeed, it's holy water from *Lourdes*. I was on a pilgrimage there only last year and this poor cow is in need of a miracle if anyone ever was. I'm away to the kitchen now to pray, should anybody need me."

Dag scrubbed up again, then collected a scalpel and prepared to make a large incision in the cow's side.

"Maria, could you come a step or two closer with the light?" he asked.

"I'm as close as I can get," I said. "The cord won't reach any further."

His scalpel was poised over the cow's skin. Deciding not to watch this part of the operation, I looked down, only to see something far more alarming taking place close to my feet. Anxious to help with the light situation, Albert was stiffly bending over and reaching a shaky hand towards the electric cord.

"Don't!" I cried, but I was too late—he grasped the cord and tugged it towards him.

We were plunged into absolute darkness. Several seconds of stunned silence ensued, until Dag said, in a voice thick with restraint, "Could someone *please* turn on the flashlight?"

"The what?" said Albert.

"The torch," I translated.

"Turn on that torch, Michael," called Brendan Joe.

"I don't have it," said Michael. "I gave it to Albert."

"You did not," retorted Albert.

"I did so," said Michael.

"Well, I don't have it," Albert claimed, "and I don't know where it is."

"Put that plug back in," suggested Brendan Joe.

"I can't see the fecking plug!" cried Michael.

"For Christ's sake, find the torch and then we'll find the plug," said Albert.

"I gave the torch to *you*," Michael reiterated.

"You did not!" shouted Albert.

"Gentlemen, please," Dag pleaded from the gloom. "Does anyone have a match?"

"D'ye have a match?" Michael asked Albert.

"I do. In my pocket."

"Well get it out and strike the fecker then."

A match flared, the torch was located and the extension cords were plugged together. The light I was holding revealed Dag in his green rubberized gown, a baffled expression on his face, still resting the scalpel against the cow's flank.

"Is everyone ready?" he asked. "No more lights out, OK?"

As the scalpel cut cleanly into the cow's skin, she lowed in protest, lurching away from the wall and scattering the two men.

"She feels the cut, boy!" said Brendan Joe.

"She feels the cut," repeated Michael.

"Ay, she feels the cut alright," added Albert helpfully.

Dag injected more anaesthetic at the base of the wound, then quickly made a ten-inch-long incision through several different muscle layers beneath the skin. Bright red blood welled up and spilled onto his green Wellingtons and the soft brown dung he stood in. Instead of cutting the final layer of muscle, he pulled apart its fibres with his fingers. Beneath lay the peritoneum, which lines the inside of the abdominal cavity, and through which I could see various internal organs. It was strange and disturbing to be witnessing a major operation on such a large, conscious animal, but I didn't have time to really ponder over this. After hours of hard labour, and the excitement of trying to escape, the cow was understandably tired and wanted to lie down.

"Keep her standing!" rapped Dag, as her knees began to bend.

"Stay up! Stay up! Stay up!" we all yelled at her.

Brendan Joe slapped her ears while the old boys hopped about in the muck, aiming ineffectual kicks at her back legs. After several minutes of this assault, she wavered, sighed, then finally gave up and leaned against the wall instead.

When Dag cut through the peritoneum, air rushed into the body cavity, making a strange sucking noise. Even stranger noises followed, sloshes and slurps from internal organs moving back and forth as Dag reached into the cow up to his armpits, attempting to twist the uterus back into its normal position. This proved impossible, giving him no option but to open it the way it was. One slice through its pink, glistening wall, and a waxy, ghostly yellow foreleg appeared. Dag reached in for the leg next to it and began pulling on them both.

"Stay on her nose, Brendan Joe," said Dag, as the calf's head came out, its eyes glazed and preoccupied. A stretched-out torso followed, and the old men rushed around and placed their hands underneath it, lending what little strength they had to Dag's efforts. Grunting under the weight, he backed away from the cow, holding up the hundred-pound baby as he pulled it to prevent ripping the uterus too badly. The body was stretched to almost five feet before the hind legs appeared. Suddenly it was all out: a slick, slippery brown and white calf, sprawled on the ground and gasping for air. Its appearance heralded a new litany from Michael and Albert.

"It's a bull calf!"

"He's a fine calf!"

"He is!"

"God bless him!"

Dag dragged the calf into the yard. He asked the two old men to rub him with straw while he began the long job of stitching the mother. First, he stitched the womb, while Brendan Joe held it for him. Then, after he had reached into the cow's body cavity and scooped out handfuls of fluid and blood, he stitched the individual muscle layers.

"By God," said Brendan Joe forty-five minutes later, as he admired the final line of neat stitches down the cow's flank. "You'd make a great tailor. Would you have the time to sew me suit?"

All that remained to be done was to reunite the cow with her calf. Out in the yard we found him with his head up, looking bright and alert despite having to cope with Michael and Albert fussing around him and shining their torch into his eyes.

"His breathing is very hoarse, boy," said Albert worriedly.

"Would you say he's warm enough now?" asked Michael.

"He'll be fine in a minute," Dag reassured them. He dragged the calf back to his mother, who sniffed him hesitantly for a minute, before starting to warm and dry his body with her long tongue.

Eileen insisted we come inside the farmhouse for a drink. The wood-panelled walls of her living room were painted a bright, glossy pink and were hung with paintings of the Virgin Mary, St. Bernadette, St. Theresa and St. Francis of Assisi. Although it was past four-thirty in the morning, the kitchen table was laid as if for high tea, with plates of ham sandwiches, a sponge cake, a tin of biscuits and a round of soda bread.

"Gather in!" she cried, wielding a teapot. "You'll all have a whiskey too, of course."

"Only a small one for me, I'm still on call," said Dag.

"Nonsense," scoffed Eileen, filling a small tumbler to the brim with Powers. "You're a big man, this won't do you any harm."

The tea she poured out had been stewing on the range and was dark brown in colour and acrid in taste.

"This is a good strong cup, Eileen," said Albert approvingly.

"Strong, nothing," said Brendan Joe. "There's a man who works my shift at the sock factory, he likes his tea so strong that he puts three bags in the mug and leaves them floating in the tea while he's drinking it. Then, when he finishes, he takes one of the bags into his mouth and sucks on it. It's a terrible thing to have to look at, first thing in the morning."

The bottle of whiskey went around a second time.

"That was a marvellous experience, boy," Albert told Dag. "I've never seen the like of it. How we managed in the old days, I just don't know."

"We managed because we had to, Albert," Eileen reminded him. She turned to Dag. "Would you say the cow needs a drink?"

"Make sure she always has a bucket of water," he said.

Michael cackled at this. "She means a *real* drink, boy. Did you never try the whiskey cure on a cow?"

Dag shook his head. "I've only heard it mentioned."

"When I was a young man, I knew a vet who swore by it, especially for the milk fever," Michael recounted. "I called him out one night for a cow that was terrible sick. It was gone one o'clock by the time he came, and a fine night it was too, with a big full moon. By then the cow was blown up with gas and stretched out on the ground. So the vet let the gas out of her, then he says to me, 'Have you a half pint of whiskey, Michael?' 'I don't ,' says I, 'but I know where I can get one.' I ran down the hill until I came to my neighbour's house and I knocked on the back door until his wife came out and I shouts, 'Can you give me a half pint of whiskey for my cow, missus?' 'Away home with you,' says she. 'It's only yourself you want whiskey for, and you'll get none here at this hour of the night.' Ah, she was a bold woman, but when I put my hand on my heart about the cow she sent me back up the hill with the bottle. I went as fast as my legs would take me, but it was past two by then and the cow was fierce sick. The vet took the whiskey and drenched her with it, he poured the full measure of it down her throat. 'She'll be sound as a clock by morning,' says he, and leaves. At four I looked in at her, and I could not believe what my eyes were telling me. Wasn't she standing up already, swaying about on her legs, with her eyes rolling around in her head. Take it from me, boy, for I've had plenty of experience in the matter—that cow was well drunk! I went back to bed and I got up again at eight and there she was, just like the vet had said, sound as a clock. There was not a sign of sickness on that cow."

"Did she have a hangover?" asked Dag.

"Well, that I couldn't tell you!" chuckled Michael. "Whiskey's a great medicine, it is indeed." He held up his glass to Eileen. "I'll have another one in there, when you're ready."

"My father had a nip of whiskey in his tea every day until he died," I told him. "And he lived to be eighty-four."

"Well, and I had a friend, a good strong man still at eighty-six. He was taken sick, and in the hospital he was shouting for a drop of whiskey and they wouldn't give it him and he died. If he'd had that drop it would have kept his ticker going, and by God he'd still be here today."

The talk turned to old cures for sickness in humans and animals.

"My mother swore by feeding a cow some of its own bee-stings to prevent it getting milk fever," said Eileen. "And she beat our cows with a white cloth, to rid them of the worms."

"Did it work?" asked Dag curiously.

"It did!"

"Why?"

"Well, that I don't know. You don't question these things, you stick with them without asking."

Albert told us there was nothing like bread soda to treat cows for "timber tongue," when the base of the tongue swells and prevents the animal from eating. And Brendan Joe said that when his father's sheep got swollen ears as a result of eating St. John's Wort, they clipped the ends of them.

"What does that do?" asked Dag.

"It lets out the poisons. It never fails." He smiled slyly at Dag. "But if the vet happens to be around, we give them some penicillin afterwards."

As we drove home, the moon sank on the western horizon, and the sky began to pale and take on hues of mauve and pink in the east. Halfway down the lane towards our cottage, the car's headlights picked out the back end of a badger. Dag braked sharply, and we watched the animal lumber along ahead us. Before he disappeared into the ditch, he turned to look at us, giving us a glimpse of his striped, startled face.

Another set of lights was heading up towards us. Dag pulled in close to the hedgerow to let Kevin O'Shea go by on his tractor. Attached to the front end of it was a large bucket, with a ewe and two lambs cuddled up comfortably inside.

"It's a fine dawning," Kevin greeted us.

"New lambs?"

"They're just born, and I found the three of them up the mountain. I'm away off to the field with them now."

"They're fine lambs, Kevin," said Dag.

"They are, they are! You're busy, I see."

"I hope there's not another call waiting for me when I get home."

"If it is, it won't be from me. Good luck now, good luck!"

✦

CHAPTER TWENTY-SEVEN

At last, I heard a cuckoo. It was calling from a copse of sally trees that grew on the lower slopes of Knocknadobar Mountain.

"Did you hear her with your right ear first or your left?" asked Dennis. "If it was the right, you'll have luck in the next twelve months."

Dennis had stopped off to visit me on his way up to feed the ponies. We were out in the garden, sitting on the stone wall.

"That same cuckoo is in those trees every spring. Sometimes in the summer, I'll see her on a branch, in the company of another little birdeen. I've heard two cuckoos now, this year. Last year, I watched a cuckoo grow up in a lark's nest. He grew to a savage size altogether."

He lit a cigarette, and as he smoked it he studied Dora. She was grazing in a clump of bluebells, busily tearing off their heads.

"That lamb should be weaned by now," he said.

From the pocket of his jacket he pulled out a paper bag and handed it to me.

"Sheep nuts," he explained, as I looked at the small, brown pellets inside. "Instead of the bottle. I brought them for you to try with her. She won't like them at first. But she'll grow accustomed to them in time."

Dora was now a hefty lamb, almost too heavy for me to lift, yet she was still demanding a bottle first thing in the morning and last thing at night.

"She seems to need the comfort of the sucking, as much as the milk," I explained defensively.

Dennis fixed me with his watery blue eyes.

"I'd say it's a comfort for you, too. You'll hate to see that pet lamb grow up and away into a sheep."

I gazed at the sky. The morning was sunny, but a chill wind was blowing from the north, teasing the clouds into feathery patterns.

"In Ireland we call the north wind the *scariveen*," Dennis told me. "It often blows in May. There's no grass in that wind. It's a terrible thing for the new growth and the lambs."

Despite the wind, the landscape of the Iveragh Peninsula was becoming more lush and colourful by the day. All over our garden, montbretia was in bud and the stout new stems of foxgloves had begun to rise imperiously from their downy leaf cushions. Along the hedgerows, the fuchsia was out in all its glory, ox-eyed daisies were about to burst into flower and there were dense yellow heads of Irish spurge, tiny blue speedwells and creeping strands of tormentil and birdsfoot trefoil. In fields saturated with greenness, cows grazed on buttercups, daisies, red clover, cowslips, larkspur and bladder campion. The lambs danced among stands of yellow irises. Silverweed and marsh marigold blossomed along the stream banks, pink sea thrift bloomed among grey and purple rocks above the harbour, while on the grassy headlands close by the rare and delicate Western Marsh orchid shivered in the *scariveen*.

These days, I could hardly bear to stay indoors. I told Dennis about my plans for the afternoon, to pack a picnic lunch and cycle to the beach called White Strand, six miles away. The route would take me through several layers of history: past the medieval stone fort of Cahergael, the fifteen-century Ballycarbery Castle and the ruins of an old "big house" in an estate owned last century by a gentrified Irish landlord. I'd been reading about these places, I told Dennis, and was excited to learn of their connections through time. The Corcu Duibne, a gifted tribe who controlled the Iveragh Peninsula between the sixth and twelfth centuries, probably built the stone fort. Later, their kingdom was divided between the Anglo-Normans in the Dingle and the MacCarthys in the Iveragh, and Donal MacCarthy Mor built Ballycarbery Castle for his son, Tadhg. In 1565, the head of the MacCarthy Mor pledged his loyalty to Queen Elizabeth in return for being granted an earldom. The catch in this agreement was that if MacCarthy died without an heir, his lands would be confiscated by the Crown. This happened at the end of the seventeenth century, when the land around Ballycarbery was handed over to Trinity College, Dublin. They leased it to a wealthy landlord, who built the mansion, known as the "big house" and rented the holdings to local farmers.

"How well you know our history," said Dennis. "But I wonder if your books spoke of the cruelty of that landlord. He was of the Mahoney clan. Hanged a young lad for the sake of a sheep."

He lit another cigarette, then let it burn down between his fingers as he told the story.

"One of the landlord's flock went missing. He accused the lad of stealing it. If the sheep wasn't back within two days, he said, he'd hang him from the tallest tree on his land. That lad searched day and night for the sheep. The people from the townland searched with him, but it wasn't to be found. So the landlord did as he'd said. He hanged that poor boy, early one morning. And while he was still swinging from the tree, wasn't the missing sheep found at last, drowned in a drain."

Ash tumbled off the end of his cigarette; in the distance I heard the steady call of the cuckoo.

"There's another part yet. When the young man's mother saw her son hanging from a bough, she cursed the landlord. She said no crows would ever nest in his trees again. They'd leave for good, she promised, and they'd take his luck with them. Soon after, all the crows left. I don't know what happened to the landlord. This was before my time, you understand, but while I've been alive I've never seen a crow in that place."

The remains of the big house stood high above the road at the top of a sloping field. I stowed my bike behind a stone wall and walked up through a stand of old sycamore trees. The graceful, two-storied mansion had lofty windows and arched doorways. Its roof had fallen in and its exterior walls, covered in crumbling ochre plaster, were being colonized by ivy. Unlike many of the "big houses" across Ireland, this one had escaped being burned down during the Troubles. But it had stood empty since early this century, when the Land Act transferred huge tracts of land from landlords to tenants, ending the tradition of an Irish gentry. I couldn't get inside the house; a fence topped with barbed wire guarded its environs. As I walked around the fence, two jackdaws appeared on a high wall. They hopped along, threatening me with raucous calls, perhaps in defence of a hidden nest. Leaving them in peace, I walked back towards my bicycle, scanning the treetops as I went, searching in vain for a crow.

I could see Ballycarbery Castle, its turret and the remains of its castellated walls standing clear against the sky, still on guard over the estuary where Spanish ships used to sail. But before I reached the lane that led towards it, I noticed our car parked at the top of a track, by a farmhouse on the other side of the road. Dag's familiar figure appeared, striding towards a shed. Deciding to surprise him, I pushed my bike up the track and popped my head around the shed door. What I saw didn't inspire me to hang around; helped by a farmer, Dag was using a jack to deliver a dead calf.

"My parents are inside," the farmer called to me. "Go into them, they'd be delighted to see you."

The cottage was traditional in design, long and low and gable-ended. An old couple welcomed me into a kitchen filled with the smell of baking. They were astonishingly sprightly for their age; eighty-two-year-old Mrs. O'Connell served me with warm scones straight from the oven, while her ninety-one-year-old husband plumped up cushions for me on the rack, from where I could look through the window and across the estuary. They sat either side of me, taking obvious pleasure in watching me eat.

I praised the scones, which were light and delicious, then had to restrain Mrs. O'Connell from immediately serving me with two more. It was safer, I reckoned, to praise the splendid view.

"Ah, you never get tired of looking at it," said Mr. O'Connell. "But it was better when I was a boy, on account of all the ships sailing into the harbour. They were a grand sight. My mother would go down to the pier and buy animal feed and flour they'd brought in. She'd load up our donkey with sacks and bring them home. We'd have a hundred-and-twenty-pound sack of flour sitting here in the kitchen. There was no such thing as buying bread when I was a boy. We made it ourselves. We milked our own cows and churned our butter, too, and we had our chickens for our eggs."

Below their cottage, on the other side of the lane, was a small house surrounded by trees. Nesting in the tops of these trees were dozens of crows, whose loud cawing had filled my ears as I pushed my bike up to the track.

"That's John Joe Moriaty's house," said Mr. O'Connell, when I inquired about it. "They say the crows came to him after a curse was put on the big house down the way. Ah, but it's nothing but *piseog*."

"What's that?" I asked.

"Superstition. Make-believe. We're big on it in Ireland. But they say the crows brought the luck with them. That might be true alright, for John Joe was the first person in all the townlands round here to get a tractor. This is fifty-one years ago I'm talking about. He'd be travelling all the time, up and down the lanes, for everyone wanted him to take them about on his new tractor. Until he died, a tractor was his only vehicle. He'd often go to town in it. It's strange not to see it there, parked along the curb. We buried him less than two months ago, God rest his soul."

"I remember that tractor," I said. "I used to see it parked outside the bank."

"Which bank?" asked Mrs. O'Connell.

"The AIB."

"That could have been Bridie from down by the castle. She goes into town on her tractor, too. But if it was the AIB you saw the tractor outside, I'd say it was John Joe Moriaty's, alright."

Dag had no more calls. Things were quiet at the surgery; Mike had told him to take off the rest of the day and evening. We stowed my bike in the back of the car and drove to White Strand. Sitting on the pale sand, we shared the sandwiches I'd brought. The tide was low. Bull kelp bobbed and turned in the shallows, their heads catching the sunlight and seeming to wink as they turned with the current. Long, flat strands of seaweed

254

curled around exposed boulders. Cormorants, shags and gulls winged by. The air was filled with birdsong and the gentle wash of waves.

"The ocean's really calm today," said Dag. "Maybe we could make it to the Skelligs."

During the past couple of weeks, whenever he'd had time off and the weather was settled, we had enquired about chartering a boat to the Skelligs. So far, we'd had no luck. Even when the sea in Dingle Bay looked like glass, the boat owners told us, the wave action around Skellig Michael's tiny, exposed pier could make landing there impossible. Back at our cottage, Dag phoned Des Lavelle, who ran trips to the islands from May to September. Conditions, he said, were perfect. Then Dag called Frank O'Leary, who liked to get out to the Skelligs whenever he could, and invited him to join us.

At four-thirty we met on the pier at Portmagee, next to Des Lavelle's forty-foot, converted fishing boat. It had a small wheelhouse and benches running around a roomy deck.

"Des is a great authority on the Skelligs," Frank told me as we went aboard. "Have you seen his book about them? He was instrumental in preserving the monastic enclosure on Skellig Michael. He's probably spent more time on and around those islands than anyone else alive today. You wouldn't believe it to talk to him: he's the most unassuming man you could meet."

Frank had brought two friends with him. Tim Casey, in his seventies, was simply dressed, in an old tweed jacket, and had an air of great innocence. Jay was a tall, self-confident American. He wore a cashmere sweater and chunky gold jewellery. He had business interests, he told me, in a nearby golf club.

"I hear this is your first time to Skelligs, Maria. You're going to *love* them. Have you seen the movie *Raiders of the Lost Ark*? That's what it's like out there."

I sat next to Tim Casey. As we motored out of the Portmagee Channel, he told me that for the past twenty-five years he had been the parish clerk at the Daniel O'Connell Memorial Church in Cahersiveen.

We were passing the steep cliffs of Bray Head on Valentia Island. Ahead of us, across an expanse of shining sea, the twin pyramids of Skellig Michael and Small Skellig stood clear against the horizon, bathed in the slanting light of late afternoon.

"I read somewhere that Skellig Michael resembles two hands pressed together in prayer," I said. "And that's exactly right."

"Are you a Catholic?" he asked.

"Long-lapsed," I admitted.

"Ah, you can always come back. Pentecostal Sunday is almost upon us. Do you remember the feast? It commemorates the Holy Spirit descending on the apostles."

As a child, I had been entranced by religious paintings depicting this event: the apostles dressed in flowing robes, with expressions of joy and amazement as yellow and blue flames issued from their heads. Eagerly, I'd looked forward to the Holy Spirit inflaming *my* being at Confirmation. But when the moment came, nothing transformational occurred: no flames, no surge of joy, just the bishop's cold dry finger grazing my cheek.

"A lot has changed in the church since you were a child," said Tim. "You'd find it quite different now."

"My mother keeps telling me that. She really misses the Latin Mass."

"So do I! Truly, I mourn its passing. Would you tell your mother that from me? I love Latin. I love the ancientness of it, the history in its words. But the words became meaningless to most people; we had to change."

We had left the protection of land; the boat dipped and rose on the swells.

"Look boys!" Des pointed starboard. A dark fin sliced through the water, then sank from sight. "A basking shark! He's the first I've seen this season. I'd say he was twenty-five-feet long."

Small black guillemots floated on the surface, diving head-first in alarm as we motored by. A flock of grey and white kittiwakes circled a patch of water, screaming and fussing over a shoal of fish. As we approached Lemon Rock, a puffin whirred past on tiny wings, fast and furious as a wind-up toy.

"Puffins spend all day at sea," said Des. "At night they go back to their burrows in the cliffs. The workmen who built the first lighthouse on Skellig Michael told the time by the puffins. As soon as they saw them coming back at the end of the day, they laid down their tools and stopped work."

After ninety minutes, we approached Small Skellig. It rose from the ocean in great vertical slabs of rock. From a distance, it had appeared snow-covered; now we saw the white birds, huge numbers of them, covering its cliffs. One flew out and circled the boat. It was the size of a goose, with a wingspan of almost six feet.

"There's our first gannet," said Des. "There are forty thousand more where he came from."

Gannets crowded onto every available ledge of this craggy island. They squabbled and courted, tussled and pushed each other and knocked their bills together. Launching themselves from the cliffs, they wheeled high in the air, then plummeted beak-first into the ocean.

"Wow," said Jay. "This puts Disneyland to shame."

Des spotted a gannet floating helplessly, trapped in a tangle of discarded fishing wire. He steered the boat close enough for Dag to reach down with a long gaff hook and haul the bird onto the deck. It was a beautiful creature, pure white with black-tipped wings and a yellow head. But its long, sharp beak looked capable of removing an eyeball in one quick thrust. Des watched the struggling bird intently, then made a sudden grab for the beak. He held it firmly while Dag and Frank cut away the net. Back in the water, the bird flapped about uncertainly.

"I don't know if he'll survive," said Frank, as we motored on. "But at least we gave him a chance."

Jay had recorded the whole scene with his camera.

"Did you see Des make eye contact with the bird before he grabbed it, Maria? That was incredible—it was like a scene from *Crocodile Dundee!*"

Half a mile away, Skellig Michael reared up straight from the ocean, to over six hundred feet and two sharp peaks.

"Some say it's named after Archangel Michael," Tim told me. "He came here to help St. Patrick rid Ireland of all its demons and snakes. They battled with them all the way to the topmost peak, and then threw them down to the sea."

"Wow," said Jay. "Someone should make a movie out of that story."

"It's only legend, of course. But the monks were here. They came eleven centuries ago in little skin boats. We'll climb the steps they built, up to their settlement."

"How did they survive out here?" I asked.

Des turned from the wheel.

"They must have had plenty of fish and sea birds and eggs. And they might have kept goats and grown a few vegetables. But that's only supposition. The old Irish manuscripts make few references to the Skellig community. They tell us the Vikings raided them a couple of times, and that the monks moved to the mainland around 1200. The rest is a mystery."

Two hours after leaving Portmagee, Des steered the boat to a pier built into the rock walls of a small cove. He offered us a steadying hand as, one by one, we scrambled up the slippery steps.

"Be back here by nine, lads," he said.

"What do you think?" Jay asked me, as I stared up at a vertical cliff. "Doesn't it remind you of the latest James Bond movie?"

Dag wanted to photograph the monk's enclosure before the light faded. We hurried on ahead of the others, following a concrete path that wound around the island towards the lighthouse. Just below a retaining wall, hundreds of kittiwakes nested, some so close we could have touched them. Soon we came to a vertiginous rock stairway that doglegged up the face of the cliff, skirting past rocky ledges and outcrops. Its steps, over six hundred of them, were constructed from slabs of split rock, wedged into place with smaller stones. They were narrow, irregularly spaced and easy to stumble on. A fall would have been disastrous: between us and the sea churning against the cliffs below, there was only space. I concentrated on my feet, only occasionally glancing up at the finger-like spires pointing heavenward above us.

We reached Christ's Saddle, a dip between the two peaks. Next to an old stone cross, a rabbit sat watching us fearlessly. Below him, a meadow of white sea campion sloped to a cliff-edge. More steps led up towards the northeast peak. The sun was dropping towards the horizon; Dag took the steps two at time, before disappearing into a low stone passageway. Ducking my head, I followed him through it.

I had expected ruins, emptiness, echoes. Instead, I stepped into a perfect little world, a high rocky eyrie with a palpable sense of peace. Six large beehive huts huddled together. They were made of flat stones, piled one on top of another to form mortared walls, several feet thick. Each hut had a low doorway, with a wide stone slab as a lintel; inside, it was high enough for us to stand up. Across a narrow stone pathway was a small oratory, also of drystone construction, shaped like an upturned boat. Behind it, the ruins of a tiny medieval church. A large cross, worn thin and irregular by weathering, faced towards the Iveragh Peninsula. It was like a figure, frozen in time, one of the monks who had stood and prayed with arms outstretched, for hours and hours on end. Next to the cross was a tiny raised graveyard, like a flower bed, with a fence of ancient headstones.

I tried to imagine how hard the monks worked to create this place: splitting stones for steps, hauling rocks up impossibly steep slopes, building walls with such painstaking care that they lasted for centuries. And how fragile they felt, clinging to this rock during dreadful winter storms, lashed by relentless winds and rain. It was killing physical labour, in the most demanding of conditions. All of it was offered up to God: the monks of Skellig gained spirituality through suffering and loneliness and pain. But sometimes the storms abated, and there were evenings such as this one, clear and calm and overwhelmingly lovely. I imagined a man, long-haired, bearded, dressed in roughly spun wool, stooping through the low doorway of a hut. He stood for a while in the golden light; he watched a gannet winging by, its head a flash of yellow; he looked over to Little Skellig with waves foaming at its feet; he gazed at the vastness of the surrounding ocean.

We ducked in and out of the huts. The interiors were cool, dank, dark. But not silent. Strange purring sounds reverberated around their domed walls. Storm petrals, the smallest of European seabirds, had sought refuge here, and were nesting deep within the ancient stonework.

Voices and laughter drifted up on the wind; the rest of our group were arriving. As the three men stepped into the enclosure, they all fell silent. Tim stood for a while, hands clasped, gazing around.

"Glory be," he said at length. "We are close to heaven."

Time slid by. Our shadows grew long; the sea turned to amber. When we left, I hung back with Tim, walking slowly down the steps behind him. We had reached the saddle when I noticed the black specks, far out at sea. There were clouds of them, steadily moving through the sky towards us. Tim stopped.

"Here come the puffins."

With high-pitched cries, they whirred up to the island, splaying out their red feet as they landed. And they landed in their hundreds, all around us: on the steep slopes below us, next to our feet on the narrow path, on rocks level with our faces. They were engaging creatures, with black and white plumage, orange legs and feet and a stout yellow beak. They showed no fear; after regarding us curiously, they turned and waddled towards their burrows, under ledges or in the soil beneath swathes of white sea campion blossoms.

"Some say these puffins are the reincarnations of the monks who lived here," said Tim. "As a Catholic, I don't believe that. But the thought is beautiful."

The sea darkened into the hues of approaching night. Across the ocean, the Iveragh Peninsula was fading into the gloom; I could barely make out its familiar cliffs and bays and mountains. Our companions had disappeared from sight. Still, we lingered on the path, in reverent silence.

Minutes passed. Gently, Tim touched my arm.

"*Procedamus in pace,*" he said quietly. "Let us go in peace."

✦

CHAPTER TWENTY-EIGHT

Our last day in Kerry dawned still and hazy. By eight o'clock the sun had risen above the summit of Knocknadobar, burning off the mist. In our garden, drops of dew gleamed on the leaves of tall, newly bloomed foxgloves, and bees busily crawled about inside the bell-shaped flowers.

It was warm enough to have breakfast outside, so we ate our toast and eggs on the picnic table where, over the past few months, I had witnessed so many operations.

Dora grazed close by; I wondered how she'd feel this time tomorrow, waking up on Peggy's farm along with Chloe, Mikey, Bess and the full complement of dogs and cats.

"Do you think she'll get used to it there?" I asked Dag.

"She'll love it," he assured me. "Where else does a pet lamb get to snuggle up to a warm fire at night?"

He was in a pensive mood. His job was over. In the afternoon he was due to go into the surgery to complete some paperwork and empty his car of veterinary equipment and drugs. Apart from that, we only had to pack, make a few final goodbyes and bring Dora to her new home.

"I feel like our life in Canada is just a dream," he sighed. "I can't imagine us not being here anymore."

"Maybe we'll come back," I said.

He stared up at the mountain.

"The O'Learys might be interested in having me again next year. I told them I'd talk to you about it."

I smiled.

"It's fine by me," I said. "That way I can see Dora again."

Dag's face brightened.

"You could raise another lamb. A mountain ewe. Or maybe couplets."

Around eleven, we drove over to visit Ted Donnelly. He was fast asleep on the sofa in his kitchen, his stockinged feet propped against the range. Carmel leaned down and shook his shoulder.

"It's the vet, Ted," she called.

He sat up, looking around in confusion.

"The vet?" he cried. "What for?"

"Relax, Ted, I'm just here for a social call," laughed Dag. "Sorry to wake you up."

"Oh, for Christ's sake, Dougeen," said Ted, rubbing his eyes. "You're very welcome. You are! But for a second there I didn't know what was happening, I had no clue at all."

"He spent a long time at prayer this morning," Carmel told me, with a wink.

"One of my neighbours had a stations," he explained. "I don't suppose you have those in Canada. The priest comes to the house to say Mass, and everyone from the townland gathers in. And then, you know how it is, after the Mass is over the bottle comes out and is poured around. Speaking of bottles, Carmel, isn't it time you showed Dougeen and Marie one of ours?"

"I'm seeing to it already, haven't you eyes in your head?" she retorted, handing us each a glass of whiskey.

"Sit down now," she said, "and make yourselves at home. You'll have a sandwich of course. How's that pet lamb of yours?"

Ted reached over to Dag, clinked their glasses together and downed his whiskey in one. Then he sat back, looking greatly satisfied.

"The gaining season is over, Dougeen! It is, thank God. We have all our lambs in now, and we only lost a few."

Carmel brought us sandwiches made from thick slices of her own soda bread and slabs of boiled ham. She poured us mugs of strong tea from a pot sitting on the range and refilled our whiskey glasses. The men talked about sheep for a while, until Dag brought up the subject of bog oak.

"There's plenty of old wood out there in my bog," said Ted. "But whether it's the kind they like in Canada, that I can't say."

He reached under the sofa, and pulled out his boots.

"I'll get a saw from the shed. Then we'll go away to the bog to see what we can find."

We followed him along the lane, through a gap in a stone wall, and into a wide area of peat bog that ran down toward the Fertha valley. We had only taken a few steps across it when a sandy brown skylark fluttered up from some reeds. Ted held his stick aloft to signal us to stop. He stepped around carefully, looking for her nest.

"Every bird as she is reared, and the skylark for the bog," he said, quoting an old saying. "I love the skylarks, and I worry about disturbing them when I'm out here in the spring."

Bending down, I picked the head off a bog cotton plant. Shaped like a tiny mop, its fibres were soft and fine as cashmere wool.

"'Like the ears of a newborn lamb, Marie" said Ted.

Growing among the bog cotton was marsh andromeda, the small woody shrub that Ted called bog rosemary. To explain the name, he pulled off a few of the pale green leaves, crushed them between his fingers and held them close to my nose to smell.

"In the old days they used this for healing," he said. "And do you see the elder blooming over there? People who suffered from fits would make remedies from its flowers and berries. They say that Christ was crucified on a cross made of elder, so in Kerry we never beat an animal with a bough from an elder tree."

We walked past an old plot that Ted had dug by hand. There were clear spade marks along the irregular troughs, where he had cut down through the different peat layers to the water-logged clay beneath. The turf bricks were piled up in a rick shaped like the oratory we'd seen on Skellig Michael.

"You arrange them so the wind blows through for good drying, and the rain runs off," he explained.

"It's a work of art," I said.

"It's a *life's* work, Marie. I've been laying turf since I was a child, so it's second nature. But I don't think my children will want to be doing it. Lots of people have the oil these days. Cutting and laying the turf takes time, and no one has time now. There's been many a day, after a poor summer when the turf wouldn't dry, that I've cursed it and said I'll get in the oil instead. But I love the smell of the turf burning, I wouldn't have anything else."

"How often do you still dig it yourself?" Dag asked him.

"Never, Doug! Never! I've had enough of that. In the old days, before the machines came in, we had no choice. The spade we used was called a *slean*. First we'd break through the top layer of sod, and take it off like a skin. We used that for the thatching; we laid it down like a roofing felt and put the reeds on the top. It's great stuff; it lasts for years. Then we'd dig. God, we nearly broke our backs with the digging. What a machine will do now in four hours, Dougeen, used to be four *days* of hard work for two men. In the 1950s, for one pony ride of turf you'd get four shillings and sixpence, and with that you could buy four pounds of sugar, a pound of tea, and maybe a pig's head. Ah, it was hard."

In an area where the mechanized turf cutters had been at work, Dag found a whole root system of bog oak, and sawed a piece off. It was black wood, dense and very hard.

"I'm glad you found what you wanted," said Ted, though he was clearly puzzled by Dag's delight.

When we got back to bungalow, Carmel was waiting for us on the doorstep.

"I've some bacon and eggs and black pudding cooked. You can't go until it's eaten."

We were in the back room of the surgery, making an inventory of drugs Dag had returned, when Ann came in. She was smiling.

"Dennis McCarthy needs a vet."

"Dennis?" said Dag. "I thought he prided himself on always looking after his animals himself."

"One of the ponies on his land has a problem. He wouldn't say what it was. He insists it has to be you who sees it, and he asked if your wife would be coming along, too. I don't think there's anything wrong with the pony. I'd say it's an excuse to see you before you go."

Dennis had never indicated that he'd like us to visit him; he was a private man, and I had been reticent about calling by his house uninvited. On the way through town, we bought a bottle of whiskey and a packet of cigarettes to give him.

The track to Dennis's farm went through several gates, all of them falling off their hinges and tied to the posts with baling twine. We arrived at a collection of ramshackle sheds next to a large field where several cows, two donkeys, a piebald pony and her foal, a couple of goats, a dozen or so sheep and their lambs grazed peacefully together. Across several more fields, we could see what we presumed was Dennis's cottage, small and white-washed and roofed with tin.

"Dennis!" called Dag, but there was no reply.

The first shed we looked in was filled with bales of silage wrapped in black plastic. In the shed next door, a cow was tethered to the wall, and four Blackface sheep stood inside a wooden pen. One of the ewes put her delicate hooves on the top rung of the pen and curiously peered out at us.

"Where the hell is he?" mused Dag.

"Not here, obviously," I said.

We both turned around, and gasped in shock at the sight of Dennis, standing very still in the doorway.

"Did I give you a fright?" he asked. "I was in the far shed with the pony, tying him up for you."

The pony was a brown yearling Dennis had recently bought. It was shy and skittery.

"He has a sore on his hip," Dennis told Dag. He pointed to a small bald patch, no bigger than a pound coin. Even I could see that this was an old wound. But Dag spent a few minutes looking carefully at it and checking over the pony to see if it had any more abrasions elsewhere on its body.

"He's fine, Dennis," he said eventually.

"What do I owe you, now?" asked Dennis, as he closed the door of the shed.

"Nothing," Dag told him. "But we have something for you."

When I handed him the bottle and the packet of cigarettes, his blue eyes expressed quiet delight.

"Well now. That's very kind of you. We'll take a drop together before you go."

We sat on the wall skirting the field of grazing animals. Dennis drank straight from the bottle, and passed it to Dag.

"I love how you keep all those different animals in the same field together," I told him.

"They're company for each other," he said. "It's the way it used to be done. I have other animals elsewhere, as you know. I've a good bit of land around here. It's important for a man to have some land for himself. I don't need anymore now. The next patch of land I'll be needing will be six feet by four, with a hole dug down into it. But I'll have drunk a few more bottles of this by then, so I will."

The whiskey had come back to me. I took a swig, then handed it to Dennis.

"I'm sorry now that you're leaving so soon," he told me. "We had some good talks together, you and I. I hope you'll both come back to us."

He replaced the top on the bottle of whiskey and stowed it in the pocket of his jacket. Then he slowly got to his feet.

"I'm very grateful that you came. I have to be seeing to my animals now, so I'll take my leave of you. Goodbye now."

He stood watching us as we got into the car. Then he leaned into my open window until his face was close to mine.

"I'd say you'll be thinking of me," he said, "when you're in Canada again."

It was late in the evening when we took Dora up to her new home. She sat between my legs in the car, her head resting on my lap. I stroked her ears as we drove up the lane, wondering what she would look like when I saw her again. Outside Peggy's house there was the usual excited scene: the cats hissing, the dogs barking and trying to lick Dora's face, and Mikey scampering about. From the back seat of the car we unloaded a bag of milk replacer powder, Dora's bottle, the sheep nuts I'd failed to interest her in, and the whiskey and sherry we'd brought as presents for Michael and Peggy.

"God, she's a weight," said Peggy, picking Dora up in her arms. "Have you weaned her yet?"

"Not completely," I admitted. "She still wants a bottle morning and night."

"That's alright. Chloe was almost six months old before we stopped giving her a bedtime bottle."

In the kitchen, Peggy set up a little folding table in front of us and laid it with plates of buttered cream crackers, sponge cake and glasses of sherry and whiskey. Mikey settled down in his spot by the fire, the dogs lay in the doorway and Dora curled up behind my chair. While we chatted, I kept turning around to scratch her head.

"There are more frogs in the field than usual," Michael told Dag. "And they say there are dolphins down by Valentia. It means we'll have a long hot summer."

"We'll be lucky if summer isn't over already," said Peggy. "You two got the best of the weather. I can't believe it's tomorrow you're leaving. The time has gone so quick, it's flown by. What way will you go?"

To Killarney, Dag told her, and from there right across Ireland to Dublin where we'd take the ferry to Wales. Then, after driving to Manchester, we would fly back to Canada.

"God, it's a journey you have ahead of you. How long are you on the plane to Canada?"

"About ten hours," I said.

"Ten hours! That's terrible altogether. I was only in a plane once, to England, and I didn't like it at all."

Around ten-thirty, Dag said he wanted a last visit to the East End Bar.

"We'll put Dora to bed," suggested Peggy. "That way she won't notice you've gone."

She prepared bottles for Mikey and Dora. We fed them outside, close to the little shed where they would both sleep. When Dora had finished, I bent down and breathed in the smell of her fleece. Then I gently pushed her into the shed. Its floor was covered with fresh hay, and she sniffed around it quite happily. But when Peggy put Mikey in next to her and closed the door, Dora broke into wild, frightened bleats. She began throwing herself against the plywood door, frantically trying to escape. I stared at Peggy, who looked totally taken aback.

"I never thought she'd fuss so," she admitted. "She knows you're leaving her, alright."

The bleating got louder and more frenzied.

"I'll look after her," Peggy assured me, as we said goodbye.

Dag put his arm around me and gently propelled me towards the car. I got in, covered my ears, and sat in abject misery as we drove down the track.

She's only a sheep, I silently counselled myself, as we turned onto the lane. You *mustn't* cry.

"You took that farewell really calmly," said Dag, when we pulled up outside the East End Bar. "I thought you'd be in pieces."

I said nothing, and followed him into the bar. The place was filled with noise and smoke and bustle. Noreen had put the word around and lots of Dag's favourite farmers had come in for a last drink with him. Pints were passed over heads to us, then big plates of sandwiches appeared, enough to feed an army: ham and cheese inside white bread, on the house for everyone. Dag was kept busy shaking hands and talking about the weather and the new grass. I stood quietly next to him, thinking about Dora. Though I knew she was in the best hands imaginable, I couldn't help but feel that I had abandoned her.

"Has that pet lamb of yours gone to her new home?" Ted Donnelly eventually asked me, shouting over the hubbub.

I nodded, then looked into my drink.

"Ah now, don't be sad, Marie," he said kindly. "By tomorrow night at the latest, that lamb will be mad about Peggy O'Sullivan, and quite happy again. The next time you see her she'll be a fine big woolly ewe, maybe with a lamb of her own to show you."

✛

CHAPTER TWENTY-NINE

Early next morning I woke with a start, convinced that something was badly amiss. It was the unfamiliar quietness that had disturbed my sleep: for the first time in two months, I hadn't been roused by Dora's insistent bleating from the haggard.

We skipped breakfast, shoved all our bags into the car and locked the cottage behind us, leaving the key under the mat for Peggy to pick up later. Then we stood for a while in our garden, among long grass sodden with dew, breathing in the mild, fresh morning air and listening to the sounds of the valley. Bees droned around the foxgloves and clover, ewes and lambs bleated, a cow coughed and a raven passing high above made a cry like a bell being struck. Only the cuckoo's call was missing, but just before we departed she flew down from the trees on the lower slopes of the mountain, and winged right past us, singing as she went.

We drove up the lane, leaving the harbour behind us. Sheep raised their heads, looking up from fields that seemed to be bursting open with new growth and colour.

"It's a pity we'll miss the montbretia flowering," said Dag sadly.

No smoke was curling yet from Peggy's chimneys, and the front door was closed. As we passed the track to the house, I rolled down my window and stuck out my head, listening for Dora's cry. But all I heard was the car's engine, and its tires on the lane as we sped away.

Acknowledgments

As always, my endless gratitude to Dag, for buoying me throughout the writing of this book with his love, laughter and soul food, for patiently checking and expanding the sections on his veterinary work and for giving me such valuable input at all stages of the manuscript.

I am also grateful to Isabelle Gutmanis, for her sensitive, insightful editorial work; to Carol and Mike Matthews, Alison Watt and Thora Howell, for always being there to offer advice; and to Joan Skogan and Karen Connelly, fellow sheep-fans and generous providers of icons and poetry.

Special thanks to my publisher, Kim McArthur—the funniest, feistiest and fairest of them all—and to her trusty cohorts on King Street West. It is a pleasure to be associated with them.

For their help with my research, I tip my hat to Maebhe Ni Bhrion of the Department of Irish Folklore at the University of Dublin and to the kind staff of Cahersiveen Library and the Barracks Heritage Centre, Cahersiveen. Of all the books to which I turned, the following were particularly informative and enlightening: *The Iveragh Peninsula: An Archaeological Survey of South Kerry*, by Ann O Sullivan and John Sheehan (Cork University Press, 1996); *Discovering Kerry*, by T.J. Barrington (1986); *Atlas of the Irish Rural Landscape*, by F.H.A. Aalen, Kevin Whelan and Matthew Stout (Cork University Press, 1997); *Sean O Connaill's Book: Stories and Traditions from Iveragh*, by Seamus of Duilearga (Comhairle Bhealoideas Eireann, 1981); *In the Kingdom of Kerry*, by Richard Hayward (Dundalk, 1945); *Irish Place Names* by Deirdre and Laurence

Flanagan (Gill and Macmillan, 1994); *The Great Hunger*, by Cecil Woodham-Smith (Hamish Hamilton, 1987); *The Skellig Story*, by Des Lavelle (The O'Brien Press, 1987); *Sun Dancing*, by Geoffrey Moorehouse (Phoenix, 1997); and *The Flowering of Ireland*, by Katherine Scherman (Little Brown, 1981).

For the Seal Line Rain City Express bags that kept these books dry as I cycled to and from Cahersiveen Library, my thanks to Cascade Designs, and especially to Tom Myers.

I gratefully acknowledge the Canada Council and the Cultural Services Branch of the Ministry of Small Business, Tourism and Culture in British Columbia, for the financial assistance that allowed me to complete this book.

Most of all, my thanks to the people of the Iveragh, Sheep's Head and Mizen Peninsulas, who over the course of three lambing seasons became our neighbours and our friends, and whose generous spirits draw us back to Ireland, time and time again.